Diagnosis precedes cure;
hope this book will help
to further your understanding
of the challenge facing
third world governments
and their people.

With compliments and
best wishes,

Courtney Smith-
3/5/95

SOCIALIST TRANSFORMATION IN PERIPHERAL ECONOMIES

To Naomi, my daughter

Socialist Transformation in Peripheral Economies

Lessons from Grenada

COURTNEY A. SMITH
School of Social and Political Sciences
The University of Hull
United Kingdom

Avebury

Aldershot • Brookfield USA • Hong Kong • Singapore • Sydney

Published by
Avebury
Ashgate Publishing Limited
Gower House
Croft Road
Aldershot
Hants GU11 3HR
England

Ashgate Publishing Company
Old Post Road
Brookfield
Vermont 05036
USA

British Library Cataloguing in Publication Data

Smith, Courtney
    Socialist Transformation in Peripheral
    Economies: Lessons from Grenada
    I. Title
    330.9729845

    ISBN 1 85972 050 1

Library of Congress Catalog Card Number: 95-76075

Printed and bound by Athenæum Press Ltd.,
Gateshead, Tyne & Wear.

Contents

Tables

Foreword

The eleventh anniversary of the invasion of Grenada last year passed virtually unnoticed in the United States which carried it out and in the Commonwealth Caribbean where its impact was most widely felt. This collective amnesia has also been evident in the memory of the revolution itself. The endeavours of the People's Revolutionary Government to transform Grenada have gone largely unrecorded with the unfortunate consequence that many of the lessons for development which the experience in Grenada is able to provide remain unacknowledged and unresearched.

Perhaps the most immediately important is the potential for development of small countries and in particular tropical island states. The PRG challenged the conventional wisdom that development in such circumstances must be dependent development. Instead, a policy which turned inward to mobilize potential was adopted along with one which sought to harness new external sources of support. In the event, the former was arguably more successful than the latter. The key successes of the revolution in social and economic terms were ones in which the Grenadian people themselves provided a significant input. Equally, the failures gathered pace as the revolution itself lost legitimacy, and the willingness to contribute time and labour to development grew less. The importance this experience provides in reminding us that development has a human dimension needs to be underlined. Popular mobilization can be a successful development technique and arguably is an indispensable one in most small tropical islands where the main resource is the people.

The organizational framework within which the PRG carried out its policies was provided by socialist experience elsewhere. The most immediately available was the Cuban experience and the PRG relied on and encouraged the Cubans to become part of the revolution. But they also went further afield and, on the way, adopted and more importantly attempted to apply the soviet theory of **non-capitalist development**. In retrospect there can be no doubt that this was a major mistake. The distinctive elements of Grenada were overlain by irrelevant ideological baggage and the insights provided by the Caribbean school of development theorists increasingly forgotten in favour of marxist-leninist formulae. Ideology took command and it is difficult to read without a sense of despair the way in which adherence to theory steadily became more important than recognition of fact. Bad theory is much worse than no theory at all and 'grand theory' which purports to explain everything is worst of all. The revolution did best when the pragmatic element was to the fore. This insight is one which is now recognised in much development literature. The fact that this applies as much to the smallest as to the largest developing countries is one of the more important conclusions to be drawn from this study.

It is also one which neighbouring states in the Eastern Caribbean might reflect on more fully. One of the unfortunate consequences of the political model adopted by the revolution was a collective dismissal by the political directorates of these countries of the Grenadian experience as a whole. This study shows that it is wholly unwarranted and exceptionally short-sighted. Grenada shares many problems with its neighbours. The way that Grenada sought to resolve them was different but not without success. The building of the international airport, as well as the broadening of the export base and the diversification of international economic relations, can be cited as steps in the right direction. So also were the attempts to reduce unemployment, particularly among the youth. Other programmes, such as the development of handicrafts and the processing of local agricultural produce were long-favoured, but had to await the PRG before they were seriously pursued. Or to put the matter somewhat differently, private capital was not developing Grenada and it was government initiatives which provided the dynamics for change. The current fashion in the region is to emphasise the private sector as the prime mover in development. The example of Grenada shows that there is a role for government and that its record, especially when measured against what was there before can be very positive.

This last point must be emphasised. The immediate years before the revolution were ones of failure and neglect. On a simple balance sheet the record of the PRG over that of the previous Gairy government can only be judged positively. Yet the PRG was opposed in its policies by the United States and Britain, as well as by the majority of Commonwealth Caribbean countries, in a way and to a degree to which the Gairy regime was never opposed. The reasons for this are many and varied and lie in the realm of geopolitics more than development. That acknowledged, their impact was nevertheless decisive and point to the necessity of getting the international policies right. There can be no doubt that the PRG failed in this decisive area and that it brought about many of the conditions which eventually led to its demise. One of the lessons demonstrated in this study is therefore the necessity of harnessing diplomacy to development. The PRG correctly understood this as a widening process but they badly miscalculated the costs it would impose on traditional links. The consequence was to make the process of development that much more difficult than it need have been.

The experience of Grenada is therefore rich in the theory and practice of development. The development record of the PRG needs to be better known for what it can tell us about the larger questions of transformation and empowerment in the developing world. It is for this reason that Dr Smith's book is particularly to be welcomed. It provides the first comprehensive overview of the development strategy of the PRG and a detailed commentary on its application in key sectors of the economy. It also provides lessons for economic and social transformation upon which to reflect. The revolution in Grenada may have been a small affair in comparison to the major revolutions in the world but after reading and reflecting on this book we are aware that it has a significance beyond its size and relatively short duration. As such, it provides insights into revolution and development which can be usefully employed not only in understanding and recommending policy for other Caribbean states but much further afield as well.

Paul Sutton
Senior Lecturer
Centre of Developing Area Studies
University of Hull

Preface and acknowledgements

This book grew out of a doctoral thesis which was submitted to Hull University, England, in 1988. I owe the idea to shape it into a book to a number of colleagues who persuaded me that it was worth bringing this work to a wider audience on account of its originality, and its potential to fill a yawning gap in the extensive literature on the Grenada revolution. Further impetus resulted from the reception to my recent contribution to A. Payne and P. Sutton, eds, (1994), *Modern Caribbean Politics*, Baltimore: Johns Hopkins University Press. Entitled 'The Grenada Revolution in Retrospect', the chapter has received appreciative comment from reviewers, and a number of requests have since been received for further information on points which could not be fully developed in this piece. The book is distinguished from previous works on the Grenada revolution by its systematic treatment of the Grenadian economy during the era of the People's Revolutionary Government (PRG), its focus on the role of economics in the demise of the revolution, and the emphasis which it places on the lessons for development which the experience of Grenada is able to provide to the rest of the Caribbean and the wider Third World. The need for such a study has long been recognised in some quarters. For example, Sutton (1988) concluded his review of a sample of the burgeoning literature on the Grenada revolution by 'pointing out the need of urgent research of the economy under the PRG'. The absence of such a study, coupled with the traumatic way in which the revolution imploded, has led many analysts to vilify the revolution and condemn it as an outright political and economic failure. Equally lamentable, it has also led some sympathisers of the revolution to draw conclusions about the PRG's achievements (and the reasons for the regime's demise) which are at variance with the facts.

It is the purpose of this book to demonstrate that economic factors contributed in large measure to the denouement of the Grenada revolution.

The argument advanced is that, by early 1981, the economy was engulfed in a profound crisis which resulted primarily from the contradictions in the application of marxism-leninism and the **theory of non-capitalist development** to Grenada's objective realities. Although it cannot be claimed categorically that this was responsible for the parallel political crisis, it is clear that the economic crisis exacerbated the political crisis. In particular, adverse economic conditions did much to alienate large segments of the social forces on which the PRG's development strategy relied for support. It is further argued that the disappointing performance of the Grenadian economy during the PRG's rule should not be allowed to obscure the important gains made by the revolution. The book documents the economic and social achievements, while drawing out the mistakes made by the PRG and the lessons which can be learned from the experiment. The inescapable conclusion is that the real failure of the PRG lie in the sphere of politics, rather than economics. Many of the reforms on the government's agenda could have been achieved within a social democratic framework. Arguably, this path would have had a greater chance of succeeding if it had been pursued by the PRG.

The analysis offered in the book rests heavily on primary data sources. These included government documents (many of which were captured by US marines during the invasion in October 1983); documents and materials prepared by regional and international organizations such as the Caribbean Development Bank, Eastern Caribbean Central Bank, Economic Commission for Latin America and the Caribbean, International Monetary Fund, World Bank, and the Commonwealth Secretariat; material drawn from the Grenadian press and regional newspapers; and indepth interviews with a number of Grenadians (comprising leading members of the private sector, politicians drawn from different sides of the political spectrum , technocrats, workers and farmers), development specialists at the Caribbean Development Bank, academics at the University of the West Indies, and 'internationalist' workers who were recruited to Grenada during the period of the revolution - many of whom held important positions in the PRG's administration.

Needless to say that the book could not have been completed without the help and co-operation received from all those who took part in the fieldwork, and a number of other individuals and institutions who helped in other ways. First, I would like to thank the British Council and Comfin Holdings Limited (particularly John Botterill and Roy Holland) for funding the field research which took me to six Caribbean territories (including Grenada) in the spring and summer of 1987. I also owe much to those who aided my research in the West Indies, whether by making materials available to me, helping me to organise interviews, or taking time from their busy schedules to supply answers to my questions. Among those who deserve special mention are

Jennifer Carneghie, Alma Tait, Ancelline Williams, Herbert Blaize, Ronnie Charles, Bernard La Corbiniere, Matthew Edwards, Justin Francis, Ovid Gill, Cecil Hypolite, Didicus Jules, Wallace Joefield-Napier, Lyden Ramdhanny, Kenrick Radix, and the staff of the Grenada Documentation Centre and Caribbean Development Bank library.

Academic support and helpful advice was provided by a number of colleagues and friends on both sides of the atlantic. I am particularly grateful to Dr Paul Sutton (who supervised the doctoral research on which the book is based), Professor Tony Payne (who was the external examiner for the thesis), Professor Michael Artis, Professor Judith Marquand, Professor Valdo Pons, Professor David Colman, Dr Michael Burton, Dr David Booth, Dr Eric Evans, Dr Joyce Bellamy, Dr Michael Witter, Scott Davidson and Bernard Vogl. Dr David Dabydeen (University of Warwick) organised a seminar at which some of the material covered in the book was discussed. I benefited enormously from the resulting discussion. Especially for moral support (and help with coping with a major personal setback experienced during the gestation of this work), I owe a debt of gratitude to Levi Atkinson, Irene Baldwin, Enola Beharie, Arthur Bennett, Rosemary Bennett, Brian Brown, Michael Chaplin, Mark Edgell, Clare Elliott, Alison Hall, Bernadette Julien, Ralph Lewars, Liz Morrey, Carol Pickering, Carron-Anne Russell, Lorraine Sutton, my parents (Monica Baxter and Gladstone Johnson-Smith), step-parents (Deloris Johnson-Smith and Kenneth Baxter) and grandparents (Evelyn Williams and Albert Williams). Thanks also to Barbara O'Leary, who has assiduously helped with the necessary, but unenviable tasks, of typing the manuscript, compiling the bibliography and checking the final draft.

For their contribution to my intellectual development during the formative years, thanks are due to my former teachers and head masters at Harry Watch All Age school and Manchester High school. Last, but certainly not least, I would also like to record my thanks to the staff at Avebury Press; particularly Josephine Gooderham and Sarah Markham (commissioning editors), Suzanne Evins (editorial manager), Steven Jarman (editorial assistant), and Tracey Daborn (promotion manager). The speed with which they responded to queries and the excellent guidance they provided on how to prepare the camera-ready copy helped to ensure that the project progressed without hiccups and undue stress.

None of the individuals or institutions mentioned above are responsible for the views expressed in this book, or for any shortcomings from which it may suffer.

List of abbreviations

AIC   Agricultural and Industrial Credit

BDD   British Development Division

BWIA   British West Indian Airways

CIDA   Canadian International Development Agency

CBI   Caribbean Basin Initiative

CARICOM   Caribbean Community

CDB   Caribbean Development Bank

CTRC   Caribbean Tourism Research Centre

CC   Central Committee

CIA   Central Intelligence Agency

CPE   Centre for Popular Education

CIWI   Commercial and Industrial Workers Union

CPSU   Communist Party of the Soviet Union

CSDP   Community School Day Programme

CMEA	Council for Mutual Economic Assistance
ECCB	Eastern Caribbean Central Bank
ECCA	Eastern Caribbean Currency Authority
ECLA	Economic Commission for Latin America
EEC	European Economic Community
EFF	Extended Fund Facility
FIC	Farm Improvement Scheme
FAO	Food and Agricultural Organization
FDC	Forestry Development Corporation
GDR	German Democratic Republic
GAIDC	Grenada Agricultural and Industrial Development Corporation
GAI	Grenada Agro-industries Ltd
GCIC	Grenada Chamber of Industry and Commerce
GDB	Grenada Development Bank
GFNC	Grenada Food and Nutrition Council
GHA	Grenada Hotel Association
GMMWU	Grenada Manual and Mental Workers Union
GNIH	Grenada National Institute of Handicrafts
GNP	Grenada National Party
GNCA	Grenada Nutmeg Co-operative Association
GRC	Grenada Resorts Corporation

GFC	Grenada Farms Corporation
GULP	Grenada United Labour Party
GDP	Gross Domestic Product
ISER	Institute of Social and Economic Research
ICAO	International Civil Aviation Organization
IFAD	International Fund for Agricultural Development
IMF	International Monetary Fund
ISER	Institute for Social and Economic Research
JEWEL	Joint Endeavour for Welfare, Education and Liberation
LIAT	Leeward Islands Air Transport
LPGC	Livestock Production and Genetic Centre
MNIB	Marketing and National Importing Board
MBPM	Maurice Bishop Patriotic Movement
MAP	Movement for Assemblies of the People
NCB	National Commercial Bank
NACDA	National Agricultural and Co-operative Development Agency
NFC	National Fisheries Corporation
NISTEP	National In-Service Teacher Education Programme
NTS	National Transport Service
NIEO	New International Economic Order
NJM	New Jewel Movement

NNP	New National Party
OECS	Organization of Eastern Caribbean States
OPEC	Organization of Petroleum Exporting Countries
OREL	Organization for Research, Education and Liberation
OPIC	Overseas Private Investment Corporation
PRA	People's Revolutionary Army
PRG	People's Revolutionary Government
RMC	Revolutionary Military Council
SWWU	Seamen and Waterfront Workers' Union
SIC	Small Industry Credit
TAWU	Technical and Allied Workers' Union
UNCTC	United Nations Centre on Transnational Corporations
UNDP	United Nations Development Programme
UNESCO	United Nations Education, Scientific and Cultural Organization
UPP	United People's Party
USAID	United States Agency for International Development
USICA	United States International Communications Agency
UWI	University of the West Indies
WHO	World Health Organization
WINBAN	Windward Islands Banana Growers Association
WTO	World Tourism Organization

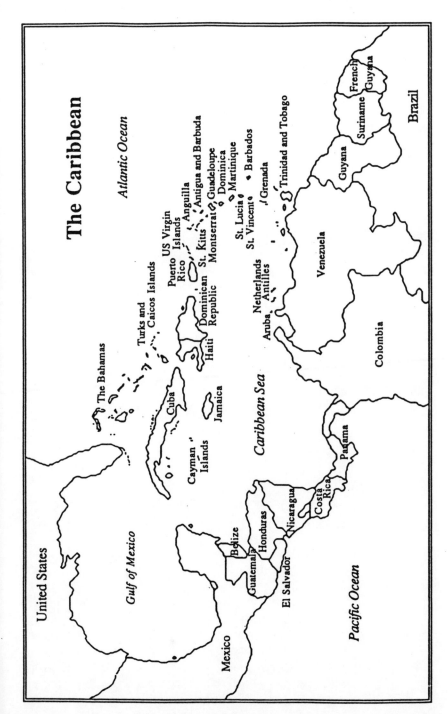

The Caribbean

United States

Gulf of Mexico

Mexico

Atlantic Ocean

The Bahamas

Turks and
Caicos Islands

Cuba

Cayman
Islands

Jamaica

Haiti

Dominican
Republic

Puerto
Rico

US Virgin
Islands

Anguilla

Antigua and Barbuda

St. Kitts

Montserrat

Guadeloupe

Dominica

Martinique

St. Lucia

St. Vincent

Barbados

Grenada

Caribbean Sea

Netherlands
Antilles

Aruba

Trinidad and Tobago

Belize

Guatemala

Honduras

El Salvador

Nicaragua

Costa
Rica

Panama

Pacific Ocean

Venezuela

Colombia

Guyana

Suriname

French
Guyana

Brazil

xxi

Introduction

On 13 March 1979, an unprecedented event took place on the tiny 133 square-mile island of Grenada (with an estimated population of 110,000 and a per capita income of US$650 in 1979). For the first time in the history of the Anglophone Caribbean a government was removed from power by extra-parliamentary means, and a Marxist-Leninist model explicitly adopted in favour of the liberal Westminster model which was bequeathed to the region. This was the regime of Sir Eric Matthew Gairy - a regime which was notorious for its repression, corruption, electoral fraud, and neglect of the Grenadian economy and social services.

The small New Jewel Movement (NJM) party which executed the coup d'état enjoyed political power for 4½ years until it met its tragic demise in October 1983, after an internecine power struggle within the party which led to the barbaric massacre of the Prime Minister (Maurice Bishop), three of his loyal Cabinet ministers (Jacqueline Creft, Unison Whiteman, and Norris Bain) and an unknown number of supporters. This crisis provided the perfect pretext for the US invasion which followed less than one week later.

These events have generated a plethora of publications from writers from both inside and outside of the Caribbean region. So voluminous is this literature that a reviewer of a sample of these books was led to pen: 'Since the revolution of 13 March 1979, and subsequent to the invasion of 25 October 1983, more has probably been written on Grenada than in **all its previously recorded history**' (Sutton, 1988, p. 134. Emphasis added). But despite this burgeoning body of writing there is as yet no substantive, definitive, and systematic study of the efforts of the People's Revolutionary Government to transform the Grenadian economy.

Questions such as the following have either not been broached or (when raised) they have been considered at a highly general and superficial level: (i) What were the main features of the development strategy of the People's

1

Revolutionary Government?; (ii) On what conceptual and theoretical premises was the strategy predicated?; (iii) What was the role of the private sector in the strategy? To what extent did they accept the role assigned to them?; (iv) what were the major initiatives undertaken in each of the leading sectors (agriculture, tourism, and manufacturing) of the economy and how successful were they?; (v) How did the economy perform on a macroeconomic scale?; (vi) What role, if any, did economics play in the demise of the revolution?; (vii) What lessons can other Third World countries (and more immediately Caribbean territories) learn from the PRG's attempt at economic transformation via the path of non-capitalist development? Is this a viable path of development for small, peripheral economies?

It is this lacuna which has prompted the present study. It is hoped that the material assembled in the various chapters will provide insights into these issues, as well as explore the problems of economic transformation for peripheral economies, especially small island economies.

Apart from this introductory chapter, the book is comprised of eight substantive chapters. The first two chapters seek to provide some background information on the type of economy inherited by the PRG. In more specific terms, Chapter one traces the type of economic structure which was implanted by the colonial powers (France and Britain), and the implications of this structure for growth and development in the domestic economy. Chapter two continues with this theme by examining the contribution of Gairyism to the country's socio-economic problems. The rise of the NJM is also discussed in this chapter. Chapter three provides an overview of the PRG's development strategy, and a critical discussion of its theoretical bases. The main focus is on the theory of non-capitalist development, and an assessment of its utility in the particular context of Grenada's economy and society.

The next three chapters examine in detail the performance of the PRG in the three critical sectors of the Grenadian economy - agriculture, tourism and manufacturing. Chapter four is devoted to the agrarian policies of the PRG. Chapter five focuses on the PRG's tourist strategy, including a conceptual discussion on the role of tourism in development. The aim of this discourse is to point out the economic, socio-cultural, political, and environmental issues which a commitment to tourism on the scale envisaged by the PRG raise for a small, leftward leaning country like Grenada and the implications of the government's tourist strategy for the transition to socialism. Chapter six provides an indepth analysis of the relationship between the private sector and the PRG. Such an investigation is necessary given the pivotal role of the private sector in the government's development strategy. As such the chapter traces the development of the relationship between the two entities - a relationship which the author has described as 'tense and uneasy'. The major sources of tensions and conflicts are identified as well as the challenges and difficulties which industrialization poses for small, backward, underdeveloped countries like Grenada.

Chapter seven pulls together the material assembled in the earlier chapters to provide a macroeconomic review of the economy. This chapter also discusses Grenada-IMF relations during the PRG era, and the role of economics in the demise of the PRG. Finally, an attempt is made in chapter eight to assess the main lessons from the Grenadian experience for countries embarking on radical economic and political change. The emphasis is on lessons for economic and social development. This chapter also examines Grenada's return to the dependent *laissez-faire* model of development in the wake of the October 1983 events, and the continued failure of this model even when assessed against its own narrow criteria.

1 The integration of Grenada into the world economy

The issues posed for economic transformation in peripheral economies like Grenada cannot be properly understood without an understanding of the structure and functioning of such economies, and how this structure has evolved over time. This account of the Grenada revolution thus begins with a discussion of Grenada's incorporation into the world economy, and the type of economic structure which resulted from this process. The chapter also traces the emergence of the Grenadian peasantry and the populist movement which began in 1951 with Gairy's return to Grenada.

The slave economy

When Christopher Columbus sighted and claimed Grenada for Spain in 1498 the island was inhabited by Carib Indians. The early writings of Europeans, particularly Columbus himself, described these people as a group of savages, nomads, and cannibals. It is believed that they wandered to Grenada and to other islands in the West Indies by land and sea from South America.

The economic, social and political organization of Carib society was quite simple. According to Franklin Knight[1]:

> it reflected both their military inclination and immigrant status. Villages were small and comprised members of an extended family. The leader of the village, often the head of the family, supervised the food-gathering activities, principally fishing and cultivating. He also settled internal disputes and served in a military group of the most experienced and accomplished in that activity, which led the raids on surrounding groups (Knight, 1978, p. 18).

In terms of mode of production analysis, this type of organization was

4

essentially a primitive communal mode. Production was oriented towards consumption rather than sale. Land, sea, and hunting grounds represented the principal means of production and these were held communally. Agriculture constituted the backbone of Carib economy. Fishing and hunting played only a supplementary role in their subsistence. Some writers contend that human flesh was also regarded as a staple food. However, it appears that the flesh of their enemies was eaten ritualistically rather than as a staple product.[2] Division of labour existed but it was mainly between the sexes.

Despite the numerous attempts of Europeans to bring Grenada into the orbit of the world economy, the Caribs managed to keep them at bay until 1650. With the advent of the French and English their society was completely transformed to facilitate the needs of European nascent capitalism. The natives were mercilessly decimated and, in some instances, expelled to Dominica and St Vincent by the end of the seventeenth century. It is recorded that the last group, comprising about 40 Caribs, jumped from a cliff (presently called La Morne des Sauteurs - translated as Leaper's Hill) into the sea to their death rather than succumb to the tyranny of the colonizers. The resistance from the Caribs was significant. It marked the beginning of a historical continuity of resistance which culminated into the brave resistance of Grenadian soldiers and workers against the well-equipped US invaders in October 1983.

Although Grenada officially belonged to Spain the Spanish did not make any attempt to settle the island. They were too pre-occupied with the extraction of gold and silver from the mines of the mainland territories of Mexico and Peru. The big islands in the Caribbean were used to provide cattle, cassava, corn, tobacco and other basic provisions. Strategically, the whole archipelago was important to Spain for the trade between Seville and Spanish America passed through the islands.

By the early seventeenth century, the Spanish hegemony in the Caribbean was seriously challenged by other European powers, most notably the French, English and Dutch, who were all desirous of gaining access to the potential wealth of the colonies.[3] They all shared this basic goal but they went about it in different ways. For Spain the acquisition of precious metals was the chief source of wealth. For the English and French the production of tropical agricultural staples for export was a more durable basis. In stark contrast, the Dutch were primarily interested in trade. They soon became the foremost suppliers of African slaves, plantation supplies, credit, and even technical expertise to their counterparts in the New World.

By the end of the seventeenth century, the British had successfully colonised several West Indian territories, including St Kitts, Nevis, Montserrat, Antigua, Barbados, Anguilla and Jamaica. The French were quick to follow suit. Their colonies included St Lucia, St Croix, Tobago, Cayenne (a part of Guiana), Maritinique, Guadeloupe and Saint Domingue. So intense was the quest for colonial wealth that these nations were prepared to go to war for control of the tiniest territory. The acrimonious rivalry which loomed between France and England during the seventeenth and eighteenth centuries is an instructive case in point. It was the English who established the first settlement in Grenada. This was done from as early as 1608 but this attempt was thwarted by the Caribs who were bitterly opposed to any form of colonial domination. In 1650, the French claimed ownership of the island. From 1756 to 1763, Britain and France fought the Seven Years' War during which Grenada was captured by the British. The island was subsequently ceded to Britain in 1763. In 1779, the French recaptured Grenada. The struggle for supremacy in Grenada between these two imperial nations continued until 1783, when the territory finally became a part of the British Empire.

The resistance of the Caribs to European intrusion as well as the struggle between the two great European powers attest to the tremendous value which was attached to the sugar colonies during this period. The situation contrasted sharply with the attitudes of these countries towards the West Indian region today. In the words of an eminent West Indian scholar: 'The West Indian colonies assumed an importance that appears almost incredible today, when one looks at these forgotten, neglected, forlorn dots on the map, specks of dust as de Gaulle dismissed them, the haggard and wrinkled descendants of the prima donnas and box office sensations of two hundred years ago' (Williams, 1970, p. 88).

When analyzed in the context of the profound social and economic changes which were taking place in Europe from the late sixteenth century onwards the rivalry between the colonizers can easily be appreciated. By this time capitalist market relations had invaded the rural manor which was the dominant institution under feudalism. These market relations put an end to the economic self-sufficiency of the manor and agriculture increasingly became a capitalistic venture in which the unceasing quest for profits became the overriding principle governing production.[4] A new epoch had begun. As Marx flamboyantly put it:

> The discovery of gold and silver in America, the extirpation, enslavement and entombment in mines of the indigenous population of that continent, the beginnings of the conquest and plunder of India, and the conversion of Africa into a preserve for the commercial hunting of blackskins, are all things which characterise the dawn of the era of capitalist production. These idyllic proceedings are the chief moments of primitive accumulation (cited in Munck, 1984, p. 46).

6

Brutal and cruel as this scenario may sound it was also believed to be simultaneously progressive. European capitalism would eventually transform these pre-capitalist societies in its own image. Obstacles to (capitalist) development would be cleared away and techniques, institutions and other pre-conditions for a "take-off" would be substituted and fostered. In this sense capitalism was also a 'modernising' and 'integrating' force. Any judgment as to whether Marx was right or wrong in his prediction must obviously take into consideration the time dimension he had in mind.

This marked the beginning of the present international division of labour. From the outset possessions such as Grenada were regarded as valuable adjuncts to the metropolitan powers. Above all, they could provide well-needed raw materials (especially those that could not be easily produced in the temperate climate of the north) for their emerging industries. The colonies could also function as an outlet for the manufactured products of the 'mother country'.[5] To cite the remark of an eighteenth century agronomist, Arthur Young: 'The great benefit resulting from colonies is the cultivation of staple commodities different from those of the mother country, that, instead of being obliged to purchase them off foreigners at the expense possibly of treasure, they may be had from settlements in exchange for manufactures' (cited in Sheridan, 1970, p. 10).

This passage by Young reflects the essence of mercantilism - the economic orthodoxy of the day. Central to the doctrine was the notion of a favourable balance of trade; i.e., a situation such that the amount of treasure or money payments flowing into the country exceeds the amount leaving. Thus government policies were geared towards stimulating the export of goods and services (particularly processed goods) and discouraging imports, especially if they compete with home produced goods. Monopoly privileges were given to traders to ensure that they could buy goods at the cheapest possible price and sell as dear as possible. Imports from the colonies were in effect an extension of the colonial power's exports. It was very important that the colonies did not compete with the metropole. Their consumption and production requirements were to be met solely by imports from the metropole.

If these policies were strictly applied then the wealth of the colonising power would be augmented. And there can be no doubt that the regulations were effective. It is for this reason that Sir Dalby Thomas could boast in 1690 that every Briton in the West Indies was many times more precious than those who remained in Britain:

> Each white man, woman, and child, residing in the plantations, occasions the consumption of more of our native commodities, and manufactures, than ten at home do - beef, pork, salt, fish, butter,

cheese, corn, flour, beer, cyder, bridles, coaches, beds, chairs, stools, pictures, clocks, watches, pewter, brass, copper, iron vessels and instruments, sail-cloth and cordage, of which, in their building, shipping, mills, boiling, and distilling houses, field labour and domestic uses, they consume infinite quantities (cited in Williams, 1970, p. 143).

In general, Grenada, if belatedly, took part in this process and followed the pattern of production which was set by the plantocracy in Barbados, one of the earliest and most successful English colonies. The settlers who went there in 1672 under the auspices of Sir William Courteen experimented with tobacco and cotton, grown on smallscale plantations with white indentured European labour. As the price of these staples declined they established largescale plantations for the production of sugar. By the 1640s the 'sugar revolution' was in full swing in Barbados. In Grenada the transformation came much later. Indeed, sugar did not become 'king' in the island until after 1763, the year when it became a part of the British empire.

The development of the sugar industry came to be intimately associated with slave labour in contradistinction to the wage nexus which characterised production in the metropole. This was despite the obvious limitations of the former. To cite Adam Smith: 'the work done by slaves, though it appears to cost only their maintenance, is in the end the dearest of any. A person who can acquire no property can have no other interests than to eat as much, and to labour as little as possible' (cited in Williams, 1964, p. 6).

Apart from their natural inclination to undermine (in whatever form they could) the system which oppressed them, slave labour was also inimical to the development of scientific and technological progress. There was a fundamental and irreconcilable conflict between what slave owners found to be politically expedient for their survival and what was economically desirable as far as profit augmentation was concerned. The former forced them to suppress and stultify the intellect of their labour force; keeping them ignorant, untrained, and uneducated. The latter called for polices aimed at raising productivity such as the application of scientific techniques to farming, crop rotations, and the deployment of high quality machines and agricultural implements. Moreover, unless supervision was adequate, tight, constant, and systematic (with all the implications this had for costs) there was no guarantee that slaves would carry out even the most basic of tasks. If the masters resorted to severe punishment (to encourage obedience) and poor diets (to reduce costs) they would be undermining the productivity and life-span of the very source of their wealth.

Notwithstanding these clear disadvantages slavery was regarded as a rational choice. Slaves were available in large quantities, and were relatively cheap compared to the price of free labour[6] and indentured servants. In general it was reliable so long as it was closely supervised. Since slaves were regarded as a part of the planter's capital stock they did not have formal rights. This gave their owners complete control over their destinies -an advantage which could not be procured from a free labour force. The gains sacrificed in productivity as a result of the unskilled, inefficient and unversatile nature of slave labour could at least be partially offset by the economies of scale which are associated with large-scale staple production. As one authoritative source puts it: 'the same buildings and many incidental charges are much the same for an estate that makes 50 or 60 hogsheads of sugar yearly as one that makes 100, so that little more is wanting than a greater strength of negroes and cattle, in proportion to the quantity' (Long, 1774, p. 448).

Long's remark attests to the relatively huge outlay of resources which were required to enter the business of sugar production. Apart from buildings, land, and labour, finance was needed to purchase foodstuffs, tools, animals, and to meet all expenses which were entailed in the marketing and distribution of the produce. The bulk of this capital came from the merchant class - many of whom were based in the large merchant houses of Britain. This client-debtor relationship is brilliantly analyzed by Ragatz (1928). He demonstrated quite clearly how the increasing indebtedness of the planters to the merchants contributed towards the demise of the former.

English merchants dominated the slave trade between Africa and the colonies until 1807 when it was abolished. The trade was first monopolised by the Company of Royal Adventures which was founded in 1663. In 1672 another company called the Royal African Company was established. This was subsequently replaced by a new organization termed the Company of Merchants Trading to Africa. According to Eric Williams: 'the slave trade was more than a means to an end, was also an end in itself. ... Britain was not only the foremost slave trading country in the world, she had become ... the 'honourable slave carriers' of her rivals'.[7]

The extreme openness and dependence of sugar colonies like Grenada on the rest of the world can be gauged from the fact that land was the only **indigenous** input. Since the plantations were all producing the same thing there was very little economic intercourse between them. The colonists were so eager to amass great fortunes that they devoted every inch of arable land to the production of export staples. Most of the basic food provisions were therefore imported. Towards the mid-seventeenth century an observer had this to say about the West Indies: 'Men are so intent upon planting sugar that they had rather buy food at very dear rates than produce it by labour, so infinite is the profit of sugar works after once accomplished' (cited in Williams, 1964, p. 110). This specialisation suited the plantocracy, British

9

shipping, British sugar refinery and other related industries. The tremendous growth and domination of the Grenadian economy by export agriculture can be gleaned from the following figures. In 1700 Grenada only had 3 sugar estates, 52 indigo plantations, 64 horses, and 569 cattle was recorded. By 1753 the situation changed markedly. New crops were introduced (cocoa, coffee and cotton cultivation started in 1714) and indigo production appeared to have either become relatively insignificant or went out of existence all together. By 1753 there were 83 sugar estates, 2.7 million coffee trees, 150,300 cocoa trees, 800 cotton trees, 2,298 horses and mules, 2,556 cattle, 3,278 sheep, 902 goats, and 331 hogs.[8] In 1774 the island exported 8,968 tons of sugar. This figure represented twice the amount that was exported in 1763. In 1770 the value of total exports from the island amounted to £506,709, some 90 per cent of which went to Britain and Ireland.[9] During this time this tiny colony earned the reputation of being one of Britain's most treasured possessions. Infact it was rated second after Jamaica.

What a sharp contrast to the situation of the island in 1700 and how splendid a confirmation of the remark made by Pere Labat in that same year when he visited the colony:

> The English know better than us how to profit by natural advantages. If Grenada belonged to them, it would long since have changed its aspect, and have become a rich and powerful colony, whereas, up to the present time, we have not reaped any of the benefits which ought to have been derived from it, and after so many years of possession we behold it still no better than a desert, deficient in population, void of all accommodation, without commerce, poor, and with ill-built and worse furnished hovels to represent dwelling-houses - in a word, scarcely better than it was when M. Du Parquet purchased it from the savages (cited in Gittens-Knight, 1946, p. 22).

The transformation which Grenada experienced since 1700 was also reflected in the social and demographic structure of the island (see table 1:1).

It can be easily deduced from table 1:1 that the British imported far more slaves than the French (compare the pre-1763 period with the post-1763 period). These figures reveal a tremendous disparity in the racial composition of the island. This pattern was consistent with the other sugar-producing territories in the French and British West Indies. Jamaica in 1778, for instance, had 18,420 whites and 205,261 slaves - a ratio of over 11 slaves to each white.

The rest of Grenada's population was mainly comprised of 'coloureds'. It is estimated that there were 451 coloureds in 1771. By 1787 they expanded to 1,115, rising further to 3,786 by 1829 (Williams, 1970, p. 151). The growth in the 'non-white' population was the inevitable product of the

Table 1:1
Demographic profile of Grenada for select years
in the eighteenth century

Year	Whites	Slaves	Ratio of whites to slaves
1700	251	525	1:2
1753	1,263	11,991	1:9
1763	1,225	12,000	1:10
1771	1,661	26,211	1:16
1777	1,324	35,118	1:27
1783	996	24,620	1:25

Source: E. Williams, *From Columbus to Castro*, p. 105.

plantation system; a system in which slaves provided not only free labour for their owners, but the women were also obliged to gratify their owners' sexual appetites.[10] Other social functions performed for their masters included 'brushing away flies at dinner and mosquitoes in bed' (Williams, 1970, p. 284).

What emerged over time was a 'caste-like' system with people possessing varying degrees of Caucasian blood. Each degree was jealously guarded since it had clear and direct implications for their status and privileges. The offspring of a negro woman and a white man gave rise to a mulatto, that of a mulatto and a white resulted into a quadroon, that between a quadroon and a white was termed a mustee, and that between a mustee and a white was labelled a musteefino. The distinctions did not end here. However, up to the level of musteefino the child was legally free at birth if his mother was a slave. Beyond this point manumission generally came at a later stage in the individual's life. Manumission was generally bestowed on those who provided special favours to their owners. It was therefore common for women to be freed on account of the sexual pleasures they provided. This largely explains why most freed coloureds were females.[11]

To be 'totally' black in such a society was an absolute curse. The penalty was intense, backbreaking toil, and contempt. 'Purity' in whiteness, on the other hand, generally meant dominance[12] as reflected in wealth, political power, education, and culture. This correlation between colour and class, a heritage from slavery, is one which continues to shape West Indian societies. In the contemporary period, the divide between blacks, on the one hand, and whites or 'mixed race' people, on the other, is still reflected in levels of education, speech, cultural affiliations, wealth and other indicators of class. Significantly, during the colonial era in Grenada, all non-British culture (not just African culture) was stigmatised. This was one of the reasons for the severe social and political disabilities which were meted out to the French in Grenada once the island was ceded to Britain. The Election Act of 1792 made it compulsory for candidates to the Assembly to satisfy the following criteria: white skin, being over twenty-one, male, possession of fifty acres of land, twenty-five of which must be under cultivation, or property rented in town at £400 per annum, a national born subject, and a protestant (see Epica Task Force, 1982, p. 18).

The coloured population were the buffers between the two principal antagonistic groups in the society, i.e. the whites at the top and the slaves at the base. So long as the British remained in the island and the status quo remained in existence, mobility could not transcend the rigid lines which debar the different class segments. Material circumstances may alter, the values of those at the apex of the society could be emulated, but an individual could not change his or her race. A society stratified along these lines contains the seeds of its own destruction. Its seeming stability can only be maintained by brute force and coercion. And unless vigilance of the strictest degree exists pent-up grievances and discords are likely to erupt and play themselves out in socially disruptive ways. Haiti, the world's foremost sugar producer in the late eighteenth century, provides early historical precedent of the far-reaching changes which can result from the unleashing of the revolutionary capacities of the oppressed layers of a society. The year 1791 saw the flames of revolution burst asunder when the coloured population and slave masses launched a bloody onslaught against their oppressors, under the dynamic leadership of Toussaint L'Ouverture. After 12 years of intense struggle the French were obliged to concede independence, making Haiti the first slave colony to become independent.

This successful uprising sent shock waves throughout the other slave colonies. The awakening of the slaves and coloureds shifted into high gear. Liberty, fraternity, and equality (the watchwords of the French Revolution) must either come from above or below. In 1795-96, there was a popular slave insurrection in Grenada led by the coloured planter Julien Fedon - a rebellion which resulted in severe damage to the plantations.[13] There were a whole series of other acts of major resistance in other territories such as: the revolt of the Carib population in St Vincent in 1795, the maroon rebellion in Jamaica in 1795, a slave revolt in British Guiana in 1808, a slave uprising in Barbados in 1816, another revolt in British Guiana in 1823, and the calamitous insurrection which took place in Jamaica in the Christmas holidays of 1831. In commenting on the reason for the revolts in Jamaica, the governor of the island noted '... a desire of effecting their freedom, and in some cases of possessing themselves of the property belonging to their masters - could have influenced their conduct' (cited in Williams, 1964, pp. 206-207).

Yet resistance from what was generally regarded as the 'docile', 'passive' and 'obedient' slave was not the only form of instability or threat to the plantations. Natural disasters, wars, and the polices of the metropole were just as menacing. In Grenada, for instance, the capital St George's was severely destroyed by fire on three separate occasions (in 1771, 1775 and 1792). This tragedy eventually forced the Legislature to pass an Act to prescribe the types of materials which should be used in the construction of any building in the town. Durable materials such as bricks, stones, and tiles were to replace the drab wooden buildings which predominated.

The solution to the plague of ants which destroyed many plantations in the island between 1770 and 1780 was less straightforward. An eye witness left us with the following grim report: 'Their numbers were incredible. I have seen the roads covered by them for miles together, and so crowded were they in many places that the print of the horse's feet would appear for a moment or two, until filled up by the surrounding multitude' (cited in Gittens-Knight, op. cit., p. 24). In 1780 another hurricane hit the island but this time it did not just bring disaster. The heavy rainfall which resulted completely destroyed the defiant sugar ant - a great blessing to the plantocracy. Had it not been for these natural disasters more wealth would have doubtless been generated by the island.

The two most critical blows to the plantations came in 1807 and 1838 when, first, the slave trade was abolished and, then, slavery itself. The first Act did not cause any great anxiety on the part of the Grenadian planters since the island was well endowed with slaves. The second, however, was greeted with shock and total outrage. Eric Williams has provided us with a well-documented analysis of the factors which led the British Parliament to make these critical moves. Succinctly put: 'The commercial capitalism of the eighteenth century developed the wealth of Europe by means of slavery and monopoly. But in so doing it helped create the industrial capitalism of the nineteenth century, which turned round and destroyed the power of commercial capitalism, slavery, and all its works' (Williams, 1964, p. 210).

In a word, slavery in the British West Indies had outlived its usefulness. It had no rationale in an era which called for the free and uninterrupted functioning of Adam Smith's 'invisible hand' of demand and supply. After the war of American Independence (1776-1783), bankruptcies, liquidation of merchant houses, increasing unprofitability, abandonment of estates, undercultivation of plantations were very common phenomena. In the case of Grenada, 14 estates were abandoned in 1805. The number steadily increased thereafter. By 1824, it was reported that of the 80 estates in St

Georges only 62 were engaged in production. In the same year, 22 of the 97 estates in St Andrews were deserted. Of the 342 estates in the island in 1824, as many as 86 were in bush and pasture (Brizan, 1984, p. 102).

The post-slavery period and the emergence of the peasantry

The Abolition Act of 1833 was a momentous piece of legislation but, nevertheless, it was carefully designed to preserve the status quo. The thinking of the British government is evident from the following passage written by Lord Howick in 1832:

> The greatest problem to be solved in drawing up any plan for the emancipation of the slaves in our colonies is to devise some mode of inducing them when relieved from the fear of the driver and his whip, to undergo the regular and continuous labour which is indispensable in carrying on the production of sugar ... I think that it would be greatly for the real happiness of the Negroes themselves, if the facility of acquiring land could be so far restrained as to prevent them, on the abolition of slavery, from abandoning their habits of regular industry. ... Accordingly it is to the imposition of a considerable tax upon land that I chiefly look for the means of enabling the planter to continue his business when emancipation shall have taken place (cited in Williams, 1970, pp. 328-29).

What transpired after 1833 was, on the one hand, a consistent and resolute attempt to enforce this strategy (on the part of the plantocracy and their allies in the Assembly). On the other hand, the ex-slaves were determined to resist the drudgery and rigour of plantation work which they denounced as the badge of slavery. The various clauses of the Act help us to understand the loyalty of the Colonial Authorities to the planting community and its corresponding total lack of sensitivity to the interests of the ex-slaves.

First, they found it necessary to compensate the ex-slave owners with £20 million in cash for the loss of absolute control over their slave property. In the case of Grenadian planters this figure amounted to £616,255. It did not dawn on them to offer some form of compensation - however marginal - to the ex-slaves, despite their brutal suffering and relentless toiling on the plantations for some 200 years. Any compensation to them was considered inimical to the survival of the estates during the post-emancipation era. Next, the Act made allowance for a period of 'Apprenticeship'. Again the interests of the plantocracy were uppermost in the minds of the British Crown. They could not cut them off abruptly from their traditional labour supply. A period of adjustment was deemed necessary and desirable. The former slaves were

14

compelled by law to provide unpaid labour to their previous masters for three-quarters of each working week. In effect the period turned out to be: 'a period in which masters in general had tried to squeeze the last juice out of compulsory labour before the expected ruin of freedom set in, and both masters and apprentices learned only one lesson, namely that when labour had to be bargained for, the labourers would be able to name their price' (Hall, 1959, p. 19).

Not a single provision was made to prepare this backward, unskilled, illiterate, and destitute population for genuine freedom. The basic institutions and ideas which justified slavery remained firmly intact. So did the hegemony of the traditional ruling class.

Land hunger

Ever since its incorporation into the world economy land ownership in the West Indies has taken on an unprecedented significance. For the planter class it was the chief symbol of wealth and social status. The more land he possessed the greater his social standing. The indentured servants who came to the region during the sixteenth and seventeenth centuries learned about the value of land even before they left Europe. And many were lured by promises of land acquisition, the most integral part of their contract package. For the newly freed population land ownership assumed an even more profound importance. It was equated with freedom and independence. It was this intense desire for economic independence from the plantations (symbols of slavery) which created a class of 'peasants' and 'proto-peasants'[14] almost overnight in Grenada and elsewhere in the Caribbean. Work done on the estates after 1838 was regarded as a necessary evil to the more prestigious end of land acquisition, i.e. the opportunity to be your own boss. This was recognised by no less a person than Governor Keate of Grenada: 'The planter must be well aware that every negro to whom he is paying wages has at heart a longing and determination sooner or later to possess a piece of land of his own or at all event to hire and occupy one which he can cultivate in his own way and at his own convenience and not at his employer's dictation' (cited in Brizan, op. cit., p. 135).

The peasantry and proto-peasantry expanded phenomenally despite the variety of obstacles which were placed *pari passu* in their way. Whereas under slavery planters relied principally on naked force to maintain control over their labour force their main weapon was now political authority. Vagrancy laws were passed to restrict the movements of the unenfranchised masses. A vagrant was defined simply as 'an unemployed person or any unlicensed hawker or peddler' (Epica Task Force, op. cit., p. 22). In general land was sold to them only as a matter of last resort. Wages were kept

15

abysmally low. The recruitment of large numbers of indentured servants ensured that they remained depressed.[15] In some cases, provision grounds were destroyed as well as fruit trees and anything which made for an alternative livelihood from the estates. By the same token, land belonging to the emergent peasantry and basic commodities consumed by them (imported rice, flour, salt meat and fish) were extortionately taxed. Similarly, land prices exhibited an upward trend.

The effects of these repressive measures and practices were easily countered by a series of circumstances which were largely outside the control of the planters. Colonies with low population densities and an inhospitable topography for large-scale sugar production provided excellent prospects for independent settlements. The Windward Islands, particularly Grenada, were aptly placed. The ex-slaves did not hesitate to clear the mountainous interiors and bring then under cultivation. So long as land remained idle (especially Crown lands and abandoned estates) authority was defied.

The crisis which developed in the sugar industry, especially after the imposition of the Sugar Duties Act in 1846 created further opportunities. This production crisis was not caused by labour shortage per se as planters would have us to believe. The fundamental cause stemmed from their failure to keep up with the times, especially in the crucial sphere of sugar technology. With the entry of giant latecomers on the sugar scene (most notably Cuba and Brazil) and increasing competition from European beet sugar the problem became even more acute. The sugar industry in Cuba and Brazil were distinguished from the outset by its extensive utilization of cost-saving mechanical devices, thanks to the Industrial Revolution. Steam-powered cane-rolling and juice-clarifying machines became commonplace. Yet in the British West Indian sugar factory, with the exception of British Guiana and Trinidad, steam technology and modernisation of sugar mills was the exception rather than the general rule.[16] As planters became increasingly insolvent estates became either abandoned or fell into the hands of creditors. Some of these were sub-divided and sold to small cultivators.[17] The rest was readily bought by professionals, public officers, and merchants. In some instance, a system of share-cropping known as 'metayage' was introduced or rather instituted.[18] Many used the system as a temporary expedient for acquiring land. For others, it eventually became a way of life in itself providing security in times of hardship.

The number of 'independent' producers can be inferred from the declining numbers of workers employed on estates. In 1834, the latter figure stood at 21,445. This fell to 16,835 in 1836, 10,196 in 1844, 8,349 in 1852, and 8,200 in 1871.[19] And as we would expect, land owned by the peasantry was tiny, fragmented, and of marginal quality. For instance, in 1891, 83 per cent of land-holdings in Grenada were under five acres each. This lopsided distribution continued into the twentieth century. By 1930, there was a total of 15,319 peasants in Grenada, 84 per cent of whom owned less than 2½ acres of land each.[20]

The diversification which took place in the agricultural sector after 1838 was spearheaded by the peasants. They soon discovered that multi-cropping (particularly tree crops and ground products) would minimise the risk of heavy reliance on one main product, especially in times of poor harvest. Cocoa became the 'golden bean' of the island. By 1881, it had completely eclipsed the sugar industry. According to Gittens Knight (1946), Grenada exported 5,069 bags of cocoa in 1885, containing some 900,000 to 1 million pounds (weight). And from as early as in 1856 'it was in everybody's mouth that cocoa would prove (to be) the salvation of the colony' (op. cit., p. 28). Apart from cocoa production, spices were also introduced. Extraordinary quantities of nutmegs and mace for the export market were produced. In 1889 a total of 163,520 pounds of spices, valued at £10,220, was exported. Banana production came later (i.e. in 1955).

Notwithstanding the dynamism of the ex-slaves and their numerical dominance economic and political power remained firmly entrenched in the hands of the plantocracy, merchants, professionals, and state functionaries. This concentration of power ensured the perpetual exploitation of both small producers and workers alike. The former had no control over the price of his produce. The type of relations between small and large producers may be illustrated by the way the nutmeg and sugar industries functioned before 1951. Of a total of 6,264 nutmeg producers in 1942 there were 6,070 small producers. The producer cooperative which marketed this product had a nine member board, eight of which were drawn from the large producers. Participation of the small producers was confined to growing and selling the product to the cooperative at a price beyond their influence.[21] The situation was very much the same in the Grenada sugar factory. The bulk of the cane processed by this company came from its four estates at Woodlands, Hope Vale, Bardia and Calivigny. Prices paid to suppliers reflected their status. In 1942 company estates were paid $6.03 per ton of cane, other estates received $5.40 while peasant farmers received $4.30. In 1945 the figures were $5.88, $5.72 and $4.88, respectively (see Brizan, op. cit., p. 238, currency not stated).

The lot of labourers was no better. Weak unionisation provided employers with great leverage over their subjects. Despite the labour intensiveness of the production process the wage bill bore no relationship to the cost of living.[22] As late as 1935 wages remained at the level which prevailed in 1840. For this 90 years span the labourers were paid a pitiful ten pence to one shilling per day. It was not until the 1940s that these were revised upwards, thanks to the recommendations of the Moyne Commission.[23]   Between 1940 and

17

1949 there were (all of a sudden) some seven wage increases. The statutory minimum wage reached 82 cents for males and 68 cents for females in 1950 (Brizan, op. cit., pp. 259-60).

But the fundamental issue in Grenada in 1950 was not about wage increase, regardless of its magnitude. What was required was a far-reaching and fundamental restructuring of the institutions, structures, and mechanisms which generated and perpetuated the various disabilities (e conomic, social, and political) under which the Grenadian masses continued to operate. Up to this time very little had changed in the Grenadian economy, society, and polity. And this was despite the growth and expansion of a new class of 'peasants' and 'agro-proletariats', introduction of new agricultural staples, migration of a large number of whites and the belated attempt to rationalise production techniques on the estates.

Land and other critical economic resources were still monopolised by a tiny oligarchy, comprised mainly of whites (including Portuguese) and light skinned coloured people. In Lewis' words: 'Slavery had been abolished, but the economic foundations of slavery, especially in the general picture of land ownership, had remained basically untouched' (Lewis, 1968, p. 88). The pattern of production, marketing, and consumption developed along classical colonial lines. The best resources in the island were subordinated to the production of a limited number of agricultural staples which, in turn, were narrowly concentrated in distant metropolitan markets. The bulk of Grenada's needs (including manufacturing and even foodstuffs) also continue to be imported. Closely associated with this trade structure was the perennial vulnerability of the economy to external shocks, especially price instability.[24]

Political conditions

Asymmetrical relations were also prevalent in the political arena. The constitutional arrangement which characterised the slave period remained firmly intact. This 'representative' government, as it was commonly termed, was comprised of a Governor (appointed by the Crown), an Executive Council (nominated by the Governor and appointed by the Crown), and a House of Assembly (made up of elected members). This system of government was justified by the notion that slaves were property, not free persons with rights to be observed and exercised. The change in the status of the slaves consequent on the Emancipation Act called for an appropriate constitutional amendment. But restrictive qualifications, based primarily on property ownership and other wealth-oriented criteria, ensured their exclusion.

Some of the defects of the Old Representative System as it manifested itself in Grenada in the first couple decades after Emancipation are captured in the following passage:

18

The meetings of the House of Assembly were characterised by the free use of personal invective and the subordination of public to private interest. The administration of the Government became a series of struggles to induce the Legislature to take action upon matters affecting the well-being of the colony, resulting more frequently in failure than in success, and, even when successful, the object in view was often defeated by amendments drafted upon the original scheme during a stormy passage through the House. It was evident that a sweeping change was necessary, and to this end the best efforts of all who really had the interests of the colony at heart were directed (Gittens-Knight, op. cit., p. 48).

A new constitution was adopted in 1875 with the advent of Crown Colony rule. This system of government purported to constitute a more accurate representation of the interests of the various competing classes.[25] Elections were abolished and power was concentrated in the hands of the Imperial Crown. At the local level the official policies of the Crown were carried out by his personally appointed representative, the Governor. Dissatisfaction with this system led to a partial modification of the constitution in 1925 to allow for a modicum of elective representation (five members) to the Legislative Council. But this limited electoral franchise was still based on highly restrictive criteria. Patrick Emmanuel writes:

> The fitness for the enjoyment of political rights, was gauged by whether or not individuals and groups possessed certain cultural, economic, (and ideological) qualifications. Literacy, formal education, property, a high enough income, as well as loyalty to the Crown, Empire, and British institutions constituted the core qualifications for the political emancipation of nonwhite peoples (Emmanuel, 1978, p. 36).

Thus, of a total population of over 66,302 in the island in 1924 only 2,159 were eligible to vote. Similarly, in the 'general' election of 1944 only 4,005 satisfied the criteria for voting (Smith, 1965a, p. 272). So the popular masses remained unenfranchised as late as the immediate post-war period.

Social conditions

The inequalities were also endemic in the spheres of culture and society. Grenada was a classic example of what J.S. Furnivall called the "plural society".[26] Adopting this framework M.G. Smith reached the following conclusion in his pioneering study of stratification in Grenada (undertaken between 1952 and 1953):

In Grenada, elite and folk are sharply distinguished by their behaviour, ideas, speech, associations, appearance, colour, housing, occupation, status, access to resources, and in other ways. Folk differ from elite in their use of the French Creole patois, in modes of mating, domestic organization, child-rearing, socialisation, and kinship, in their social institutions, such as maroon, jamboni, susu, "bouquet", or company dance, and in their local organization as dispersed communities. They differ also in their folklore, in their wakes, the third-night, nine-night, forty-night, and other funeral ceremonies, in their cults of shango, congo, shakerism, and the Big Drum .... They differ in technology, occupational skills and expectations, in standards of living, education, school attendance, income, type of house, dress, and so on. These modes of celebrating childbirth, baptism, and marriage are also distinctive. They place special weight on ritual, and have aspirations, beliefs, and values that contrast sharply with those of the elite (Smith, 1965a, p. 235-36).

M.G. Smith's observations are not just of cultural cleavages. They are also symptomatic of 'class' differences. Although racial discrimination was no longer legitimate the race/class divide which was a central hallmark of slave society was still strong. Thus the folk were overwhelmingly from the black strata while the elites were white and light-skinned. The dominant aspiration of the folk was to join the ranks of the elite; through the acquisition of wealth, a good education (preferably in one of the institutions of the Mother Country), and the conscious adoption of European customs and traditions. Frustration was the lot of many for they frequently encountered a 'catch-22' situation. The scholarships, awarded by Britain, were few in numbers (only two throughout the 1940s) and they normally went to people who were socially acceptable.[27] But as one commentator notes 'to be socially acceptable one had to have either fair skin, straight hair and 'good looks' or a fair amount of wealth' (Brizan, op. cit., p. 22). Education, as a route for upward mobility, was thus ruled out for the overwhelming majority of the population. Many found it easier to seize migration opportunities whenever they arose. Before 1945, the oil-fields of Trinidad, Aruba, and Venezuela provided a haven. When these outlets dried up many went further afield, especially to the United States and United Kingdom. Malnutrition, deadly diseases, overcrowding, and despicable living conditions became the lot of the vast majority.

The persistence of these conditions - conditions reminiscent of slavery - more than one hundred years after the 'Emancipation' Act was clear testimony of the incompleteness of change in the island. The economic, social, political, and institutional structures which ensured their reproduction remained firmly intact, and were not seriously challenged until Gairy's dramatic appearance on the political scene in 1950.

The plantation economy model

The economic structure which evolved from the way economies like Grenada have been incorporated into the international economy has been analyzed by the *New World Group (NWG)*[28] in terms of their *plantation background*. Founded in Georgetown, Guyana, the NWG was a loosely knit group of Caribbean intellectuals whose aim was to develop an indigenous view of the region' (Girvan and Jefferson, 1971, p. 27).

Central to the Group's analysis of the causes of underdevelopment in the Caribbean is the concept of *plantation economy*. For example, in his analysis of the structure of Caribbean economies, Brewster argued that 'although there have been some developments in mining and industry these have been achieved within the framework of an economic organization similar to that of the regional sugar plantation economy' (Brewster, 1967, p. 39). Similarly, Girvan (1971) characterised the Jamaican economy as 'a modified plantation-type economy'.

By definition, the plantation economy is a dependent economy. As we have already seen, in the case of Grenada and other Caribbean economies, it was a result of Caribbean land, African labour and European capital. The model developed by Best and Levitt (1975) illustrates that, by and large, this pattern of dependence has remained intact during the contemporary period. They identified three stages in the evolution of Caribbean plantation economy, viz, (i) Pure Plantation Economy (i.e. 1600-1838); (ii) Plantation Economy Modified (1838-1938); and (iii) Plantation Economy Further Modified (1938 onwards). This economy was developed as a hinterland of exploitation as opposed to a hinterland of settlement (such as what was established on the American mainland).

Pure plantation economy

It is the 'pure plantation' phase which represents the critical and decisive period. During this foundation era, the economy takes on characteristic modes and patterns of behaviour. It is here that Best and Levitt locate the basis of underdevelopment. Writing about this period, Best (1968) noted: 'The legacy of institutions, structures, and behaviour patterns of the plantation system are so deeply entrenched that adjustment tends to take place as an adaptation within the bounds of the established framework. By and large the economies do not experience any considerable or sustained relief from their dependence

21

on the traditional export staple' (p. 294).

This phase was characterised by the establishment of slave-based plantations for the production of export staples. Dependence on outside forces was instituted from the very outset. This was not confined to markets. Apart from land all the requirements of the plantation economy were imported. The Caribbean was relegated to the mere locus of production, albeit production of a kind which did not compete with the metropole.

Best and Levitt observed that the export-import orientation of the economy, other types of non-market dependence, for example, foreign managerial skills and capital, lack of interdependence between the production units and specialization in a limited range of unprocessed and/or semi-processed products, was replicated in phase two. The economy remained enmeshed into the imperial division of labour and continued to play a complementary and subordinate role to their metropole.

The modified plantation economy

In the first half of the nineteenth century, adjustments were forced upon the system. The period was characterised by two principal modifications: (i) the formal abolition of slavery; and (ii) the removal of the imperial preference for sugar. These developments gave rise to other adjustments most notably the emergence of a local peasantry, a new wave of indentured servitude based mainly on East Indian labour in the plantation sector.

The emancipation dispensation to the slaves was more symbolic than real; 'a condition of mind rather than a fact of life' (Lindsay, 1976, p. 51). Best and Levitt went on to demonstrate how the status quo of plantation society and economy was preserved. The ex-slaves did not have any other skill or training apart from tilling the soil. Yet there was no revolution or even reform of the ownership of resources, particularly land. Neither was there any provision for equipping them to perform 'nonplantation-type' tasks.

In this modified plantation economy phase, not only were they in conflict with the plantation sector for land but they also competed for other resources, especially agricultural equipment, credit, marketing facilities, and domestic infrastructure. But their efforts were consistently thwarted by reactionary government policies which sought to preserve the plantation sector at all costs despite its growth-inhibiting nature.[29] Consequently, the essentials of the pattern of development characteristic of the pure plantation economy phase continued unabated, and genuine economic transformation remained an illusion.

The further modified plantation economy

The period since 1938 witnessed other modifications in the plantation economy but these were merely in form rather than content. One of the most outstanding modifications was the introduction of other types of activities in the economy. This degree of diversification in the hinterland was generated by an unprecedented dependence on foreign capital, technology, and managerial skills. The multinational corporations, particularly American corporations after World War II, were the principal agencies of this metropolitan investment. Apart from the traditional plantation sector this capital penetrated mining, light assembly-type manufactures, banking and tourism, thus creating the so-called 'denationalization of the commanding heights of the economy'.

During this period the economy became even more firmly incorporated into the orbit of world capitalist development. Many of the old mercantilist features characteristic of the pure plantation economy phase are, again, reproduced. These include the extreme openness of the economy, excessive dependence on the metropole(s), disarticulation of the national economy, sharp class divisions and the exploitation of both labourers and small cultivators. For practical purposes this may be termed the era of the 'new mercantilism'. Thus Levitt penned: 'In the new mercantilism, as in the old, the corporation based in the metropole directly exercises the entrepreneurial function and collects a "venture profit" from its investment. It organises the collection or extraction of the raw material staple required in the metropolis and supplies the hinterland with manufactured goods, whether produced at home or "on site" in the host country' (Levitt, 1970, p. 471). In this critical sense the multinational corporations are no different from the joint-stock trading companies of the Pure Plantation era. Both serve just as effectively in plundering resources from the region, thereby deepening the process of underdevelopment and limiting the possibilities of transformation.

Using this critical historical/institutional/structural method Best and Levitt were able to shed much light on the incompleteness of change in Caribbean plantation economy. They located the region's underdevelopment and excessive dependence firmly in the nature of the plantation system and, in more recent times, to the domination of the region by multinational corporations. They concluded that at best multinational corporations could produce economic growth, but not genuine economic transformation.

The model pioneered by Best and Levitt received further elaboration from a number of other New World scholars; most notably Thomas (1965), McIntyre (1971), Girvan (1971, 1973) and Beckford (1972). Beckford's contribution deserves special mention. In the preface to his celebrated work *Persistent Poverty: Underdevelopment in Plantation Economies of the Third World*, Beckford made it clear that: 'This is an 'ideas' book. What we need most are studies pregnant with ideas, not studies full of sterile detail' (Beckford, 1972, pvii). In at least two important respects Beckford has helped to sharpen and enrich this body of theory. Firstly, he has a broader and more comprehensive definition of the plantation system than Best and Levitt. Secondly, he offers a more detailed treatment of the manifold 'underdevelopment biases' which he deemed to be characteristic of plantation agriculture, and appears to be more sensitive to the social and political requirements for change in plantation economies.

Beckford writes: 'Plantation Economy refers to those countries of the world where the internal and external dimensions of the plantation system dominate the country's economic, social and political structure and its relations with the rest of the world' (ibid., p. 14). Besides, a plantation economy can be identified by considerations such as the plantation's share of national economic aggregates (total output, employment, capital, land area, etc.); its contribution to income, employment, government revenues and the country's foreign exchange earnings; evidence of the effects of the plantation on social and political structure; and its effect effect on the minds and outlook of the local population. So all-pervading was the influence of the plantation that it conditioned, and still does, the behaviour of even the non-plantation type units within the system.

Beckford advanced the thesis that underdevelopment in plantation economies and development in the metropole are aspects of the same process. This is because: 'The emergence of the vertically integrated corporate plantation enterprise has really served to preserve the character of the slave plantation system. The three characteristics of that earlier institutional environment - appendage in overseas economy, total economic institution, and incalculability - have been preserved and strengthened in the period since Emancipation' (ibid., p. 48).

The legacies from the past (as reflected in the nature of economic, social, and political organizations prevailing in these societies) create several biases toward a continuous state of underdevelopment. These include: (i) inherent social instability which serves to restrict investment; (ii) the rigid pattern of social stratification which limits upward mobility; (iii) the concentration of social, economic and political power among a tiny minority which prevents the emergence of a highly motivated population; and (iv) racial discrimination which inhibits the fullest use of the society's human resources.

Yet the catalogue of indictment does not end here for the 'underdevelopment biases' resulting from sociological factors are even more pernicious. Among the sociological legacies analyzed by Beckford are the destruction of the family as an institution (hence the entire social fabric); the ethos of dependence and patronage engendered by the system (hence depriving people of dignity, security, and self-respect); and the undermining of the material, social, and spiritual advance of the majority of the population. In these circumstances, Beckford contends '... we could hardly expect to find a highly motivated population displaying the kinds of characteristics that development demands. The energies of most people are spent in trying to beat the system in one way or another' (ibid., p. 206).

Interestingly, Beckford attributes the limited development which some of these plantation economies experienced in the post-emancipation era to the growth and dynamism of the peasant sector. According to him this sector contains the real dynamic for generating development in plantation societies. This, indeed, was a major theoretical innovation. His case for unleashing the creative energies of the peasants is based essentially on the market orientation of both groups of producers. The peasant sector is believed to gear their production primarily towards the domestic market. Consequently the 'multiplier effect' of increased production is realised internally, thereby stimulating the local economy. The plantation sector, on the other hand, contributes directly to growth and development elsewhere, given their overwhelming export-orientation. This yields the conclusion that the development of the peasantry and (by extension) the development of the region is constrained, frustrated, and undermined by the plantation sector by virtue of their domination of land and other resources in the plantation economy.

This explanation of Caribbean underdevelopment was a far cry from modernization theories which explain underdevelopment in terms of 'natural' variables; i.e., factors such as size, cultural traditions, the nature of institutions and other inherent characteristics of these societies.[30] In the context of the Caribbean, the contribution of Lewis and Demas can be subsumed under this school of thought. Thus Lewis (1950, 1954) explains Caribbean underdevelopment largely in terms of capital shortage and other constraints emanating from small size (such as limited resource configuration, limited market size, lack of a dynamic and well-motivated entrepreneurial class, problems of economies of scale, etc). This pessimistic and somewhat 'deterministic' view of 'small' Caribbean-type states is even more pronounced in the work of Demas (1965). For example, Demas advanced the thesis that: 'the question of size is very relevant to the character of, if not to the possibility of achieving structural transformation' (and that) 'fully self-sustaining growth is possible only in a very large - in terms of both area and population - continental type economy' (Demas, 1975, p. 35). The strategy of 'industrialisation by invitation' which resulted from the Lewis/Demas thesis is discussed in chapter two below.

The challenge to the colonial economy and society

The first attack on the colonial economy and society was launched by an urban, educated, light-skinned middle-class politician, T.A. Marryshow. Along with his counterpart, C.F.P. Renwick, he was instrumental in founding a newspaper, *The West Indian*, which was to become his principal mouthpiece. His anti-colonial outlook was reflected in the popular slogan of the newspaper 'The West Indies must be West Indian'. Marryshow also played a major role in establishing the Representative Government Association in 1917 - an organization which campaigned vociferously for the abolition of the system of Crown Colony rule. The Association won a modicum of success when its demands were partially met in 1925 with the advent of a minority elected representation (i.e., five elected members in a sixteen-member Council).

Had it not been for Marryshow's ambivalence as a middle class politician and his deep loyalty to Britain and respect for British norms and values, it is probable that further advance could have been attained - not just political, but also economic, social and cultural advance. As the Epica Task Force put it, Marryshow (like other middle class politicians) 'wanted a liberalised expanded franchise to enlarge their constituencies, but continued to think of 'representative government' as a system in which the middle class would represent the poor'.[31] Indeed, this was an era in which politicians throughout the region were using trade unionism as a vehicle for social change. Bustamante in Jamaica, Bradshaw in St Kitts, Adams in Barbados, and Butler in Trinidad all became powerful political leaders through this route. Marryshow could also have taken this route since trade unions were legitimised in Grenada from as early as 1933. But this seemed to have conflicted with his ideological outlook - an outlook which rarely differed from the establishment. Gordon Lewis, the eminent West Indian political scientist, sums him up in these telling terms: 'Marryshow was, at the most, a West Indian Fabian, a Royalist-Loyalist who could never bring himself to fight the colonial power except on its own polite terms. His vanity, his enjoyment of Buckingham Palace garden parties and parliamentary receptions at Westminster, and his comic pursuit of royal personages all over, made it impossible for him to engage the fight in any other terms' (Lewis, 1985, p. 12).

This task was left for Eric Gairy who became the chief anti-colonial hero in Grenada during the late 1940s and the 1950s. There were two important vacuums to fill. On the one hand, there was a vacuum in the trade union movement. By 1946, Grenada had two unions, the General Worker's Union and the Grenada Worker's Union. These unions were concentrated in the urban areas. The rural areas continued to remain unrepresented and unorganised. Furthermore, these unions did not function as genuinely working class organizations. As Brizan puts it:

> They (i.e. the unions) worked within the existing colonial framework and were thus prepared to compromise with the employers of labour. In addition, the members of their executives were invariably colonial-minded Grenadians who had developed a great reverence for class, colour, and status. By 1950, these unions came to be viewed as almost synonymous with the employers of labour in attitudes, values, and beliefs, even by the very workers they represented. (Brizan, 1979, p. 30).

On the other hand, there was also a vacuum to be filled in the sphere of politics. Gairy took advantage of this opportunity and soon became the leader of a mass party. Unlike Marryshow, he had certain qualities which made him particularly suitable for the job. He was black, of peasant background, and intensely religious - a typical member of the 'folk' to use M.G. Smith's term. He did not have to imagine the meaning of poverty, oppression or social ostracism: he was a direct victim of these circumstances. At the age of 19, instead of heading for some university abroad like many of his privileged counterparts, he was obliged to leave his homeland in search of work. First he worked at an American military base in Trinidad, then in an oil refinery in Aruba. He returned from Aruba in December of 1949 at a time when the lot of the peasants and working class in Grenada was probably at its worse. This class was desperate for a leader. In the words of D. Sinclair Dabreo:

> Gairy's appearance on the scene was like a Messiah, one who came at a particular time to save his people from oppression and to open a new era of hope. An era when for the first time the 'crowd' was about to enter the political stage. No longer did the people feel themselves to be the audience, the lookers-on, they considered themselves the actors, the participants in the play, which was written, produced and directed by the 'hero' himself - Eric Gairy (Dabreo, 1979, p. 29).

By July of 1950, Gairy founded the Grenada Manual and Mental Worker's

Union (GMMWU). He did not hesitate to demand higher wages and better working conditions for the workers and peasants. In February of 1951, he proceeded to lead the biggest demonstration which the island has ever witnessed. The strike lasted for four weeks and involved all agricultural and road workers throughout Grenada. His arrest in the process raised his popularity even further. His followers prolonged the upheaval as a mark of their acclaim for their 'messiah' and brought the island to a state which not even the colonial authorities and their forces could reckon with. In the end they were obliged to release Gairy, grant his request, and then appealed to him to put an end to the violence. This he did in his characteristically personal and patronising style. The full text is worthy of quotation since from now on this would be the central hallmark of his brand of politics:

> I feel obligated morally and spiritually to do something to alleviate, to stop, and when I say stop, I mean stop, the burning of buildings and fields, interfering with people who are breaking your strikes (leave them alone), stop taking away things from the estates that are not belonging to you, particularly cocoa and nutmeg, I want you to stop, and you must stop now, every act of violence and intimidation ... I told His Excellency the Governor that I have gained your respect and your implicit confidence and you will obey me without fail. Now don't let me down. I, Eric Matthew Gairy, am now making this serious appeal to you to start leading your normal peaceful life. Take my example and be a respectful decent citizen as I say, starting now. Let me make this point, however, everyone knows that I am a serious young man and when I say "no" I mean "no", and when I say "yes" I mean "yes". Now listen to this: I am now in search for gangsters and hooligans, I ask everyone of my people to help me, and if anyone is found setting fire to any place, breaking down or robbing or in any way interfering with people who are working, there will be nothing to save you, because the law will deal with you most severely, and "Uncle Gairy" will turn you down completely. So join me now in saying no more violence. Come on now, together "no more violence", "no more violence", "no more violence". Thank you' (cited in Jacobs and Jacobs, 1980, pp. 57-58).

Another general strike ensued in 1952. These events were parallel to the wave of revolutionary outbursts which swept throughout the region in the 1930s.[32] The oppressed in Grenada were calling for a change of the unjust colonial status quo, just as their counterparts in the other West Indian territories did in the 1930s. That their revolutionary entry on to the historical stage was delayed was largely due to the system of paternalistic and semi-feudal relationships which were established between the estate owners and their dependents soon after 1838 (see Smith, 1965b; Rottenberg, 1953). The 'privileges' of these 'worker-tenants' included free rent for dwellings on the estates, concessionary rates for small plots of land, first claim on any job the proprietors had going, and easy access to any unmarketed crops and fruits. This arrangement allowed the workers a modicum of security - notwithstanding low wages. For the estate owners it provided a reliable supply of labour, especially during crop time.

The debilitating effects of the Great Depression of the 1930s on the island spurred the plantocracy to substitute full-fledged capitalist relations for paternalistic relations. As the Moyne Commission advised in 1938: 'Faced with increasing competition and low prices for primary products, the agricultural community is faced with disaster unless estates are managed on modern and scientific lines - not only must every acre be made to produce its maximum, but the land and its appurtenances must be properly conserved and every superfluous overhead charge cut out' (Mandle, 1985a, p. 10).

The progressive dismantling of the traditional relationships now led to uncertainty, mutual distrust, and, eventually, to open revolt - as witnessed by the 1951 disturbance. This successful labour revolt signalled the dawn of a new era. Gone were the days when the downtrodden masses would allow themselves to be overawed and overwhelmed by the establishment, even in times of extreme oppression. Their leader, Gairy, was the perfect epitome of this qualitative leap in consciousness and defiance. Power for the people became the touchstone of his demands. Thus after forming the GMMWU he established a parallel political party the Grenada People's Party, which subsequently became known as the Grenada United Labour Party (GULP). Further constitutional change in 1951, with the introduction of Universal Adult Suffrage, provided another important milestone in the island's political economy. The poorest Grenadian could now vote on the principle of 'one person one vote' - a fundamental departure form the previous elitist and discriminatory franchise.

In less than two years, Gairy had become the leader of the two largest organizations in Grenada. He was undoubtedly the most influential man in the island in terms of the number of followers he commanded and the extraordinary reverence they held for him. The result of the 1951 election was another clear sign of his popularity. His newly organised party won a resounding victory - 66 per cent of the total number of votes casted and six of the eight Legislative Council seats. Gairy and his party were to become the nucleus of subsequent developments in Grenada until the collapse of his government in 1979. His compromising course with the Colonial Authorities in 1951 (i.e. to end the strike), however, was ominous as premonition of what was to come. From being a champion of the cause of the downtrodden poor he was to become their chief oppressor.

Notes

1. Knight (1978) provides a comprehensive discussion of other aspects of Carib economy, society and polity.

2. See Devas (1964), p. 23; and Bullbrook (1959), especially p. 15. Bullbrook writes: 'That he was a cannibal has to be admitted but he did not eat human flesh because he preferred it. It is even possible that he did not actually like it. He ate no one save a brave enemy, and he ate him entirely for the purpose of gathering to himself that enemy's bravery' (p. 15).

3. A.P. Newton describes this intense drive graphically: 'After 1625 swarms of English and French colonists poured like flies upon the rotting carcass of Spain's empire in the Caribbean, and within that year the West Indian scene was changed for ever' (cited in Sheridan, 1970, p. 11).

4. This quest for wealth must be seen against the economic and social recession which hit Europe in the seventeenth century. This point is developed in Hobsbawm (1954).

5. See Williams (1970), especially pp. 140-155, for a lucid discussion of the economic significance of colonies. Note that during these **formative** years of West Indian economies everything was looked at from the standpoint of the needs of the metropole. The colonies were not expected to have divergent objectives. Thus questions such as the effects of mercantile policies on the development of manufacturing industries in the colonies were ignored.

6. Since such a supply was not available locally it would have to be imported, presumably from Europe. But Europe suffered from a limited expansion in population during the sixteenth century. It was therefore difficult to attract Europeans in large enough numbers at competitive wage rates. Note, the decision to resort to slave labour was governed primarily by economic factors rather than racism. Eric Williams develops this point quite well in his opening chapter of *Capitalism and Slavery*. As he puts it: 'Slavery was not born of racism: rather, racism was the consequence of slavery' (p. 7).

7. See Williams (1964), p. 34. The profitability of this trade is also comprehensively documented in Williams (1970).

8. See E. Gittens-Knight (1946), p. 22. Gittens-Knight also notes that an unknown quantity of high quality tobacco was grown which, at around the first two decades, commanded two and three times the price fetched by growers in other islands (p. 23).

9. A lucid discussion of the value of this trade to Britain is given in Sheridan, 1975. See, especially, p. 95.

10. See Williams (1970), p. 151; and Green (1976), p. 12 for further details.

11. A European couple who spent four years in Tobago remarked that during all this time his wife had managed to come across only one solitary white woman. European women who resided in the West Indies were believed to be deficient in social grace and skills. This point is elaborated in Green (1976), especially p. 11.

12. The exception to the race/class 'rule' was the status of the poor white - many of whom were transported to the colonies as indentured servants. This did not mean they were on the same level with the servile blacks or the coloured population. They were simply on the lowest rung of the white segment of the population.

13. Today Grenadians commonly regard Julien Fedon as their first revolutionary. To the People's Revolutionary Government, he was what Jose Marti and Simon Bolivar were to the Cuban revolution. It must be stated, however, that - unlike Marti and Bolivar - Fedon did not set out to topple colonialism in any fundamental way. His revolt began as an attempt to re-assert French control over the island. The revolt was later joined by a substantial proportion of the slave population who used the opportunity to destroy plantations and kill as many of their owners as they could. Fedon eventually succeeded in gaining control over most of the island for some 15 months, before the British successfully reclaimed the island in June 1796. Although most of the rebels were either killed or deported, it is believed that Fedon was never captured. One hypothesis is that he drowned as he tried to escape to neighbouring Trinidad. See Schoenhals and Melanson, 1985, especially p. 5 for further discussion of this point.

14. Brizan (1979) uses the term 'proto-peasantry' to capture the fact that many of the newly-emancipated were not peasants in the strict sense. They had a foot in both the labour market and own-account

31

production. Many were also engaged in paternalistic arrangements with estate owners. This is discussed in chapter two below. See, also, Frucht (1967). For Frucht the concept of 'wage-proletariats' was the most appropriate category for describing and analyzing the newly-emancipated.

15. Between 1836 and 1885 over 10,000 immigrants were brought to Grenada alone. These were recruited from Africa, Malta, India, and Portugal (Brizan, 1984, p. 183).

16. See Williams (1970), p. 369. Of a total of 79 estates in Grenada in 1876, there were 6 ploughs and 7 steam-engines (Brizan, 1984, p. 139).

17. It has been reported that purchases of 1-5 acres at an average of £10 per acre were quite common in one district in Grenada (Mathieson, 1932, p. 86).

18. See Brizan (1984), especially p. 233, for an exposition on the terms and conditions of *metayage*. Note by 1940, estates had allotted 15,078 acres to 12,937 persons to work on this share-rental arrangement, since estate owners were not able to provide full-time employment for all their workers for a five-day working week. In fact, only 1,549 worked for the full week of the 5,036 who were employed on states in 1940. Around this time approximately 70 per cent of the peasants participated in this system of paternalism (Brizan, 1984, p. 256).

19. A small producer is here defined as one operating on 10 acres or less. See Brizan (1984), chapter 16, for further information on the structure and operation of the producer cooperative, Grenada Cooperative Nutmeg Association (GCNA).

20. Sec Brizan (1984) for further details (especially p. 238).

21. See Brizan (1984) pp. 235-239 for information on the cost of living, particularly the price of basic food-stuff.

22. The Commission headed by Lord Moyne was sent to investigate the causes of the violent demonstrations which shook virtually the whole West Indies in the 1930s. The Report and recommendations of the Commission constituted a powerful indictment against the plantocracy. The conditions they reported were so appalling that for

the sake of prudency the full report was withheld until after the War. For further details, see West India Royal Commission (1940).

23. The 1946 census recorded the following population distribution: 630 whited (0.9 per cent of the total population), 3,500 Indian (4.8 per cent), 15,000 coloured (20.9 per cent), and 52,800 negroes (73.4 per cent). See Smith (1965a), p. 95.

24. See E. Gittens-Knight (1946) for some quantitative insights into this phenomenon for the first half of the twentieth century.

25. Although the principle of Crown Colony rule is theoretically non-partisan and was intended to protect the unenfranchised workers and peasants against the encroachments of the monied class, the evidence suggests that (in practice) it failed to achieve much of the stated goals. Its policies were overwhelmingly biased toward the propertied class. This was admitted by no less an authority than the West Indian Royal Commission (see *Report of the West India Royal Commission*, 1939-1940).

26. The term was used by Furnivall to characterise colonial societies of the Far East, with special reference to the Indonesian and Burman experience. Of the Plural Society Furnivall writes 'It is in the strictest sense a medley, for they mix but do not combine. Each group holds by its own religion, its own culture and language, its own ideas and ways. As individuals they meet, but only in the market place, in buying and selling. There is a plural society, with different sections of the community living side by side, but separately, within the same political unit. Even in the economic spheres, there is a division of labour along racial lines. ... The plural society is in fact held together only by pressure exerted from outside by the colonial power, it has no common will' (quoted in Smith, 1965b, pp. 1-2).

27. See chapter four of Oxaal (1982) for an insightful discussion of the 'scholarship boy' phenomenon. The 'scholarship boys' typically studied medicine and law. Many of them remained in Great Britain.

28. The New World Group was formed in Guyana in 1962 but later shifted to the Mona campus of the University of the West Indies. Many of the articles produced by the Group can be found in Girvan and Jefferson (1971).

29. As one analyst put it 'though people might now be free - the land remained in bondage' (Tinker, 1974, p. 2).

30. These views are exemplified in the work of Rostow (1960).

31. See Epica Task Force (1982), p. 29. See, also, Emmanuel (1978), especially chapter two.

32. See Lewis (1968) and Post (1978) for a detailed treatment of the general revolt which hit the region in the 1930s.

2 The Grenadian economy on the eve of the revolution

On the eve of the March 1979 revolution, Grenada was an agrarian appendage of the international economy - fragile, dependent, and vulnerable to the prevailing economic conditions in metropolitan economies. Of course, this is not to deny the modicum of diversification the economy experienced during the 1960s and 1970s with the advent and growth of tourism, banking, insurance, commerce, construction, and light manufacturing. But the economic contributions of these sectors lagged considerably behind the agricultural sector. This chapter discusses the phenomenon of Gairyism, the management of the Grenadian economy under Gairy, and the emergence of the Grenada revolution.

Gairyism and the Grenadian political system

Very few leaders in the history of the West Indies have had a more pervasive impact on their society than Gairy. And none have provided more tangible and incontrovertible evidence of the assertion made by one observer that 'West Indian leaders are carbon copies of the European slave master' (Lowenthal, 1972, p. 253). This man and his party dominated Grenadian politics from the advent of Adult Suffrage in 1951 until his demise in 1979. Of the eight general elections held during this period to elect candidates to the Legislative Council and later the House of Representatives the GULP lost only two (1954 and 1962), thanks to the Westminster System of 'first past the post' and a series of fraudulent electoral tactics, especially during the latter years. The GULP developed as an extension of Gairy's GMMWU, as a party to articulate and defend the interests of the working class. In the early days the party relied mainly on the dues from the union to finance much of its electoral activities. The intimate link between both organizations was

loosened in the last years of the regime but was never completely severed.[1]
Gairy never made any serious attempt to solicit the support of the urban-based workers. They remained unrepresented throughout much of the 1950s. But by 1960 this omission was absorbed by the three St George's-based unions, the Seamen and Waterfront Workers Union (SWWU), the Commercial and Industrial Workers Union (CIWU), and the Technical and Allied Workers Union (TAWU). Although they were in the minority numerically this failure to mobilise them was to prove critical in the years when opposition began to mount against his administration.

The other contending party was the Grenada National Party, (GNP) first established in 1953 under the middle class leadership of Dr John Watts. The leadership subsequently fell into the hands of another middle class politician, Herbert Blaize, a lawyer from Carriacou. The thinking of those who formed and led this party was reminiscent of the colonial authorities. Both shared the conviction that politics and trade unionism were separate and distinct activities. The party thus made no pretensions to appeal to the particular interests of workers and peasants despite their numerical dominance. Instead it projected itself as a multi-class organization. With this posture it naturally attracted the support of the middle and upper classes from the very outset, particularly the urban bourgeoisie and landed gentry.[2]

The party subsequently never lost its image and reputation as the party of the well-to-do (an explanation for its frequent misfortunes at the polls). In contesting the 1972 elections it tried to remedy this by making an explicit and direct appeal to the lower segments of Grenadian society, but its promise of political and economic power to the people fell on deaf ears. Gairy thus emerged from that election as the first Grenadian leader to savour power in an independent nation state. Curiously enough, memories of his early gains for the Grenadian working class (including their political awakening) were never obliterated, especially among women and the older members of the population.

By 1972 the traditional differences (real and imaged) which existed between the two parties had evaporated. Their power base, social composition, economic policies, political philosophy and practices were now practically indistinguishable.[3] They were carefully groomed by Britain to accept the 'virtues' of the capitalist system and all the attendant structures and institutions which were implanted during the colonial era. So complete was the socialization process that at no time did any of these parties consider the question of transforming these legacies. They were chiefly content with pursuing limited reformist goals within the inherited framework. On more than one occasion Gairy openly disclosed the true orientation of his party. In 1967 he revealed to the propertied elite (his previous enemies): 'At no time do we contemplate the taking of properties from individuals with the hope to nationalise those properties. We feel that our taxation system is so geared to allow individuals to establish their individual enterprise. We are supporting employers, we are supporting industrialists to the fullest' (cited in Jacobs and Jacobs, 1980, p. 66).

Those who doubted the sincerity of his proclamation were further reassured by his deeds. Not only did he become a member of the Chamber of Commerce and a director of several businesses, but he also became the proprietor of a number of private enterprises; including several hotels and restaurants, a night club, and a beauty parlour. Such moves finalised his repudiation of the working class, notwithstanding the rhetoric which continued to fill the pages of election manifestos.[4]

Another central hallmark of the Grenadian political system was the importance assigned to clientelism.[5] Political education, development of ideological consciousness, the virtues of active and direct participation of the masses into the country's affairs, were never articulated. Under these circumstances it was natural that most Grenadians came to regard politics as the art of dispensing patronage. The leaders were the dispensers (patrons) and their supporters were the seekers (clients). The patronage typically took the form of job appointments, promotions, tax concessions, gifts of money, land, contracts, monopoly privileges, and invitations to government functions. As the class character of the two parties converged many Grenadians were prepared to oscillate between them, depending on their subjective evaluation of any one party's ability to deliver largesse. This helps to explain why Gairy was able to successfully penetrate the traditional power base of the GNP in the 1972 elections. In that year GULP won all four seats in St George's.

The entire history of GULP is replete with examples of how Gairy managed to sustain himself in power through a well-established and very extensive system of patronage, aided and abetted by corrupt practices and repression. His personal and arbitrary approach to politics is captured in the following passage from the seminal work of Singham (1968): 'He had developed neither a coherent policy nor a group of leaders around him, there was no "inner circle" in the party. Any type of inner circle that did exist was heavily dependent on Gairy's personal support in maintaining their electoral strength .... Loyalty at the constituency level was to him, not to the constituency candidate or member' (p. 174).

The 'Hero' was addressed by his followers, 'the crowd', as 'Uncle Gairy'. They in turn were termed 'my people'. Having first hand knowledge and experience of their deep attachment to christianity (and matters spiritual) Gairy made sure not to forget to add a religious dimension to his meetings and rallies. Hymn singing, praying, bible reading, promises to legitimise witchcraft were all used as devices to retain their loyalty. Politicising his followers was unnecessary from his point of view. In fact, once he consolidated his personal power and became a member of the propertied class it could even prove dangerous.

The reputation of his government first received official scrutiny in 1962 when he held the posts of Chief Minister and Minister of Finance under the Ministerial Constitution. The Commissioners, who were appointed by the Administrator to carry out an investigation into the scandal known in local parlance as 'Squandermania', found overwhelming evidence of unscrupulous conduct on the part of Gairy.[6] These included the contravention of the laws and regulations governing public finance in Grenada and the victimization of civil servants who did not condone his corrupt practices. Some of these financial irregularities were designed to benefit Gairy directly while some were apparently intended to either maintain or attract political loyalty to him and his party. According to the Jacobs brothers Gairy's real intention was to create a new capitalist class which could successfully compete with the old elite and ultimately displace them (Jacobs and Jacobs, p. 63). Significantly, many of those who triggered off the commission's enquiry and gave evidence against him belonged to the traditional elite - his arch enemies.

The gravity of such improprieties led to the termination of his government from office and the suspension of the constitution, with the Administrator taking over his duties until the next election. In the wake of 'Sqandermania' Gairy lost the September 1962 election. Blaize's party won six seats while GULP won four. Of the 21,107 unspoilt votes which were cast, the GNP polled 54 per cent while the GULP polled 46 per cent. These results are significant. They show that a considerable proportion of the electorate must have been convinced by Gairy's counter argument that the 'Squandermania' charges were prompted out of envy and jealousy. Bluntly put, his opponents did not want to see a black man of lower class origins indulging in the type of life-style which had come to be associated with white and light-skinned people.[7] Plausible as this 'class' argument is at one level, it is highly probable that the 'Squandermania' charges were well-founded. For Gairy had earlier demonstrated a highly dubious history with regard to financial matters (Smith, 1988, especially chapter two).

After an intense campaign Gairy's party was back in power in 1967. Predictably, the GNP's exploration of Unitary Statehood with Trinidad and Tobago met stiff opposition from various groups within what was then a petroleum-rich state. This bitter failure by the GNP was skilfully manipulated by Gairy to his party's advantage. Besides, after putting Blaize in power for two terms (1957-1961 and 1962-1967) Grenadian workers and peasants had no economic or social benefits to show for their support.

From 1967 to 1979: mounting corruption and repression

Gairy's next 12 years in office were to prove critical to the subsequent political history of the island. During this period the worst features of the phenomenon, 'Gairyism', came to the fore. This was to manifest itself in abject poverty for the overwhelming majority of the population, arbitrariness in government, various forms of corruption (especially with respect to the use of public funds), mounting repression, sexual exploitation of all categories of women (including the wives of the elites), and buffoonery at home and abroad. Some of these dimensions of 'Gairyism' were operative in the pre-1967 period but, apart from the misuse and misappropriation of public funds as epitomised in the *'Squandermania'* issue, the situation did not warrant any cause for public alarm. Indeed, up to the time of *'Squandermania'*, Gairy could still be regarded as an advocate of the interests of the oppressed layers of the society. But after the suspension of the constitution in 1961 and GULP's defeat at the polls in 1962 he underwent a profound transformation. According to observers in Grenada who know him personally this transformation was motivated in part by the personal misery he suffered whilst he was out of power between 1962 and 1967.[8] During this time Gairy sustained himself mainly by borrowing and hand-outs from friends. It is commonly said in Grenada that he vowed that he would never allow himself to fall into such penury should he become leader of the country again. More ominous, he also vowed that he would maintain the command of government by any means.

To Gairy, it seems as if this new stance necessarily meant the subordination of the rights and interests of the peasants and working class to those of the property-owning class. It also seems to have meant a firmer commitment to the capitalist ethic and a further opening of the economy to external domination. The thinking behind his economic policies were largely influenced by the work of W. Arthur Lewis. On account of Lewis' impact on development policy in the region during the post-1945 period, it is worth summarising his approach to economic development, before moving on to examine the performance of the Grenadian economy during Gairy's tenure in office.

A dependent model of development: Arthur Lewis as prophet and guide

The need to devise policies and strategies for engineering economic development in Grenada and its other colonies ran counter to the requirements of the British economy. As long as they were in direct control of the administration of the colony Britain would therefore ensure that the division of labour imposed during the era of open slavery remained intact.

The official view was that the size, resource configuration of these territories, coupled with the racial and cultural features of their inhabitants, militated inexorably against their development.[9] Invoking the notion of comparative advantage, it was further argued that the destiny of the Caribbean lies in the deepening of their traditional specialisation in the production of agricultural staples. Industrialisation, diversification of economic activities, and structural transformation in the wider sense, were thus ruled out. These views were clearly articulated in the report produced for the Jamaican colonial government in 1945. The chief author of the document, F. Benham, was the chief economic adviser to the comptroller for the West Indies. Its contents set in motion a vigorous debate between Dr Benham and Professor Lewis, a distinguished West Indian economist from St Lucia, over the scope and prospects for industrialisation in the British West Indies. Lewis' challenge was successful.

His views eventually became orthodoxy for the region as a whole. His strategy, derisively dubbed 'Industrialization by Invitation', was pursued with great enthusiasm by various West Indian governments throughout the 1950s and 1960s.[10] The strategy was heavily influenced by the Puerto Rican experience:

> A visit to the British West Indian islands at the present moment is a depressing experience. Everyone seems to be waiting for something to happen, but the traveller is never quite able to discover what it is that they are waiting for. Some key is needed to open the door behind which the dynamic energies of the West Indian people are at present confined. The key has obviously been found in Puerto Rico, where the drive and enthusiasm of a people hitherto as lethargic as the British West Indians, warms the heart, and inspires confidence in the future. The British West Indians can solve their problems if they set to them with a will. But first they must find the secret that will put hope, initiative, direction, and an unconquerable will into the management of their affairs. And this is the hardest task (Lewis, 1950, p. 53).

The secret was thought to lie in the establishment of an Industrial Development Company (IDC), with the critically important tasks of supporting, attracting, and encouraging private capital to the maximum extent possible. The pioneers of the new manufacturing industries would have to be foreign capitalists since the local capitalist class was believed to be lacking in experience and knowledge in this area. In Lewis' words: '... the local capitalists know very little about industry. They are specialists in agriculture and in commerce. They think in terms of import and export rather than of production. Some would even be hostile to domestic manufacture, which they see as a threat to their wholesale import business' (ibid., p. 40).

Foreign capital should be induced by providing a host of incentives including tax holidays, duty rebates on imports, subsidised industrial sites (provided with adequate and reliable utilities - water supplies, electricity, telecommunications services, etc.), accelerated depreciation allowances, subsidies, low wages and an inter-sectoral trade favourable to the industrial sector: 'The new arrival should feel free to cast on to the shoulders of the Corporation any difficulty that crops up. All this costs money, but it pays a wonderful dividend. For, if the new arrival writes home to say that all is well, it will not be long before others come after him' (ibid., p. 52).

The anticipated dividends to the host economy, according to Lewis, would include much needed capital, technology, organization, market connections, job creation, foreign exchange, and provision of certain categories of consumer goods based chiefly on domestic raw materials. Despite the overwhelming emphasis placed on industrial development he did not, however, regard industry as a substitute for agricultural development[11]. Industrial and agricultural development were to be complementary: 'If agriculture is to give a higher standard of living, then industry must be developed. But equally, if industry is to be developed, then agriculture must give a higher standard of living, in order to provide a demand for manufactures. The agricultural and the industrial revolutions thus reinforce each other, and neither can go very far unless the other is occurring at the same time' (ibid., p. 16).

The new industries were expected to cater primarily for the export market, rather than pursuing a strategy of pure import-substitution. The latter was not possible any way since these economies were characteristically small with limited domestic markets. This market size was not sufficient for the scale of industrialisation that was necessary to alleviate the unemployment which these societies faced. Once the industrialisation process starts it will proceed on its own momentum. Moreover, the indispensability of foreign capital will lessen as local capitalists learn the 'tricks of the trade' and become conscious of the importance of capital accumulation on a rapid scale:

'Industries are like sheep, they like to move together. In consequence, a place which has no industries is unattractive to new industries, while a place which has plenty of industries attracts still more. The analogy of the snowball is even better than that of the sheep. For once the snowball starts to move downhill it will move of its own momentum, and will get bigger and bigger as it goes along' (ibid., p. 36).

The theoretical bases for this strategy was developed in a subsequent article (Lewis, 1954). For the purpose of analytical rigour he dissected the economy into two sectors, viz, (i) a modern, advanced capitalist sector; and (ii) a backward, traditional, subsistence sector. The former is distinguished from the latter by its use of reproducible capital. The principal assumption is that marginal productivity of labour in the subsistence sector is negligible, zero, or even negative. This low productivity is a direct consequence of an overabundance of labour relative to capital availability in the particular society. To raise output in the subsistence sector it is therefore necessary for this sector to shed labour to the more productive capitalist sector. Moreover, more industries can be created since labour does not constitute a bottleneck. Skilled labour may be scarce initially but 'the capitalist or their government will soon provide the facilities for training more skilled people. The real bottlenecks to expansion are ... capital and natural resources' (Lewis, 1954, p. 406).

To attract labour to the capitalist sector (and thus fuel the process of capital accumulation) it is necessary to pay a wage which exceeds that prevailing in the subsistence sector. A useful rule of thumb is to pay a wage which is equivalent to the average product per worker in the subsistence sector, plus some 'margin'. The magnitude of the economic expansion in the economy will be critically dependent on the size of the capitalist surplus and the extent to which this surplus is being reinvested. Here Lewis makes the rather naive assumption that capitalists (whether local or foreign) will automatically reinvest their profit. As this profit is reinvested more employment is created in the capitalist sector, hence labour will increasingly be drawn from the subsistence sector. The accumulation process continues to 'snowball' until a labour surplus no longer exists in the subsistence sector. At this critical point wages will now begin to rise beyond the subsistence level and thereby impinge on the size of the capitalist surplus. But the capitalist can still continue to accumulate, though not within the constraints imposed by the closed economy. Lewis thus opens up the model to allow for the dual possibilities of (i) encouraging immigration (i.e. to check wage increases); and (ii) exporting the surplus capital to other territories which have an unlimited supply of labour (available at a subsistence wage).

Some theoretical and empirical objections

Any one who reads Lewis' work cannot fail to be impressed by the clarity and logical consistency of the arguments employed. Despite this brilliance the arguments suffer from certain important theoretical and empirical defects (not, it should be stated, much appreciated at the time). First, the observation is made that despite his trenchant critique of the colonial view of development his analysis and policy recommendations have much in common with that view. The colonial powers, for instance, had long insisted on the benevolence and 'development-promoting' role of private capital inflows. It is this which explains the 'marriage' of the capital markets in the colonies to those in the metropole via Currency Boards, exchange rate regimes and other banking and currency facilities. Lewis went on to provide further ideological and theoretical support for foreign capital.

He did not regard foreign capital as one of the central obstacles to underdevelopment in the region, a major manifestation of which was the crisis in the subsistence sector. Curiously enough, he hinted at this in an important passage of his 1954 contribution but he did not develop it:

> Thus, the owners of plantations have no interest in seeing knowledge of new techniques or new seeds conveyed to the peasants, and if they are influential in the government, they will not be found using their influence to expand the facilities for agricultural extension. They will not support proposals for land settlement and are often instead to be found engaged in turning the peasant off their lands .... This is one of the worst features of imperialism, for instance. The imperialists invest capital and hire workers, it is to their advantage to keep wages low, and even in those cases where they do not actually go out of their way to impoverish the subsistence economy (even by taking away the people's land, or by demanding forced labour in the capitalist sector, or by imposing taxes to drive people to work for the capitalist employers) they will at least very seldom be found doing anything to make it more productive (ibid., p. 410).

Instead of developing this important strand of reasoning he went on to focus on the 'natural variables', viz, overpopulation relative to resource endowment, shortage of capital, market size, etc. By giving these issues analytical and theoretical primacy he missed the role played by foreign capital and foreign decision-making in undermining development in Caribbean economies. Not only did he fail to analyze the impact on external forces on domestic accumulation but the analysis dismissed social relations and conflicts between different classes in the 'capital-starved' economy. Rather, he invoked the experience of a totally different historical and social milieu, namely the Western European experience and particularly the England of Adam Smith and David Ricardo. His opening sentence (1954) thus reads:

> This essay is written in the classical tradition, making the classical assumption, and asking the classical question. The classics, from Smith to Marx, all assumed, or argued, that an unlimited supply of labour was available at subsistence wages. They then enquired how production grows through time. They found the answer in capital accumulation, which they explained in terms of their analysis of the distribution of income (ibid., p. 400).

The principal objection to the above is not whether an unlimited supply of labour exists (and at a subsistence wage) in the case of the Europe of the classical era or in contemporary Caribbean economies. The objection lies in the causes of this unemployment and underemployment of labour. Certainly there are different historical and structural reasons for this phenomenon.[12] Moreover, the analysis of the classical economists was not hinged on a prominent role for foreign capital. It was the interests of the burgeoning indigenous capitalist class which was central to their problematic. Once dependence on foreign capital comes into play a whole complex set of issues is raised: will foreign decision-making lead to a misallocation of resources in the host society (e.g. a bias towards a particular sector, say the profitable mining sector)?; Will it marginalise or eventually displace the less powerful local capitalist class?; Will the growth and development process be internalised?; Will dependency be reinforced?; Will the surplus be reinvested or will it be repatriated? In sum, will foreign capital frustrate or promote development in the host country? Rather shortsightedly, Lewis was of the view that growth and development would be promoted. The surplus generated in the capitalist sector would be automatically ploughed back into domestic investment to the point where unemployment and underemployment are completely eradicated.

These theoretical criticisms raise doubt on the capacity of the Lewisian strategy to resolve the dilemma of Caribbean economies. Yet this became the development model in vogue in the Commonwealth Caribbean since the 1950s. In the context of Grenada, Gairy pledged his commitment to this model in his 1969 Budget Speech: '(We will) ... take the necessary action to encourage local (and international) capital to participate in the very necessary industrialization programme of the state. This capital, once invested in Grenada, will get the maximum incentive allowances from the Government for its protection and encouragement' (cited in Jacobs and Jacobs, p. 66).

But despite the obvious weaknesses in the Lewis' strategy we cannot attribute the crisis and impoverishment which beset the Grenadian economy under Gairy's administration exclusively to Lewis. Lewis did not assign the role of corruption, repression, institutional rigidities, arbitrariness in government, and (in a word) all the phenomena which define Gairyism to the state. The *raison d'etre* of the Lewisian state is to create the perfect environment for the smooth and uninterrupted operation of capital of all kinds. Notwithstanding this disclaimer, it should be stressed that the other governments in the region which pursued polices which were largely consistent with Lewis' recommendations typically produced results which were contradictory to Lewis' own expectations. According to one authoritative source (Commonwealth Caribbean Regional Secretariat, 1972) the result was essentially:

a continuation of the centuries - old pattern of West Indian economy: growth without development, growth accompanied by imbalances and distortions, growth generated from outside rather than within, growth without the fullest use of West Indian manpower, entrepreneurial, capital, and natural resources, growth resting on a foreign rather than indigenous technological base, and growth accompanied by imported consumption patterns (cited in Payne, 1981, p. 4).

Economic trends under Gairy

The net effect of the policies pursued in Grenada during the Gairy era was the reinforcement and consolidation of the economic structure which was implanted by French and British colonialism. Although other sectors (most notably, tourism and light manufacturing) had emerged in the 1960s and 1970s to complement agriculture, their contribution was negligible; especially in the critical areas of gross domestic product, employment generation, and foreign exchange earnings. For example, despite the setback that the agricultural sector experienced during the Gairy year, it still accounted for 30 per cent of the island's gross domestic product in 1978, provided employment for some 40 per cent of the workforce, and consistently generated over 90 per cent of total visible exports between 1971 and 1978.

Although constituting the backbone of the economy, agriculture was constrained by legacies of the plantation economy era, most pronounced in the pattern of land ownership. Of the 14,039 farm holdings existing in 1975, the vast majority (12,265, or 87.4 per cent) were small farms of five acres or less, accounting for only 28 per cent of the farm acreage. At the other end of the scale, 99 farms (0.7 per cent of the total) accounted for approximately 33 per cent of cultivable acreage. Yet the contradiction went further. The best land was concentrated among the larger holdings, while the small farmers subsisted on the rugged and mountainous terrain left uncultivated by the plantocracy. Despite this severe land hunger, thousands of acres of arable land remained idle (see table 2.1).

The situation called for a radical land reform programme, not the piece-meal, patronage-ridden programme of Gairy's so-called 'land for the landless'. The Jacobs brothers observed that by 1972 (i.e., four years after the land reform scheme was introduced) the agrarian structure of the country remained essentially the same.[13] This is not surprising because by this time the GULP government was overtly pro-capitalist. It would therefore be unrealistic for the regime to redistribute land belonging to large estate owners to small land-hungry farmers. According to Jacobs and Jacobs the 'land for the landless' programme was aimed not so much at land reform but, more

Table 2:1

Distribution (nos. and acreage) of holdings (farms) by size group, 1961

Size group	No. of holdings	% of total holdings	Acreage (acres)	% of total acreage	Proportion cultivated (acres)
L1	6,458	45.8	2,476	4.1	95.2
1-L5	6,062	42.9	11,907	19.8	88.6
5-L10	934	6.6	5,998	10.0	79.5
10-L25	418	3.0	5,867	9.8	70.7
25-L50	100	0.70	3,367	5.6	72.0
50-L100	42	0.29	2,814	4.7	61.1
100-L200	28	0.19	3,618	6.0	67.9
200-L500	52	0.36	15,098	25.0	61.5
500+	12	0.08	9,052	15.0	46.6
Total	14,096	100.00	60,197	100.00	69.6

Source: National Census, Grenada 1961. ('L' denotes 'less than')

fundamentally; it was Gairy's strategy for victimising non-GULP farmers, mainly from the middle segment who were known to be enemies of his government. As for the land confiscated, these were not redistributed in economical units. Some 50 per cent comprised half-acre lots. Some was also used to establish state farms, which consistently operated at a loss (Chernick, 1978, p. 124).

In keeping with tradition, the large estates were predominantly involved in commercial, export-orientated agriculture, comprising three primary crops - nutmeg (including its by-product, mace), cocoa, and bananas. These crops were exported in an unprocessed state, as in the days of plantation agriculture. The value and volume of exports of these crops between 1975 and 1978 is shown in table 2.2. The concentration of this limited range of unprocessed products into a few markets (including that of the old 'mother country') was also indicative of lack of structural transformation and peripheral status in the world economy. The low elasticity of demand for its few agricultural staples also made for a paucity of foreign exchange earnings. Although small farmers were also involved in the production of these staple crops, their main output was geared for the domestic market. In 1975, for example, they provided 85 per cent of all the food and vegetables produced on the island.

But small uneconomic parcels of land, limited access to credit facilities and agricultural inputs, and ignorance about soil conservation, irrigation methods,

Table 2:2

Exports of major agricultural commodities from Grenada, 1975-1978

Commodity	1975	1976	1977	1978
Bananas:				
Volume ('000 lbs)	29,700	33,800	30,900	31,500
Value (EC$ 000)	6,600	7,900	8,586	9,288
Price per 1b (¢)	0.22	0.23	0.28	0.29
Cocoa:				
Volume ('000 lbs)	5,100	5,900	4,600	5,300
Value (EC$ 000)	7,100	8,883	8,883	19,575
Price per 1b (¢)	1.39	1.50	1.93	3.69
Nutmeg and Mace:				
Volume ('000 lbs)	3,800	7,000	7,100	5,000
Value (EC$ 000)	9,900	15,984	17,577	12,293
Price per 1b (¢)	2.60	2.28	2.48	2.48

Source: Government of Grenada, *Economic Memorandum on Grenada*, Vol. 1 (February 1984), p. 12.

and agronomical practices in general inevitably led to low yields and low incomes. In addition, small farmers had to contend with lack of a market infrastructure. This factor did much to undermine domestic agriculture, since guaranteed markets were provided only for the three export crops. Given these deep-seated problems in the agricultural sector, it is not surprising that the economy was consistently beset by a net deficit in agricultural trade. In 1972, for instance, total foreign exchange earnings from agriculture amounted to EC$9.2 million, while imported food items stood at EC$13.3 million (cited in Ferguson, 1974, p. 97).

The retention of features of the old plantation system could also be seen in the tourist industry, Grenada's second major source of foreign exchange. This sector expanded throughout the 1960s and 1970s on account of the steady and rising demand for holidays in this tropical Garden of Eden. Hotels were designed to meet the desire for ostentation of tourists from affluent backgrounds. The bulk of the trade was from North America, making the island vulnerable to developments in the US economy and the foreign policies of the US government. Although some of the hotels and guest houses were owned by local businessmen, the industry was dominated by foreign interests. For example, the Holiday Inn alone accounted for 60 per cent of the total bed space in the sector. Typically, hotel owners were also involved in complementary services, such as transport and restaurants. In addition, foreigners also invested in holiday and retirement housing settlements, thereby reinforcing their hold on the island.

The growing investment in real estate also exerted inflationary pressure on land prices and further exacerbated the problems in the agricultural sector. A further constraint on this sector was inadequate infrastructure and air transportation. The limited interrelation between the tourist industry and other sectors, particularly agriculture and construction, also placed a severe strain on the country's balance of payments. The principal bottleneck was the lack of an international airport, equipped with night landing and instrument landing facilities and capable of accommodating large wide-bellied jets. The impossibility of night landing was a drain on the economy, since visitors often had to stay overnight in the neighbouring islands of Barbados and Trinidad. According to one estimate, some 50 per cent of the visitors to Grenada stayed overnight in other islands, at approximately US$85 per visitor, causing an annual loss of US$1.3 million to Grenada (Government of Grenada, 1981c, p. 5).

A somewhat similar picture emerged for the financial sector. The banking system was dominated by foreign ownership, mainly Canadian and British interests. The lending policies of these banks were instrumental in deepening the structural problems of the economy. Short-term borrowing, especially by merchants, was favoured at the expense of long-term strategic loans. For example, of the EC$27 million loaned to the agricultural, tourism, manufacturing, and distribution sectors in 1977, 55 per cent was allocated to the distributive trade, 22.2 per cent to agriculture (mainly export agriculture) 14.8 per cent to tourism, and 7.4 per cent to manufacturing (Smith, 1988, p. 86). By financing merchandise activities, the banks were simultaneously securing the Grenadian market for foreign goods and services. In the words of Maurice Bishop: 'They (the banks) are lending money left and right to buy cars and radiograms and other things which cannot produce food for us to eat, and which we have to buy at fat prices from the same countries the banks came from. But our farmers and small businessmen catch hell to get a loan from them.... On top of all this, they rake fat profits out of the country daily. We will put an end to this *bubul*' (Manifesto of the New Jewel Movement, 1974, pp. 148-149).

Dependence was also acute in the island's fledgling manufacturing sector. The contribution of this sector to the gross domestic product averaged a paltry three per cent throughout the 1970s. Agro-industries were still regarded as an activity beyond the capacity of the economy. As late as 1974 the country only had three such industries - 1 sugar mill, 1 animal feed plant and

48

1 food processing plant. The absence of a wide range of processing plants and storage capacity meant that much of the abundant supply of fresh tropical fruits and vegetables with which the island was blessed were either wasted or had to be hastily consumed, especially in times of abundance.

Among the main manufacturing operations during the prerevolutionary period were food, drink, and tobacco processing, garment factories, and furniture making. These activities were based overwhelmingly on imported raw materials and capital equipment. In the case of the tobacco and beer brewing industries, all the inputs were imported. This dependence contributed to the uncompetitive nature of many of the goods, notably furniture. As one government source noted, 'It is quite common to find cheaper imported products on shop shelves. In cases where some raw materials are obtained locally, these are so highly priced that the finished products is beyond the range of the ordinary consumer' (Government of Grenada, *Manufacturing in Grenada*, n.d., p. 2). Finally, Grenada's manufacturing sector was distinguished by the lack of a functional, formal, and systematic organizational structure along company lines, largely a reflection of the size and ownership structure of these businesses. The majority were small, family-owned, cottage industries, typically employing fewer than five people. Manufacturing also operated with considerable excess capacity; capacity utilisation in food and beverage processing, for example, averaged only 56 per cent.

Given these structural problems in each of the main sectors, we can begin to understand why the economy performed so sluggishly under the Gairy regime. The period from 1960 to 1978 was one of uninterrupted and growing balance of trade deficits, reaching a record level of EC$50.5 million in 1978. A substantial part of the import bill was comprised of foodstuffs, many of which could be produced locally (especially carbohydrates-based products). In 1972, for example, Grenada imported food items to the tune of EC$13.3 million.

Before 1974 the deficit was financed primarily be grants from Britain, but after independence this source of finance diminished in importance. Increasingly, the deficit was financed by commercial loans which soared after 1973. Between 1973, the year of the OPEC price increase, and 1978 public debt increased from EC$23.8 million to over EC$51 million. This would doubtless have been higher had it not been for the government's poor debt-service record and its mounting corruption. For example, the tendency for money to disappear from the treasury led the Caribbean Development Bank in 1977 to refuse to grant further loans and aid to the country. For the same reason, some EC$19 million from other foreign sources was also withheld in 1977 (Ambursley, 1983, p. 200).

The drying up of all forms of foreign inflows, allied to the deteriorating foreign exchange situation of the country, produced a number of predictable consequences; an escalation of unemployment, the deterioration of social services (especially health care, education, and housing), a net depreciation in the island's capital stock (particularly its transportation infrastructure and other public utilities), and an acute reduction in the national saving ratio. There was also a marked decline in business confidence, as witnessed by the pattern of investment growth during the last years of the Gairy regime. In 1976 total domestic investment amounted to US$13.6 million, rising marginally to US$14.7 million in 1977, and falling to US$11.8 million in 1978 (Government of Grenada, *1979 Abstract of Statistics*, p. 8).

Impact on the masses

These developments had a particularly deleterious impact on Grenada's workers, small farmers, and the unemployed. According to one source the unemployment rate in 1960 was as high as 42.6 per cent of the total labour force. A decade later, instead of decreasing it rose further to 44.6 per cent. Of the 55.4 per cent who worked in 1970 as much as 30 per cent of them were seasonally employed, i.e. employed for less than ten months per year.[14] By early 1979 open unemployment was believed to be as high as 50 per cent. When examined in terms of sex and age the picture was even more gloomy; i.e., 69 per cent for females and some 80 per cent for those who were under 23 years old (Thorndike, 1985, p. 48). Had it not been for significant net emigration the unemployment situation would have been even more intractable (Smith, 1988, table 2.16).

Although obviously not as worse off as their unemployed counterparts, the employed segment of the population nevertheless had to content themselves with poor and insecure working conditions and low and relatively stagnant wages. Despite a proliferation of trade union organizations the cause of employees as a class went unnoticed. The GMMWU which continued to monopolise the unionisation of workers, contrary to the wishes of many of the workers, was by now blatantly anti-working class in outlook and in practice.[15] Since Gairy was now inextricably bound to capital and property, being an employer himself, it would be unrealistic to expect him to strengthen the power and bargaining capacity of workers. Wage rates for the majority of workers thus remained low, a situation which was suggestive of the general dominance of capital over labour in Gairy's Grenada. Government ministers, senior civil servants, secret police and other personnel close to Gairy, on the other hand, received colossal remunerations (tax free in many instances).

The lot of workers and peasants was made worse by the exploitative pricing policies of Grenada's merchant class. According to figures published in the

50

Grenada Abstract of Statistics, between 1964 and 1975 the price of basic foodstuffs escalated by 200 per cent, clothing by 164 per cent, and housing by 135 per cent. It is believed that the markup on a bag of rice, for example, was in excess of 200 per cent (Epica Task Force, 1982, p. 44). Many of these price increases were caused by indirect taxes and the corrupt practices of the merchant class, which in turn were generally attributable to corruption at a higher level (i.e., the monopoly privileges which Gairy bestowed on his political cronies). Jacobs and Jacobs write:

> It is no secret that up to 1975 one individual had the sole right to import sugar which he did at a cost of EC$53.00 per 200 pound bag, yet that same sugar was allowed to be sold to the general public within Grenada at EC$113.00 per 200 pound bag. Moreover, this is only one example of a situation that applied to other commodities and as such it is clear that the open exploitation of Grenada's working class, which was there from the start of the twentieth century, was still there three quarters of the way through that century (Jacobs and Jacobs, p. 47).

The lot of the Grenadian masses was further exacerbated by the limited and deteriorating social services which existed. Provision of housing, health and educational services, manpower development, maintenance of physical infrastructure (especially, roads, telecommunication, electricity, and water supplies) all took a backseat on the government's list of priorities. In an address to the Caribbean Development Bank (CDB) in April 1979 Bernard Coard pointed out that the percentage of homes without pipe-borne water exceeded 60 per cent. Those who had these facilities received very little water in actual fact because of the age and quality of the piping system. For example, as much as 70 per cent of all water entering the capital town, St George's, was lost before it reached the homes of Grenadians.[16]

The scarcity of general practitioners and the rising cost of medical services (in the case of private doctors) and drugs deprived poor Grenadians of medical attention. The three medical clinics which existed were described as 'unsatisfactory and ill-equipped'. Basic items such as bandages, tablets, ambulance services, sheets, and pillow cases were nonexistent. According to one source: 'Women gave birth on cold concrete floors as cockroaches scurried through the filthy wards. Even these services cost more than most people could afford, and many rural Grenadians received no health care at all. Dentistry was virtually an unknown science in pre-revolutionary Grenada, where not a single public clinic existed for those who could not pay private dentist fee' (Epica Task Force, p. 86).

A similar picture emerges for the education sector. The training of teachers, upgrading of buildings, provision and maintenance of school furniture, were all left unattended. In as much as ordinary Grenadians were conscious of the importance of education as a tool of upward mobility their aspirations were shattered. Many could not afford the cost of books, uniform, transportation and lunch for their children. The abysmal state of the economy compelled many to shorten the period spent at school (usually at the third or fourth grade level) so that they could contribute to the livelihood of the family. Small wonder functional illiteracy afflicted as much as 33 per cent of the population in 1978 (Epica Task Force, p. 82).

Gairy even terminated Grenada's contribution to the regional University, the University of the West Indies, thereby depriving promising Grenadians, especially those from humble backgrounds, access to a subsided education at the tertiary level. The pressing need in the island for trained human resources was never recognised. According to one source this was a carefully orchestrated policy since Gairy felt threatened by well-educated Grenadians: 'Gairy knew that educated Grenadians held him in contempt, and he feared - correctly - that University-trained youths might pose a future threat to his control' (Epica Task Force, p. 44). The growing confrontation which Gairy encountered from the intelligentsia during the 1970s makes this view plausible (discussed below).

Such moves, coupled with the increasing shortage of employment opportunities, made Gairy the *bete noire* of the youth segment of the population. Unlike their parents, who could recount a few gains in the early years of Gairy's rule, they could only remember, or see, mounting misery and social discontent. The impact of the international crisis on what has always been an ailing agricultural sector drove many to the urban areas in search of material betterment. But they soon learned that without good social connections it was virtually impossible to get paid employment outside the stagnant agricultural sector.

In sum, the post-war experience of the Grenadian economy thus bore many of the trends and features which characterised other Caribbean economies. But in the case of Grenada the situation was further compounded by the practices associated with Gairyism. This led to the peculiar result of stagnation and retrogression in contradistinction to the norm elsewhere of 'growth without development'. Assessing the state of the Grenadian economy on the eve of the revolution, the World Bank noted that 'the country was plagued by a low standard of living, heavy unemployment and under-employment, inadequate production of basic foodstuffs, inflation and persistent deficits in the balance of payments' (World Bank, 1984, p. 8).

The insurrection

To maintain political power in the face of such economic and social adversities, Gairy stepped up his repressive apparatus and his mysticism. The former was geared against any one who opposed or agitated publicly against his government. Although he genuinely believed that he possessed mystical powers his appeal to the power of God was an attempt to exploit the fears, superstitions, and backwardness of the Grenadian masses.

The brunt of the oppression unleashed by his specially selected security forces fell on activists from the New Jewel Movement (NJM). The NJM was established in March 1973 by the merger of the Movement for Assemblies of the People (MAP) and the Joint Endeavour for Welfare, Education and Liberation (JEWEL). MAP was predominantly urban-centred and was the brain-child of Maurice Bishop and Kenrick Radix, both of whom had studied law in the United Kingdom and had recently returned to their homeland. JEWEL, on the other had, was rural-based and was founded by Unison Whiteman who, too, had recently returned home after studying economics at Howard University.

The merging of the two groups into one coherent organization seemed to them to be a logical step at the time since they both had similar aspirations, namely, the liberation of Grenada from 'Gairyism' and all forms of oppression and domination. Hardened by their experience abroad where they came into direct contact with racism, and galvanised into action by the concrete developments in their country, they were determined to shunt their society on a different course of development. Many were inspired by the Cuban Revolution and the activities of the Black Power Movement. Bishop's return to the island was well-timed. He had the fortune of witnessing large black power demonstrations in Trinidad in early 1970 (discussed in Sutton, 1983). Although he also observed that many demonstrators were savagely arrested by the police, that did not deter him from engaging in confrontational politics in his native Grenada.

Sensing that these uprisings in neighbouring Trinidad could easily influence his opponents in Grenada, Gairy publicly declared his government's intention to use violence as a policy for 'stabilising' his society:

> It is said that when your neighbour's house is on fire, keep on wetting your own house. We are now doubling the strength of our Police Force, we are getting in almost unlimited supplies of new and modern equipment. ... Opposition referred to my recruiting criminals in a reserve force. Does it not take steel to cut steel?.... Indeed, hundreds have come and some of the toughest and roughest roughnecks have been recruited (cited in Epica Task Force, p. 45).

True to form, he proceeded to strengthen the power of his infamous 'Mongoose Gang', 'The Night Ambush Squad', 'The Green Beasts', and 'The Iguanas' by a range of repressive legislations[17] and large supplies of arms and ammunitions from foreign allies - Pinochet's Chile, South Korea, the United States and South Africa.

The 'Mongoose Gang' soon proved how 'rough' and 'tough' they were when six prominent members of the NJM - Maurice Bishop, Unison Whiteman, Selwyn Strachan, Hudson Austin, Simon Daniel, and Kenrick Radix - were brutally beaten on Sunday, 18 November 1973, and then jailed (an event subsequently commemorated as 'Bloody Sunday').[18] This incident sent shock waves throughout the island. The Committee of 22 which comprised organizations embracing the whole class spectrum of the society (most notably, the Chamber of Commerce, the Employers Federation, the Civil Service Association, churches, schools and trade unions) publicly condemned the savagery and demanded an enquiry into the circumstances surrounding it. The upshot was a Commission set up under Herbert Duffus, a Jamaican jurist. But the recommendations of the Commission went unheeded.[19] Innocent Belmar, for instance, who was debarred from all public duties, was subsequently made a minister of government. Moreover, about two months later (21 January 1974), 'Bloody Monday' followed, with the wanton murder of Rupert Bishop, father of Maurice Bishop. Rupert was shot at the entrance of a building along the Carenage (St George's waterfront) as he tried to appeal to Gairy's secret police for the safety of the women and children who had taken up refuge in the building in the wake of the violence in the street. This incident served further to intensify the tensions in the society. The island-wide strike which was in progress at the time of Rupert's death continued for another two months with very crippling effects on the already fragile economy.

In the midst of this profound crisis the British government proceeded to grant independence to Grenada under Gairy's leadership in 1974. Predictably, the tensions escalated and these were greeted with mounting repression from the state. Nevertheless, the NJM continued to maintain a visible and increasingly powerful profile. Of the six seats won by the People's Alliance[20] in the 1976 election, three went to the NJM and Maurice Bishop became the leader of the opposition. With Bernard Coard's return to the island in 1976, the NJM underwent a qualitative leap. Apart from continuing to protest against the economic, social, and political conditions in the island, the NJM began to place special emphasis on organization, tactics and strategy for acquiring power. They were convinced (after the 1976 election) that Gairy's corrupt and dictatorial regime could not be removed by parliamentary means.

The opportunity for coming to power by an alternative route came in March 1979. Gairy left the island on 12 March 1979 for New York to discuss, further,[21] the subject of Unidentified Flying Objects with the Secretary - General of the United Nations (UN). Meanwhile it was alleged that orders were left with members of his security force to carry out the assassination of eight of the leading members of the overwhelmingly popular NJM.[22] The information was leaked to the NJM leadership on the same afternoon of Gairy's departure by disaffected members of the police force. At 4 am on 13 March, 46 NJM combatants, under the leadership of Hudon Austin, launched a successful attack on the army barracks at True Blue. One hour later, the radio station was captured from where Grenadians were mobilised to come out and support the revolution. The response to Bishop's appeal was overwhelming.

Within 12 hours, at the expense of only three lives, the long-awaited revolution became a reality and a People's Revolutionary Government (PRG) was established. The daunting task of transforming the legacies left in all spheres of the economy, society, and polity by centuries of colonialism and years of economic mismanagement under the Gairy regime now fell on a new generation of leaders. Apart from these constraints, the young revolutionaries had no practical experience in managing the complex affairs of a country. What they had, however, was energy, enthusiasm and, very importantly, popular support from all segments of the population - all of which were absolutely critical to the survival of the revolution and the realization of their goals.[23]

Notes

1. Membership in the GMMWU in 1951-2 stood at 16,000 (6,000 paid and 10,000 unpaid). The number fell to 7,700 by 1959 (3,600) paid and 4,100 unpaid) and then to 3,000 by 1962 (Singham, 1968, p. 185.

2. Between 1957 and 1972 the GNP nominated 52 candidates for general elections and, with the exception of one (a shoemaker), they were all drawn from the elite strata. See Jacobs and Jacobs (1980), p. 73 for the full list and their respective professions.

3. See Jacobs and Jacobs (1980), especially pp. 61-63, for a discussion of the class implications of the various legislations which were passed during their administration. Both parties embraced and adopted the dependent model of development ('Industrialisation by Invitation') propounded by W.A. Lewis. This model is discussed later in this chapter.

4. The 1972 manifesto, for instance, boldly notes:

   We seek to change the system which ensures that those who have, have more and those who have not, have less. We are determined to redistribute the economic potential of this country so that all may benefit. We will ensure that there is a more equitable distribution of income. Bitterness and frustration will not deter us and we ask all those who, like ourselves, want change by action and progress to join with us so that we may give economic power to the people (cited in Institute of International Relations, 1974, p. 131).

5. Although this patron-client style of politics was very pronounced in Grenada, especially under GULP, it was by no means peculiar to this island. It was a Caribbean-wide phenomenon. See Stone (1980) for a discussion of this point.

6. See Government of Grenada (1962) for details. The currency was not stated but it is likely to be local dollars.

7. The main issue in the 1962 election campaign was not so much '*Squandermania*' as the constitutional future of the island following the collapse of the West Indian Federation. The GNP proposed the integration of Grenada with their petroleum-rich neighbour, Trinidad

and Tobago. Most Grenadians favoured this highly unrealistic proposal to Gairy's less attractive option of federating with the other seven small territories in the Eastern Caribbean. See Payne (1980) for details of the failure of the attempt at federation.

8. Author's interview with a number of Grenadians in June 1987. Having squandered his earlier gains on his characteristically extravagant and flamboyant life style, he was now reduced to begging. According to one interviewee, Errol Berkeley, Gairy was forced to sell some of his personal possessions in an effort to obtain money to maintain and run his car. This interviewee also pointed out that Gairy became a laughing stock in Grenada on account of the frequency with which his car ran out of petrol.

9. This view was propounded with so much force and consistency (even during the contemporary period) that policy-makers in these societies came to accept such arguments, consciously or unconsciously, almost without question. For a development of this theme see 'Colonialism and the Myth of Resource Insufficiency in Jamaica' in Lewis (1976).

10. By this time the pace of constitutional decolonisation was rapidly increasing. Jamaica and Trinidad became independent states in 1962. Guyana and Barbados followed in 1966. Many other territories were at the stage of Associated Statehood, for example Grenada in 1967. The responsibility for employment creation, economic growth, social services, etc. now became the responsibility of the new leaders.

11. The main rationale for industrialisation was over-population and mass unemployment. 'The islands already carry a larger population than agriculture can absorb, and population are growing at rates of 1.5 to 2.0 per cent per annum. It is, therefore, urgent to create new opportunities for employment off the land' (Lewis, 1950, p. 1).

12. In the case of Europe, for instance, the transition from feudalism to capitalism (and the dispossession of the peasantry which it brought in its wake, e.g. the enclosure movement) was primarily responsible for this labour surplus.

13. Jacobs and Jacobs (1980), p. 47. For example, the authors note that there were 51 estates in 1968. The number fell to 50 in 1972.

14. This is based on *The 1970 Population of the Commonwealth Caribbean*. See Appendix J of Jacobs and Jacobs, 1980, p. 157.

15. In 1978, for instance, the *Essential Services Act* (Amendment) and *Grenada Port Authority Act* (Amendment) were passed, designed to suppress the militancy of workers, and to curb their ability to use the strike weapon for material advance.

16. See Statement by Bernard Coard, delivered on 26 April 1979 at a Conference hosted by the Caribbean Development Bank, pp. 133-134.

17. For example, *The Emergency Powers Act* of 21 May 1970. This made it legitimate for the police to search a home without a warrant, curtailed the movement of people, and undermine the right to convene public meetings.

18. Their heads were shaved with broken bottles, after which they were thrown behind bars without bail and medical attention. Some of them, particularly Bishop, never completely recovered from the injuries sustained. See Epica Task Force, 1982, p. 46 for further information on 'Bloody Sunday'.

19. The Commission recommended, among other things, the disbanding of the police aides, a reorganization of the police force (including the superintendent Innocent Belmar who should not be allowed to hold any public office whatsoever), the termination of the duties of certain magistrates who were deemed to be incompetent and unfair in their duties (see G. Brizan, 1984, p. 344 for other recommendations).

20. This Alliance was comprised of the NJM, the GNP and the United People's Party (UPP), which had defected from the GNP. If this election was contested fairly it is highly probable that the Alliance would have emerged victorious. But as was characteristic of Gairyism the election was marred by all type of frauds - 'multiple-voting', removing the names of known anti-GULP supporters from off the voter's lists, denying the opposition access to the media, and other electoral machinations.

21. Since the achievement of complete constitutional independence, Gairy has raised the subject of Unidentified Flying Objects in international fora on more than one occasion. In his address to the Thirty-Second Session of the General Assembly of the UN in October 1977, he

argued in earnest: 'Man must reckon with himself to recognise that on this plant we are simply the guests of a benefactor - The Universal Divine God, the Great Supreme Architect. ... All Ceremonies ... should commence with the acknowledgement of God and the Invocation of His Blessings on the event' (cited in Jacobs and Jacobs, 1980, p. 107). He also urged delegates at these fora to support his motion for the granting of resources to carry out research into these cosmic phenomena.

22.   This account of the seizure of power is based on the semi-official account of the revolution provided by Jacobs and Jacobs (1980). See, especially, pp. 124-127.

23.   The coup was overwhelmingly popular. O'Shaughnessy (1984) notes 'the coup was enormously popular with Grenadians and it seemed as if the whole of the island was coming out into the streets to celebrate' (p. 79).

3 The PRG and the theory of non-capitalist development

The strategy of development which the People's Revolutionary Government formulated, and sought to implement in Grenada between 1979 and 1983, was a product of several theoretical and intellectual currents - some intra-regional and some extra-regional. With respect to the latter, the **theory of non-capitalist development** or **socialist orientation** was particularly influential. This chapter examines the main features of the PRG's development strategy, with emphasis on the conceptual foundations of the strategy.

Economic strategy

From the very outset the architects of the Grenada revolution made it clear that the revolution was for material betterment - not the socialization of poverty and underdevelopment: 'People of Grenada, this revolution is for work, for food, for decent housing and health services, and for a bright future for our children and great grandchildren' (Radio Broadcast Address by Maurice Bishop, 13 March 1979). An economic strategy for accomplishing these goals was worked out long before the PRG came to power, the essence of which was articulated in the party's 1973 manifesto. Some of the tasks for transformation were dictated by the immediate problems afflicting the country. Among those mentioned in the manifesto were: (i) chronic maldistribution of income and means of production; (ii) mass unemployment and underemployment; (iii) high and rising cost of living; (iv) poor (and in some cases inappropriate) standard of housing, clothing, education, health, food, recreational facilities and other general social and economic infrastructure; (v) irrationalities in the utilization of resources, especially agricultural land; (vi) disjuncture among the sectors of the economy; (vii) excessive dependence on a small number of countries for markets, capital, technology, aid, ideas, and even for goods and services which the country can produce for itself at competitive prices; (viii) foreign ownership and domination of critical sectors of the economy (banking, insurance, and tourism); (ix) an inadequate motivation to work; and (x) severe political apathy, aggravated by a backward patronage-ridden political system that engendered a get-something-for-nothing mentality.

The analysis of the origins of these problems was more controversial. Drawing upon the insights into Caribbean underdevelopment provided by the *New World Group*, the PRG attributed these problems to colonial domination, neocolonialism, and the ill-fated development policies of Grenada's traditional political leadership. As noted before, these policies were partly guided by the Lewis model of 'Industrialization by Invitation'. Contrary to conventional wisdom, the physical size of the country was regarded as a secondary constraint. Prime Minister Maurice Bishop summarised the party's thinking on this question in telling terms:

'The real problem is not the question of smallness per se, but that of imperialism. The real problem that small countries like ours face is that on a day by day basis we come up against an international system that is organised and geared towards ensuring the continuing exploitation, dominating, and rape of our economies, our countries, and our peoples. That, to us, is the fundamental problem' (Bishop, 1982a, p. 190).

Consequently, several far-reaching structural and institutional changes at the national, regional, and international level were called for. In the spirit of the economic strategy espoused by Thomas (1974),[1] the manifesto articulated an economic programme predicated, first and foremost, on the resource endowment of the country. To provide more houses it thus advocated a national low-cost housing plan, utilizing as much as possible indigenous materials such as wood, clay, and river sand. Similarly, to improve the problem of insufficient and inappropriate clothing, it called for a revitalization of the cotton industry in Carriacou to supply the raw material requirements for a textile and garment industry (Manifesto of the NJM, p. 144).

The manifesto identified three sectors for catalysing growth and development, viz, (i) agriculture and fisheries; (ii) agro-industries; and (iii) a 'New Tourism'. It was recognised that each sector required fundamental transformation in order to generate the maximum possible benefits to the society. For instance, in agriculture, land (particularly idle land) would have to be radically redistributed into cooperative farms of at least 40-50 acres in size.[2] Emphasis was to be placed on the establishment of linkages (backward and forward) between the various sectors of the economy. As an example of what was possible once the structural contradictions in the economy were eliminated, an impressive list of products that could be made from Grenadian raw materials was compiled. Included in the list were: (i) jams, nutmeg oil, jellies, liqueurs, marmalade, juices, spice powder, pharmaceuticals, and preserves from nutmegs; (ii) flour, baby foods, cereals, and farine from cassava; (iii) animal feeds, baby foods, flour, chips, and cake-mixers from bananas; (iv) ice-cream, confectionery products and chocolate beverages from cocoa; (v) oil, animal feeds, and plastics from cotton; (vi) fruit-juices, nectars, liqueurs, and wine from Grenada's abundant supply of fresh fruits.[3]

The manifesto also emphasised the need for state control of essential sectors, agrarian reforms, price controls, wage reforms, heavy investment in social and productive infrastructure, and the creation of a National Importing and Exporting Board empowered to handle Grenada's import and export trade. On the international plane, it made a plea for diversification of international relations to include the Third World and socialist states, a strong commitment to regional cooperation, a New International Economic Order, and respect for the sovereignty, legal equality, and territorial integrity of all states, however small.

A number of complementary institutional changes were also proposed. Since it was contended that foreign entrepreneurs were notorious for reinforcing the structural underdevelopment of the economy, the party promised to undertake a wholesale nationalization of those sectors of the economy under foreign control. Banking was to be the prime target: 'The new banks would be controlled and directed by a Central Bank. One of the main functions of this Central Bank will be to make sure that the loans available in these banks are provided for housing, small farmers, fishermen, cooperatives, the setting up of agro-industries, and the expansion of the new tourist industry' (Maifesto of the NJM, p. 149). Apart from the creation of a National Importing Board and a National Exporting Board, a Wages and Prices Board was also proposed. The latter was designed to control price increases and to ensure that wages kept pace with price increases. Minimum wages for different categories of workers was also proposed.

Heavy emphasis was placed on the need to improve and extend the country's physical infrastructure. As regards roads and transport, the following problems were identified: (i) poor and inadequate roads; (ii) no properly organised service to satisfy the requirements of the people; (iii) uneconomical vehicles and operations; (iv) unaffordable fares to poor local passengers; and (v) high cost of petrol and spare parts for vehicles.

Among the proposals for alleviating these problems were the establishment of a Cooperative Bus Service, and the opening of new agricultural feeder roads. With respect to harbours and (what was to become a very thorny issue between Grenada and Washington) the airport, the Manifesto called for a modest upgrading of existing facilities. To quote: 'What is desperately needed now is not an international airport but ownership of LIAT (Leeward Islands Air Travel) or some other regional airline by the Governments of the region, including Grenada, so that we could regulate efficiently flight schedules and the cost of flights' (Manifesto of the NJM, p. 149).[4]

These programmes were to be financed by internal and external sources; particularly, (i) revenue derived from taxation; (ii) government revenues from the profits of banks, insurance companies, and hotels; (iii) finance raised from the local private sector; (iv) commercial loans from foreign sources (to be repaid from profits generated from the use of such loans); (v) loans from regional and international financial institutions, especially the Caribbean Development Bank; (vi) 'untied' aid from fraternal countries; (vii) profits from the various sectors of the economy (these should be re-invested in the same sectors (i.e. agriculture, fishing, agro-industries and tourism) so that they can go on to generate even greater profits); (viii) finance raised from organizations such as Credit Unions, Friendly Societies, and Cooperative Associations (e.g the Nutmeg Cooperative Association); and (ix) savings derived from operating more efficient and less patronage-ridden organizations.

Mixed economy

Once in power, the PRG set out with vigour to implement these policies. It was decided to retain a mixed economy, albeit with a dominant state sector and a newly-established cooperative sector. Some critics, most notably Ambursely (1983) and Watson (1985), construed this pattern of ownership as evidence of the regime's commitment to the capitalist ethic. However, this interpretation is erroneous, since it fails to realistically appraise the utter impracticality of a total state sector model in the context of Grenada's objective conditions. As revealed by Bishop's **'Line of March'** address in 1982, the PRG opted for the mixed economy model in the hope that it could continue to draw on the skills, experience, material resources, and market connections of the private sector. In addition, it was recognised that 'the capitalist prefers to deal with the capitalist and capitalist governments allow other capitalists to come in, even when their government is a socialist-oriented government like our government in Grenada' (see US State Department and Department of Defence, 1984, p. 20).

The alliance was therefore conceived in tactical terms. By assuming leadership of the development process the state could guide and influence the process and pattern of economic and social development to ensure that capitalist relations did not dominate at the expense of socialist-collectivist forms. Simultaneously, it also sought to enlist the cooperation of private sector interests by granting them economic incentives and engaging them in constant dialogue as a means of assuring them of their continued role in the new society. The hope was that they would boost production and hence offset the constraints of the inexperienced and under-capitalised state sector. As Bishop put it: 'The state sector alone cannot develop the economy, given the very low level of technology available, the limited human resources, the lack of capital, the lack of marketing expertise, the lack of promotional capacity. So, we must stimulate the private sector generally, but also of course in agriculture, and in particular among the small and medium farmers' (ibid., p. 19).

Despite this farsighted remark the PRG lost no time in developing and extending the state sector. Among the areas of the economy demarcated for state control were all financial institutions, foreign trade (both import and export), certain aspects of domestic trade, and all public utilities - including the assets belonging to the British Company, Cable and Wireless. Although some of these plans did not reach further than the conference table, by mid-1983 the spread of the state sector was considerable (see table 3:1). Indeed, it bore very little relationship to the technical and managerial capacities of the state. Some of these state enterprises were acquired from the previous government (e.g. farms, night clubs and hotels) and the private sector (Holiday Inn, Royal Bank and Canadian Imperial Bank of Commerce). Others were either new initiatives (e.g. Grenada Agro-Industries) or were set up to manage machinery and equipment received as aid for the government's investment programme. A striking feature of these enterprises was that they gave the state a foothold in each of the pivotal sectors of the economy.

An important rationale for creating a large state sector was to effect central planning of the economy. In making the case for planning Coard enunciated:

> Our economy has suffered from years of colonial exploitation and Gairyite exploitation. And we are still poor and underdeveloped. Now this is where planning becomes critical. Because of our scarce resources, we need to mobilise those which are available and use them most efficiently to benefit ourselves. To reach this goal, we must try to plan the most efficient use of our resources. We must try to order our priorities and to balance our needs against what is available - our available supplies (Government of Grenada, 1982e, p. 59).

To this end the Ministry of Planning was restructured. It was subdivided in November 1982 into a macro-planning unit, a projects development unit, a physical planning unit, a technical and economic co-operation unit, a national computer centre, a central statistical office, an administrative and training unit, comprising a Registry and a Documentation Centre. Before 1979

64

Table 3:1:
Spread of state enterprises by 1983

Agriculture

1. Grenada Farms Corporation, Grenada Sugar Factory Ltd, Livestock Production & Genetic Centre, Forestry Development Corporation, National Fisheries Company, Marketing & National Importing Board, and Grenada Dairies Ltd

2. Grenada Agro-Industries

Banking and Utilities

1. National Commercial Bank Grenada Bank of Commerce

2. Grenada Development Bank

3. Grenada Electricity Services Ltd, Grenada Telephone Co. Ltd, Central Water Commission, National Transport Service, Grenada Port Authority

4. Free West Indian, Radio Free Grenada

Tourism

1. Grenada Resorts Corporation

2. Grencraft

Source: International Monetary Fund, (1984b); and Kirton (1983).

(Note:This list excludes those ancillary enterprises which were established mainly for the purpose of meeting the needs of government departments. The list includes Quintana Asphalt plant, carpenter shop, petrol station, G.Y. machine shop, gravel and concrete plant, emulsion plant, telescope quarry, Sandino Complex and Cocoa Rehabilitation Project. It also excludes the National Housing Authority).

planning was virtually non-existent in Grenada. It is commonly said in Grenada that Gairy worked according to dreams and visions rather than plans. Whatever planning took place was carried out in the Ministry of Finance. According to Qureshi (1966) 'There (was) only one planning officer at a junior staff level. Most of the planning (was) ad hoc. Systematic quantification of tasks, goals, and target setting, prioritising and programming (was) not yet undertaken' (cited in Kirton, 1983, p. 25). Besides, there was a manifest lack of reliable statistics on the different aspects of the economy.

These critical constraints to effective planning were somewhat alleviated between 1979 and 1983, thanks to the tremendous emphasis which the PRG placed on education and training, and the large influx of foreign technocrats (especially from the Caribbean) who flowed into Grenada during this period. These 'internationalist workers', as they were often called, were instrumental in reorganising the Ministry of Planning and computerising all relevant statistical data. Attempts were made to utilize the input-output method as a technique for planning the economy. At the enterprise level emphasis was placed on plan proposals for investment, labour, and technical and material supplies.[5]

The importance of beginning with a short term planning horizon (i.e. under five years) was recognised:

> You can call anything a plan. You can call it a 5-year or 10-year or 15-year plan, but those are games for school children. You are really fooling yourself if you believe that that is planning, unless you have control over all the variables, or most of the variables. In a situation where you have an open, dependent economy, on which fluctuation in the world economy have a devastating effect to a degree that you cannot fully predict and cannot control, and when you don't even have reliable data upon which to base anything, talk about planning is merely to impress people (cited in *The Courier*, No. 61, May-June 1980, p. 27).

The one-year budget plans which were prepared for 1982 and 1983 were thus predominantly concerned with current production problems. The goals for the medium and long-term were more ambitious. As articulated in a Government document these embraced five basic tasks:

1   the amelioration of the constraints imposed by the anachronistic gold exchange standard (e.g. automaticity between domestic growth and export receipts, chronic leakages - especially on imported consumption goods - engendered by the financial system, and impotence of discretionary monetary policies);

2   to lay the basis for structural transformation of the economy, economic diversification, self-sufficiency and greater employment of the country's limited resources through the rehabilitation of all usable capital stock and a concerted effort to construct new physical and social infrastructure;

3   to implement measures geared towards establishing backward and forward linkages between the major pillars of the economy, to demonstrate to the private sector the various opportunities and outlets for profitable investment in the productive sectors of the economy, and to utilize all idle resources - material and human - for the development of the economy;

4   to maintain strict control over the public accounts, to eliminate misappropriation and misallocation of public funds, to expand the revenue base of the economy, and to rationalise and economise on current expenditure; and

5   to create a vibrant and dynamic agricultural and tourism sectors (Government of Grenada, 1982g, p. ii).

The second and third goals were considered to be of extraordinary significance. As bluntly stated by Coard:

> For us the most important aspect in building an economically independent country (which is the only way that you can truly say that you are politically independent) is the method of diversification - in all ways and in all respects. First, diversification of agricultural production, secondly, diversification of the markets that we sell these products to, thirdly, diversification of the sources of our tourism, the variety of countries from which our tourists come. The maximum diversification, the minimum of reliance upon one country or a handful of countries means the greater your independence, the less able certain people are able to squeeze you, pressurise you and blackmail you (cited in *Race and Class*, vol. 21, No. 2, 1979, p. 179).

Consistent with this thinking was the need for a dynamic foreign policy - as a means not only of diversifying international economic relations and maximising aid, but also to harness political support to help stave off what the PRG regarded was an imminent invasion from the United States. The PRG thus quickly became a member of the Non-Aligned Movement (in September 1979) advocating legal equality, mutual respect for sovereignty, non-interference in the economic and political life of nations and other well-known principles of the Non-Aligned Movement.

Although plans were made to develop the major pillars of the economy - tourism, agriculture, manufacturing and fisheries - the emphasis on each sector was to vary with different time periods. Thus for the first five years of the regime the emphasis was to be placed on tourism. The next five years (1984-89) would emphasise agriculture and fisheries development, followed by manufacturing - especially non-agro based industry (see *Line of March for the Party*, op. cit., p. 20). Despite this prioritization of tasks, a great deal of both thought and action went into the development of each of these sectors. Before examining and evaluating the main initiatives undertaken in these sectors, a discussion of the conceptual basis of the PRG's development strategy is offered.

The theory of non-capitalist development

The policy thrusts and ideological orientation of the regime were an outgrowth of the theory of non-capitalist development. The pioneers of Marxism - Marx, Engels and Lenin - had long realized that in order to establish socialism in certain historical circumstances and material conditions certain transitional steps and stages are necessary. The theory of non-capitalist development or 'socialist-orientation' is offered as one of the many possibilities (usually portrayed as the most appropriate) for reaching the ultimate stage of scientific socialism in present-day peripheral social formations.

The theory is believed to have originated in the writings of Marx, Engels and, particularly, Lenin. At the Second Congress of the Communist International in 1920 Lenin declared unequivocally that it was possible for economically backward nations to bypass or significantly interrupt capitalist development in their quest for socialism. The importance of this theoretical principle to the current debate about the utility of non-capitalist development in peripheral societies warrants its full quotation:

> The question was posed as follows: Are we to consider as correct the assertion that the capitalist stage of economic development is inevitable for backward nations now on the road to emancipation and among whom a certain advance towards progress is to be seen since the war? We replied in the negative. If the victorious revolutionary proletariat conducts systematic propaganda among them, and the Soviet Government came to their aid with all the means at their disposal - in that event it will be mistaken to assume that the backward people must inevitably go through the capitalist stage of

development. Not only should we create independent contingents of fighters and party organizations in the colonies and the backward countries, not only at once launch propaganda for the organization of peasants' soviets and strive to adapt them to the pre-capitalist conditions, but the communist international should advance the proposition, with the appropriate theoretical grounding, that with the aid of the proletariat in the advanced countries, backward countries can go over to the Soviet system and, through certain stages of development, to communism, without having to pass through the capitalist stage (cited in Solodovnikov and Bogoslovsky, 1975, p. 23).

This celebrated remark underlines three critical factors for the successful treading of the non-capitalist road, viz: (i) adequate aid from the proletariat in the advanced countries and the Soviet Government; (ii) organization of peasants' soviets which must be appropriate for the productive forces and the corresponding social relations. These organizations should be placed under the hegemony of the peasants and workers; and (iii) further development of theory to inform the struggle for socialism. In other words, creative innovations must be made to the classical theory of scientific socialism to reflect both the internal and external milieus in which the process of change is launched.

The fact that after Lenin's death history unfolded in a way significantly different from his prognosis bring into question not so much the relevance but the feasibility of a non-capitalist strategy in backward, underdeveloped societies. Notable among these developments is the 'yet to be materialized' proletarian revolution in the developed West which he believed was imminent. On the contrary, revolutions in the name of socialism have become something more of a 'Third World' phenomenon. This scenario poses innumerable problems for the question of 'appropriate theoretical grounding'.

Lenin's 'disciples' were quick to respond to the challenge; as witnessed by the voluminous literature generated on this subject during the 1960s and 1970s, and the various conferences convened to discuss the route to socialism in newly independent states. The meeting of Communist and Workers' Parties, held in Moscow in November 1960, was particularly significant. Notwithstanding the objective constraints posed by the economic and social structures of the newly, or about to be, independent societies, delegates concluded unanimously that socialism was the only system which could cure the ills of these nations and put them on the road to genuine economic and social development. As the Declaration candidly put it:

After winning political independence the people seek solutions to the social problems raised by life and to the problems of reinforcing national independence. Different classes and parties offer different

69

solutions. Which course of development to choose is the internal affair of the peoples themselves. As social contradictions grow the national bourgeoisie inclines more and more to compromising with domestic reaction and imperialism. The people, however, begin to see that the best way to abolish age-long backwardness and improve their living standard is that of non-capitalist development. Only thus can the peoples free themselves from exploitation, poverty and hunger. The working class and the broad peasant masses will play the leading part in solving this basic social problem.[6]

For modern proponents of the noncapitalist path, most notably, Andreyev (1974), Solodovnikov (1969), Solodovnikov and Bogoslovsky (1975), and Ulyanovsky (1971; 1974), Lenin's theoretical conclusions hold *a fortiori* during the present period. The experience of the Central Asian republics of the former Soviet Union and the Mongolian People's Republic is often cited as examples *par excellence* of pre-capitalist or semi-feudal societies which have successfully interrupted capitalist development in their march to socialism. In more recent times countries such as Mozambique, Angola, Ethiopia, Tanzania, Zimbabwe and Algeria are regarded as examples of countries which are on the non-capitalist route.

Main characteristics and tasks

The notion of non-capitalist development recognises that the objective and subjective economic, social, political and cultural conditions which are indispensable to the construction of socialism are not yet present in these societies. Not only are their productive forces undeveloped but their social structures are dominated numerically by various semi-feudal elements. These objective constraints warrant a transitional stage which may last for 'a whole historical epoch'. The process begins with the success of the national liberation revolution and the creation of a revolutionary-democratic state. As the name implies the state is under the hegemony of revolutionary democrats or elements of "progressive" petty-bourgeoisie - usually drawn from the intelligentsia. However, this class is also aligned to the oppressed layers in the society (typically regarded as workers, semi-proletarians and peasants) and even certain sections of the national bourgeoisie. As Ulyanovsky (1971) put it: 'At this particular stage the national democrats upholding the non-capitalist path of development are coming to grips with tasks of an anti-feudal, anti-imperialist nature, i.e. general democratic tasks the implementation of which is also in the interests of a certain section of the national bourgeoisie' (p. 39).

70

It is significant that this particular remark makes no reference to anti-capitalist tasks per se. This may be interpreted as a recognition of the strategic importance of the domestic capitalist class in helping to create the material basis for launching a socialist transformation in the long run. During this phase (i.e. non-capitalist) the national democratic state proceeds to lay the socio-economic basis for effecting a socialist revolution. In this very crucial sense the non-capitalist road may best be regarded as 'a form of approach and ultimately of transition to socialism, the connecting link between national liberation revolution and socialist revolution' (Solodovnikov and Bogoslovsky, p. 247).

Success along this path requires the consistent and resolute pursuance of the following programme:

1   The granting of democratic rights and freedom to the peoples (especially freedom of speech, press, freedom to become members of trade union organizations, to establish political parties and to participate in government policy). In brief, all aspects of social life should be democratised. This implies that authoritarian forms of government must be rejected, and political mobilization encouraged.

2   Improve the social and material well-being of the popular masses, particularly in the areas of health and education.

3   Carry out agrarian reforms, including the abandonment of exploitative social relations, establishment of cooperatives and allocation of land to the peasants.

4   Create a mixed economy in which the state sector becomes increasingly dominant. This calls for the 'limiting' and control over the activities of the private sector, particularly foreign corporations. This control may be obtained by nationalization measures and comprehensive economic planning.

5   Reduction of economic dependence through greater self-reliance, inter-sectoral linkages, control over the national economy, and diversification of international economic relations.

6   Abolition of all foreign military bases.

7   Pursue a foreign policy which reflects a firm and unconditional anti-imperialist stance, non-alignment, Third World solidarity and co-operation, and support for a New International Economic Order.

8   Fight against all forms of oppression - nationally and internationally (e.g. support and solidarity for campaigns against racism).

Success along this path also depends on the extent to which the national revolutionary democrats (despite their overwhelming petty-bourgeois origin and character) assimilate the fundamental tenets of Marxism-Leninism. Although many would question the revolutionary potential of this class, the proponents of non-capitalist development are confident that the revolutionary democrats possess the capacity for achieving the mission of eventual socialist construction. 'They do not follow Marxist-Leninist ideology in its entirety even though they have borrowed much from it and have learned much. Most important of all, many of them show, under the impact of historical development, a willingness to learn, to continue drawing nearer to scientific socialism' (Ulyanovsky, 1971, p. 39).

The resolution of the class struggle, externally and internally, is also important. Countries following a non-capitalist approach to social change find themselves in the precarious situation where objective circumstances oblige them, in certain cases, to court foreign and local capital, in pretty much the same way as countries which are unequivocally pro-capitalist. There can be no doubt that this chronic dependence has far-reaching implications for the autonomy of the state. The more dependent the state is on the forces of international capitalism then the more likely it is to become an instrument of those forces. The autonomy of the state can be so reduced to the extent that foreign classes can literally dictate the policies of the government.[7] The role of the International Monetary Fund in the destabilization of the Manley regime in Jamaica is a case in point. Studies abound on both overt and covert intervention of particular imperialist powers in the domestic affairs of dependent economies, especially when the policies or posture of the latter threaten the interests of the former (e.g. Pearce, 1982).

The class struggle is further compounded by the behaviour of the indigenous capitalist class. Excessive dependence on the technical expertise and capital of this class can also prove to be counterproductive. There is no guarantee that they will provide the degree of co-operation which the process requires. If they perceive that their interests are threatened by the 'socialist' posture of the state then they are likely to respond with resistance. This can take a variety of forms ranging from reductions in the rate of investment to outright capital flight. In circumstances where the popular masses are not properly mobilized the political repercussions of this offensive can thwart the entire process. On the other hand, it may not be too difficult to negotiate an accommodation with this class. There may be some room for state autonomy. Writings on the Third World state reveal that local capitalists are very dependent on the state for a whole range of services - infrastructure, security, management of external affairs (including protection against competition from foreign capital), subsidies, and policies which generally enhance capital accumulation (Gold et al., 1975; Skocpol, 1980).

But given that an accommodation has been worked out with domestic and foreign capitalists it is difficult to see how a government can advance further along the delicate path of non-capitalist development without intensifying the class struggle to the point where it either fall from the tight-rope or triumph over reactionary classes. The current evidence gleaned from countries on this path is increasingly pointing in the direction of the former. That is to say, governments find themselves in the uncomfortable position where they are obliged to grant more and more concessions to the private sector, especially the local bourgeoisie. This observation has led many analysts to be sceptical of the very notion of non-capitalist development, let alone its practicality in the present era. Others have been led to characterise such regimes as 'state capitalist', on account of the their failure to bring about fundamental changes in the relations of production and the difficulties they face in deepening the whole process of socialist construction.

Pitfalls

The previous section anticipated some of the underlying weaknesses of the path of non-capitalist development. Much of the criticisms of the non-capitalist road hinge on the commonly observed tendencies of these states to practice dictatorial and despotic methods of government - contrary to the recommendations of theorists of the non-capitalist path. Despite their numerical dominance workers and peasants are often excluded from active independent participation in the socio-political life of the country. Trade unions are made subordinate to the state as strikes are not generally regarded as part of the class struggle. Workers are urged to work assiduously in the interest of the state; portrayed as 'their' state. The right to form political parties and other social organizations to foster their interests is often violated. In sum, disaffection of the masses is commonly greeted with persecution and increasingly repressive measures.

The record of regimes on this path has attracted a number of critics of the theory of non-capitalist development. Thomas (1978) offers one of the most incisive critiques of the theory. The brunt of his critique focuses on the role of political democracy in non-capitalist development. He dismisses categorically the widely held misconceptions in these regimes that 'political democracy is a **bourgeois illusion** based on so-called bourgeois freedom' - on the grounds that these so-called bourgeois freedoms were 'won on the basis of mass struggle - (and) not the product of bourgeois, colonialist, or imperialist generosity' (pp. 22-23, emphasis in original). Thomas sums up:

> political democracy and civil rights therefore cannot be put to stand counterpoised to socialism or to non-capitalist development. Any such argument or line of thinking is fundamentally anti-Marxist. Rationalizations of the need to curb freedom in order to further so-called progress have no place in the building of a socialist society. On the contrary, socialist theory advances two fundamental arguments in direct opposition to this view. In the first instance, socialist theory argues that the weakness of freedom and political democracy, as it has developed in these societies, is not that it is too much, and therefore should be curtailed, but that it is in fact too little (p. 23).

In short, workers and peasants must be socialized to wield political power, control the means of production and participate in all aspects of the development process. Unless the class struggle is resolved in such a way that the national democratic state comes under the firm hegemony and direction of the toiling masses there can be no advance to the higher social order of socialist development.

Another pitfall of the theory centres on the role of the petty bourgeoisie in the broad-based class alliance. Even the staunchest protagonists of the non-capitalist way recognise the historical tendency of the petty bourgeoisie to vacillate, especially under circumstances where they have to make crucial choices between hastening and slowing down the pace of change as objective circumstances dictate. As Ulyanovsky (1969) observed: 'Vacillation, change of heart and fence sitting as between the workers and peasants and the bourgeoisie are the mark of the petty bourgeois intellectual' (p. 46).

In the case of Grenada and a number of other Caribbean economies, the 'petty bourgeois mentality' of large segments of the population does not square easily with the theory of non-capitalist development. This stems from the historical experience of these societies - particularly the way the ex-slaves adjusted to emancipation after 1838. In the case of Grenada we have already emphasised the significance of land (however small and marginal in quality) to the peasants and 'agro-proletariats'. Patrick Emmanuel (1983) has spelt out in direct terms the implications of this reality for the success of non-capitalist development. The central problem, in Emmanuel's words, is:

> **the peasantry was born out of proletarian conditions**, and not the other way around.... The very substance of emancipation was enjoyed for the first time in the form of the mass experience of control over land. This almost uniquely Caribbean sociology of property produced, over a long period of time, a peasant state of mind or outlook, which

is unreceptive to socialist conceptions of collectivization (pp. 210-11, emphasis is in the original).

Emmanuel also made some pertinent remarks on the revolutionary potential of the petit bourgeoisie which is placed at the helm of the alliance. Not only do they have a historical tendency to vacillate between class interests (as Thomas, Ulyanovsky, and others have pointed out) but 'petty bourgeois radicals can outdo themselves with new kinds of infantile disorders on the far left' in their overwhelming enthusiasm 'to pass the stern Soviet tests of ideological development' (p. 203). In a later section he further noted 'The fact that party cadres have to be built after, rather than before, revolutionary takeovers can seriously compound this tendency' (p. 226).

Apart from the absence of a collectivist tradition in the Caribbean (unlike in Africa and Asian societies), and the reservations about the leadership potential of the petty bourgeois radicals, there is also the absence of an authoritarian tradition in the Anglophone Caribbean. Any attempt, therefore, to smash or restrict the institutions or practices associated with democracy will certainly incur the displeasure, if not the vengeance, of those affected. In the English-speaking Caribbean the institutions of Westminster parliamentarism are a definite sore spot. If a case can be made against this political structure (such as its 'divisive' as opposed to 'integrative' nature as stressed by the NJM) a case can certainly be made for it. After a long process of socialization Britain made sure it carefully groomed its subjects into accepting the virtues of parliamentary democracy. Above all, its constitutions enshrine property rights and the conditions for capitalist reproduction. Political competition and economic competition are thus regarded as inseparable. And the 'true' test of democracy (often portrayed as the only one) becomes the holding of national elections.

Another major weakness in the theory stems from the lack of an explicit economic strategy. As Thomas (1978) puts it: 'The literature has not considered in anything like enough detail the conceptualisation of an economic strategy consistent with the development of socialism in these societies .... It is therefore not altogether surprising to observe how closely economic strategy in the non-capitalist societies follow the classic colonial lines' (p. 26). Thomas argues, further, that his own study *Dependence and Transformation* represents the only attempt to fill this gap. Given the impact of this work on the PRG and its contribution to Marxist scholarship on the transition to socialism in peripheral social formations, a brief exposition on its main tenets is offered in the next section, before we move on to examine the PRG's embrace of the theory of non-capitalist development.

The 'Thomas strategy'

As suggested by the title of Thomas' book *Dependence and Transformation: the economics of the transition to socialism*, he is concerned with the economic aspects of the transition process to socialism. The book is specifically concerned with the circumstances of small nations struggling to overcome economic, social and political backwardness. No doubt Thomas had the Caribbean in mind, but he was also concerned with a substantially wider class of economies. He was particularly impressed with the wind of change which was initiated by President Julius Nyerere, shortly after Tanzania attained constitutional independence from Britain.[9] Referring to the changes in Tanzania, Thomas (1974) wrote 'I believe that this single circumstance, more than any other has been responsible for the unique form and conception it (i.e. his book) has taken' (p. 7). But the work was also an elaboration of an earlier book written with Havelock Brewster, *The Dynamics of West Indian Economic Integration* (1967).

In part one, Thomas devotes his attention to a critical analysis of issues relating to underdevelopment, dependence, neo-colonialism and transformation. Here he confronts, and ably dispels, many traditional neo-classical and socialist views on the fate of small economies. In rejecting the former (over-population, geographical and modernization theories) Thomas noted their underlying methodological flaws:

> despite the apparent diversity of these theoretical formulations, there is indeed a common methodological unity in that they all purport to explain underdevelopment as a phenomenon **independent** of the historical process. They are therefore fundamentally anti-historical theories, explaining underdevelopment in terms of innate characteristics of peoples and their environments, or in terms of self-perpetuating cycles of poverty (p. 48, emphasis is in the original).

For Thomas, underdevelopment (whether in small or large economies) is fundamentally an expression of both class relations and the subordinate position in which these societies were integrated into the world capitalist system. Size (smallness) is merely the physical context in which social relations are established and the mode of production is organised (ibid., p. 30). It becomes a problem when the small economy remains enmeshed in the international capitalist system and attempts to pursue the same goals as the developed countries.

Although he posits a more sophisticated analysis than most *dependency theorists* (especially his treatment of class) his thesis on underdevelopment is strikingly similar to that enunciated by Andre Gunder Frank (1967, 1969, 1972), who is usually credited as the 'High Priest' of the dependency

76

paradigm. Like other subscribers to this paradigm, he attributes the problem of underdevelopment to the effects of international capitalism. As Thomas (1974) puts it: 'European development generated the underdevelopment of the rest of the world by destroying those indigenous social forces which otherwise might have led to the transformation of their pre-capitalist modes of production' (p. 58). In their place colonies like Grenada were offered participation in the global division of labour as suppliers of raw materials and consumers of manufactured goods; leading to the long-term consequence of a profound divergence between the structures of production, consumption, and economic activities in underdeveloped societies.

In true neo-Marxian spirit he thus argues for a fundamental disengagement of underdeveloped countries from international capitalism and the adoption of a comprehensive socialist strategy of development. It is in this context that he postulates his famous two 'iron laws of transformation', namely: (i) convergence of resource use and demand; and (ii) the convergence of need with demand. This convergence is a *sine qua non* for the economic transformation of small, peripheral societies during the transition to socialism.

The rest of Thomas' book is concerned with the technical issues and problems which are central to the transformation process. Broadly speaking, these include the role of different sectors in the accumulation process (particularly agriculture); role of the state (in structural transformation, ownership of the means of production, relative balance between private and public sectors, attitudes towards foreign capital, foreign trade, comprehensive planning, reliance on the market as a mechanism for allocating resources, transformation of social relations and international economic relations, land reform); the role of aid and the general financing of the transformation process; and the importance of regional integration.

The economic and political strategy outlined by Thomas is, arguably, the principal innovation in his contribution to the debate on underdevelopment. For the most part, his colleagues in the Caribbean and Latin America were principally preoccupied with diagnosing the cause(s) of dependence and underdevelopment. Very little attention was devoted to offering concrete policies for transforming the structures and growth-inhibiting institutions which underlie their analyses. Unlike Thomas' work, their analyses displayed very little awareness of the relevance of class and politics to the discussion of underdevelopment and transformation. Referring to the theoretical bankruptcy of the Caribbean variant of dependency theory, Blackman (1980) noted:

> To this day I believe that 'dependence theory' provides a useful **descriptive** analysis of underdevelopment in former colonies. Unfortunately, having developed a useful theory of underdevelopment,

the scholarship of the New World economists fell apart. As some of them now admit, they omitted the next logical step - the development of an **operational** model of economic development. ... By operational, I mean 'likely to succeed in real world conditions' (p. 45, emphasis in the original).

Although the analysis offered in Thomas' book represents a major advance on New World scholarship, it, nevertheless, suffers from a number of limitations. It underplays the dependence on external inputs which would still be encountered in the process of implementing the two 'iron laws of transformation' and other important aspects of his strategy. Like theorists of the non-capitalist path, Thomas also fails to address the political difficulties (both at the national and international levels) which such a model would encounter on account of its socialist orientation. This radical posture in itself constitutes a barrier to development, especially in the context of Caribbean economies. Oxaal (1982) captures the seriousness of the geo-political constraint when he wrote 'the intellectual's question, "which models of the future are **desirable**?" (becomes) quickly transformed into the politician's question, "Which models of the future are **possible**"' (p. xiv, emphasis added).

The PRG's embrace of non-capitalist development

Despite the problems with the theory of non-capitalist development the leaders of the New Jewel Movement pledged their unconditional allegiance to it. Although very little was said about the theory in public top members of the party admitted on more than one occasion that they were guided by it; a view confirmed by the documents captured by US marines during the October 1983 invasion and sources close to the party.

In their study of the Grenada revolution, Jacobs and Jacobs (1980) argued that 'The (party) did not fit the pro-capitalist mould of either the GNP or the GULP. Indeed, the party emerged as a non-capitalist one, displaying certain selected scientific socialist tendencies, especially in the area of democratic centralism' (p. 78). Jacobs and Jacobs further noted that the drive towards firm Marxist-Leninist principles of party building and organization was not contemplated until after the 'independence sell-out' of 1974 when Gairy's party was restored to power despite the intensive campaign of the New Jewel Movement to prevent this occurrence.

The analysis offered by Jacobs and Jacobs was further supported by public pronouncements made by prominent members of the PRG. Thus, in

November 1979, Selwyn Strachan declared in an interview that Grenada was undergoing a process similar to Cuba's:

> We believe that our course of development will be more or less the same as the Cuban revolution. There may be one or two minor differences, but nothing dramatic'...If we have taken a decision to socially transform our society, and we are adopting the correct approach according to the laws of historical development, we should more or less go through the same process, with slight differences because of the unevenness, since some countries are more developed than the next. But basically, the approach will be the same, if we are moving to socialism (cited in Bishop, 1982b, pp. 15-16).

In an interview two years later, Bishop himself pointed out that the revolution was at the 'national democratic stage, the anti-imperialist stage of the process we are building' (cited in *Granma Weekly Review*, 12 July 1981). Bishop also went on to list a number of tasks which were required on the political and economic fronts to effect this disengagement from imperialism. He also noted that his government has already taken some of these steps. Among the tasks stressed was the need for 'revolutionary democracy' to ensure constant participation of the people.

The 1973 manifesto also contained clear hints that the NJM was committed to an alternative political system to the one bequeathed to Grenada by Britain. For example, a passage in the manifesto noted:

> To create the new life for the new man in the society, it is necessary that we reject the present economic and political system which we live under. More than this, we need to construct an entirely new system of values where the lust for money, power, and individual selfish gain are no longer the motivating factors. The creation of this new man demands the transformation of the minds and hearts of each and every one of us (Manifesto of the NJM, p. 156).

Indeed, on international affairs the manifesto affirmed 'we stand firmly committed to a nationalist, anti-imperialist, anti-colonialist position'.[10]

The Westminster model was denounced on account of its divisive and 'undemocratic' nature:

> Firstly, parties divide the people into warring camps. Secondly, the system places power into the hands of a small ruling clique. That clique victimises and terrorises members of the other party. Thirdly, the ruling elite seizes control of all avenues of public information, for example, the radio station, and use them for its own ends. Finally,

and most importantly, it fails to involve the people except for a few seconds once in every five years when they make an "X" on a ballot paper (Manifesto of the NJM, p. 143).

Accordingly, the Westminster model was to be replaced with a system of 'People's Assemblies' on the Tanzanian *ujamaa* model. The People's Assemblies would include four sub-assemblies, viz, (i) Village Assemblies; (ii) Parish Assemblies; (iii) Workers' Assemblies; and (iv) a National Assembly. Members of the Village Assembly would be drawn from those who are 18 years old and over.

The party's pro-socialist stance was also reflected in its statement of principles (1976); which pledged for: (i) people's participation, people's politics, and people's democracy; (ii) people's cooperatives for the collective development of the people; (iii) health care based on need; (iv) maximum development of the people's talents, abilities, and culture; (v) full control of Grenada's natural resources; (vi) employment for everyone; (vii) a decent standard of living for everyone; (viii) preservation of democratic freedoms (including freedom of expression and religion); (ix) the emancipation of black and oppressed peoples throughout the world; and (x) a united people ... a new society ... a just society (cited in Bishop, 1982b, p. 23). These ten principles were clearly consistent with the non-capitalist path of development, and radical plantation theory.

Composition of The People's Revolutionary Government

In keeping with the requirements of the non-capitalist path, the party set up a government (known as the People's Revolutionary Government), which was comprised of an alliance of different social classes with special emphasis on the propertied class. 'We need the alliance', Bishop told party members in September 1982, 'to hold power in the first few days and weeks' .... 'to consolidate and build the revolution and to ensure the defeat of imperialism', ... 'because we don't have enough managers, because we don't have enough international contacts, because we don't have enough markets' (*Line of March for the Party*, op. cit., p. 19).

Of the 14 people who comprised the ruling council of the People's Revolutionary Government when they initially took power most were non-party members. For instance, Sydney Ambrose and Simon Charles were described as members of the peasantry, Bernard Gittens and Lloyd Noel belonged to the 'professional middle strata', Palm Buxo and Norris Bain were 'middle capitalists', and Lyden Ramdhanny was 'big capitalist'. The rationale was to reassure imperialism so that they "won't get too excited and would say 'well they have some nice fellas in that thing, everything alright' and as a result wouldn't think about sending in troops" (*Line of March for the Party,* p. 21). But Bishop was not prepared to allow the revolution to degenerate into some form of state capitalism. Thus, after weathering the storm in the critical period of the revolutionary process another seven party cadres were appointed to the government (only two of whom were drawn from the propertied class).

While conceding the need for democracy they also saw the need for firm control. The result was a dictatorship of the small party.[11] So much so that Bishop could boast in 1982 that the party enjoyed more than '90 per cent direct control of the government' (*Line of March for the Party,* p. 23). This hegemony was also extended to the multiplicity of mass organizations and committees which were established, in the spirit of the 1973 manifesto. These included parish and zonal councils, the National Student's Council, Farmer's Unions, trade unions, community work brigades, the Pioneer Movement, the National Youth Organization (NYO), the National Women Organization (NWO), New Jewel Movement party support groups, the People's Militia - and a bewildering variety of committees which included investment, workers, organizing, discipline, education, emulation, production and defence committees.

Contrary to the manifesto the 'organs of democracy' now began to function differently. Power no longer flowed from the bottom up but, rather, it was the other way around. This is not to say that the mass organizations were not consulted on policies. This took place, but as Mandle (1985a) correctly noted 'The Party, ultimately, expected to be obeyed. Its rule was not open to challenge. The ruling party could listen to the people but would reserve to itself the right to adjudicate the conflicts and choose among alternative policy options' (p. 66). The Party defended this system of rule since it was claimed that the people did not yet understand the science of Marxism-Leninism. It was therefore necessary to act in their name.

Although other parties were not legally abolished they were rendered 'silent' by the New Jewel Movement. They were only too aware of the divisive role of 'opposition' parties. Meetings and demonstrations by non-party members were thwarted by the People's Revolutionary Army (Mandle, 1985a, p. 63). The assumption of total power by a Leninist vanguard party - despite the size of Grenada - was to have its problems, since it had tremendous implications for the workload of the party members. The strict criteria for party membership did not help the situation. As late as October 1983 the NJM party had a mere 72 full members. The other 278 members were 'Candidates' and 'Applicants', working hard to pass the arduous test for full membership.[12]

Before turning directly to the implementation of the PRG's development

81

strategy, it should be recalled that initially the government commanded the co-operation, if not the support, of the overwhelming majority of the population. Without this co-operation the revolution would probably not have survived the early days. On the morning of the revolution Bishop called on 'the working people, the youths, workers, farmers, fishermen, middle class people, and women to join our armed forces at central positions in your communities and to give them any assistance they call for'. He also assured Grenadians that: 'all democratic freedoms, including freedom of elections, religions and political opinion, will be restored to the people. The personal safety and property of individuals will be protected. Foreign residents are quite safe, and are welcome to remain in Grenada. And we look forward to continuing friendly relations with those countries with which we now have such relations' (Radio Address, 13 March 1979).

But dissatisfaction was not long in coming to the fore since the party was overwhelmed by the reactionary use to which democratic freedoms could be put. To safeguard the revolution it chose to introduce what to them were 'revolutionary manners', but to those affected by them (and their external allies) these were expressions of the repressive and undemocratic nature of the regime. The list of measures included indefinite imprisonment, press censorship, and a hesitancy to hold elections in the spirit of Westminster parliamentarism. These measures were to have an adverse impact on their attempt to transform the economic base of the economy to begin the process of socialist construction proper. The logic of the path requires that the party 'use' the bourgeoisie rather than the other way around.

In Bishop's words:

> We bring them in for what we want to bring them in for. They are not part of our dictatorship because when they try to hold public meetings and we don't want that, the masses shut down the meeting. When we want to hold zonal councils and we don't want them there, we keep them out. When they want to put out newspapers and we don't want that, we close it down. When they want freedom of expression to attack the Government or to link up with the CIA and we don't want that, we crush them and jail them. They are not part of the dictatorship. In fact, if the truth is to be told, they have been repressed by the dictatorship (*Line of March for the Party*, p. 24).

As we will see in chapter six below the private sector was fully aware of this dictatorship which Bishop spoke about. Its frequent resort to 'revolutionary manners' did much to poison the investment climate, and hence undermine the material base of the revolution. This in turn made it more difficult for the regime to advance on the non-capitalist development path. And this was despite the emphasis which Anreyev and other proponents of the theory of non-capitalist development placed on pragmatism and the avoidance of authoritarian forms of government. However, the PRG was more consistent and resolute in its formulation and implementation of the type of economic policies proposed by Clive Thomas and other New World scholars. As we will see, these were evident in the policies pursued in the key sectors of the economy - agriculture, tourism, and manufacturing. The policies pursued in each of these three sectors are critically evaluated in turn in chapters four, five and six below.

Notes

1. Clive Thomas was a prominent member of the *New World Group*. Professor Thomas is now Director of the Institute of Development Studies at the University of Guyana.

2. It should be noted that very little was said about compensation except that they intend to negotiate with the owners in order to organise this scheme successfully. See 1973 Manifesto of the New Jewel Movement, p.147.

3. For a list of other economic activities which were believed to be feasible and how these can be developed to help meet Grenada's needs, see p. 146 of the manifesto.

4. Note LIAT denotes Leeward Islands Air Transport. LIAT is the principal air carrier between the Windward Islands and the rest of the Caribbean.

5. Details of the **Materials Balance** approach in the Grenadian context are outlined in a government document (written in 1982), bearing the title *System for Planning Grenada's Economy.*

6. Modern proponents of the theory of non-capitalist development have legitimised the theory by linking it explicitly to the writings of Marx, Engels and Lenin; and the various declarations of the world communist movement. See 'Statement of the 81 Communist and Workers Parties, December 1960' in *The African Communist* (No. 4, 1961).

7. See Frank (1979), especially pp. 4-5 for a lucid discussion of this point.

8. Note the theory of non-capitalist development provides no concrete insights as to how this happy marriage can be brought about. The vagueness of many of the formulations of the theory is one of its main drawbacks. This is partly due to the fact that the theory is designed to appeal to leftist regimes in all parts of the Third World, even though there are huge variations in their current economic, social, and political profiles.

9.   See Nyerere (1968) for an elaboration of the government's strategy for building a socialist society.

10.   This position is remarkably similar to the tenets of the theory of non-capitalist development. Perhaps the authors of the manifesto had access to this body of writing before it was 'officially' brought to the region in 1975. See Gonsalves (1981) for a general discussion of the theory in the context of Africa and the Caribbean.

11.   Real power resided in the Central Committee which was established in September 1979. It had a membership of 16 in September 1983. The members were Hudson Austin (Commander of the People's Revolutionary Army, Minister of Communications), Fitzroy Bain (Trade Union leader), Tan Bartholomew (People's Revolutionary Army), Maurice Bishop (Prime Minister, Minister of Defence, Interior, Information, and Carriacou Affairs), Phyllis Coard (Head of National Woman's Organization), Leon Cornwall (People's Revolutionary Army, ex-ambassador to Cuba), Ewart Layne (People's Revolutionary Army), Chris De Riggs (Minister of Health), Liam James (People's Revolutionary Army), George Louison (Minister of Agriculture), Kamau McBarnett, Ian St Bernard, (People's Revolutionary Army), Selwyn Strachan, (Minister of Mobilisation), John 'Chalkie' Ventour, and Unison Whiteman (Minister of External Relations).

12.   Applicants had to wait for one year before they could be considered to be a 'candidate member'. To be accepted, they were required to pass a number of tests; embracing five points: (i) acceptance of Marxist-Leninist principles and willingness to pursue further development; (ii) dedication to party work, (iii) attitudes towards criticisms and party discipline; (iv) relations with the masses; and (v) possession of 'proletarian' qualities such as modesty and respect for the masses. If accepted as a candidate member, after working satisfactorily for one year, the individual could submit a further application to become a full member. Acceptance was conditional on the applicant excelling in a number of areas. These included possession of good Marxist-Leninist leadership qualities, ability to guide junior party comrades, technical and professional skills to carry out political work (including an application of Leninist standards of discipline, consistency and rigour) and good relations with the masses. See chapter six of Thorndike (1985) and *Line of March for Party* for details on the workings of party life under the NJM).

4 Agrarian reforms and rural development

The arduous task of transforming the agricultural sector was an integral part of the revolutionary programme. This is not surprising given the resource endowment of the country. In this chapter, we discuss the PRG's agrarian policies and assess the success or otherwise of these policies.

The agrarian strategy

It was patently clear to the revolutionary government that the development and transformation of the agricultural sector was an important prerequisite to attaining the economic goals of the revolution. In recognition of this fact, Deputy Prime Minister Coard described agriculture as 'the base, the bedrock of anything we do'.[1] Appropriately enough, 1981 was officially declared as the **Year of Agricultural Production and Agro-industry**.

The objectives set for this vital sector were: (i) to serve as a major generator of foreign exchange; (ii) to provide the main basis for industrialization and the building of agro-industrial development; (iii) to serve as the main creator of jobs to overcome unemployment; (iv) to supply as much food for the population as is economically and technologically feasible;(v) to increase the country's self-reliance by utilizing to its fullest extent all agricultural land (Government of Grenada, 1982b, p. 95). Implicit in these objectives was a predominant emphasis on export-orientation rather than a policy of mere import-substitution. As experts in the People's Revolutionary Government put it:

> ... the moment we start to produce anything in our economy in a serious way or even half serious way, if we don't find export markets for it, we dead. A very simple reason is that our population is

110,000. The experts told us that we only need 300 acres of our rich and fertile soil to produce all of the fresh foods required to feed all the people of Grenada. Therefore, even for the lettuce, tomatoes, carrots, and cabbage, not to mention manufactured items, we have to find external markets in order to satisfy the needs to employ our people and to raise their income and hence their material standard of living (Government of Grenada, 192b, p. 44).

But apart from the problem of economies of scale the government was conscious of a myriad of deep-seated problems plaguing the island's agricultural sector. To recapitulate some of these, we may note: (i) the rugged and mountainous nature of the terrain; (ii) the chronic inequity in the distribution of land among the farming community; (iii) the numerical dominance of this sector by small-scale producers with a predominantly subsistence mentality; (iv) extreme fragmentation of the holdings of farmers, especially those with under ten acres; (v) the relative dearth of young people with managerial and agronomic training employed in this sector; and (vi) absence and/or underprovision of allied infrastructure and services (roads, transportation, drainage facilities, market, credit and technical advice).

These gave rise to other problems. For instance, fragmentation frequently occasioned loss of time and energy in transporting tools, seeds and other inputs from one fragment of land to another, difficulties in guarding against praedial larceny and supervising paid labourers when employed, loss of land to create boundaries between fragments owned by different people, and the need to solicit the co-operation of owners of neighbouring fragments when introducing certain farm improvement schemes.[2]

A Census carried out in July 1981 by the PRG in collaboration with the Organization of American States (OAS) provided a wealth of empirical data on the structure of Grenada's agrarian sector. This agricultural census had five aims, viz: (i) to develop a farm register in which names and addresses of farmers were recorded by 'enterprise' (i.e. cocoa, nutmeg, bananas, sugar cane, vegetable, fruits, roots and tubers, peas and corn, small livestock, large livestock, coconuts, minor spices, cotton, peanuts and bees); (ii) to furnish information on pertinent aspects of agriculture - tenure, population of full and part-time individuals involved in agriculture, types of crops produced for sale, and the importance of agriculture to the livelihood of the family; (iii) to ascertain the total acreage of land under agriculture and the amount lying idle; (iv) to find out the main problems confronting farmers; and (v) to provide a frame for regional agricultural survey.

The Census provided information which is indispensable to any successful planning in this all-important sector. Two of the most worrying findings for the PRG were: (i) the apparent decline in the total farm acreage relative to the findings of the last two censuses (total farm acreage declined from 50,693 acres in 1961 to 38,942 acres in 1975, and 34,243 acres in 1981); and (ii) the apparent reduction in the total population engaged in farming activities - 15,319 in 1961, 12,565 in 1975, and 8,202 in 1981. And this was despite the overwhelming importance of agriculture to the national economy. With respect to problems facing farmers (in order of magnitude), the Census revealed that the single most important problem for farmers in all districts was praedial larceny. This was followed by labour shortage.[3] These two problems were most acute on larger farms. In fact the figures revealed a direct relationship between farm size and the existence of these two problems (see table 4:1).

Table 4:1
Problems experienced by farmers by farm size

Problems	0-2 Acres	2-10 Acres	Over 10 acres
Praedial larceny	23.23	26.00	30.22
Plant material	13.31	8.67	4.99
Marketing	5.77	5.18	2.87
Extension help	8.55	6.89	4.99
Labour	17.43	20.90	21.46
Water	7.71	5.26	1.97
Roads	9.33	13.55	19.33
Disease	12.61	11.63	12.83
Credit	2.06	1.92	1.34
N (per cent)	100	100	100

Source: 'Final Report on Grenada Agricultural Census', p. 39.

The Census report ended on the very insightful note that: 'Regardless of the effort placed in planning and implementing agricultural projects, benefits would never accrue to the farmers unless their present problems are identified and solved'. With regard to the severe problem of praedial larceny two adverse consequences were noted: 'In the short or immediate run, it reduces farmers income. In the longer term, the psychological impact on farmers would lead to less and less acreage cultivated and a fall in overall agricultural production' (Government of Grenada, 1982a, p. 46).

The significance and implications of these findings for agricultural planning cannot be over-emphasized.[4] Technical assistance was sought in this area (i.e. agricultural planning) from the Food and Agriculture Organization of the United Nations (FAO) in 1980. The team which came in its wake noted in their report the chronic lack of skilled manpower in the island's Ministry of Agriculture. For example, not a single trained economist was employed in the Ministry. Nor was there any one with the expertise to prepare project documents in a manner suitable for presentation to donor agencies. At best appointees in the Ministry were only able to prepare crude 'shopping lists for aid'. If these lists were approved by donors further problems were created since there was no one with the required knowledge and experience to implement the project(s) (FAO, 1982, p. 4).

The FAO document also made the obvious, but important, observation that the present structure of the Ministry of Agriculture was created during the colonial era - a period when the Grenadian economy was shunted on a completely different path from what the PRG was embarking on. In the words of the consultant:

> the priorities were mainly directed towards promoting and enhancing the production of what have become regarded as the traditional export crops ... It was the larger and more affluent land owners and producers who were the main beneficiaries of this policy: the smaller farmers, i.e. those who would be responsible for the production of crops for local consumption, were in general passed over with regard to extension services, credit, marketing, etc (FAO, ibid., p. 4).

Against this background, a proposal was prepared for a three-year project for the government's consideration. Among the immediate objectives specified were: (i) to improve the effectiveness of the Ministry of Agriculture by helping in its reorganization so that it can exercise more effective follow-through of its programme and plans; (ii) enhance the planning capability of the Ministry of Agriculture by helping in the organization and placement of a planning unit within the Ministry, preparing its terms of reference and setting up its posts (including job descriptions); (iii) provide training to planning staff in essentials of agricultural planning, project identification, preparation, implementation and monitoring; (iv) establish and operationalize a mechanism for monitoring all capital projects; (v) provide assistance in the development of cooperatives, especially at the level of training; (vi) assist the Ministry to obtain its own 'in-house' capability to develop and operate a computerized data-bank and retrieval system as well as undertaking selected programming exercises (FAO, ibid., p. 5). Recommendations were also made for the granting of fellowships and consultancies to Grenadians from international donors, especially in the areas of computer programming, development planning and agricultural economics.

The long term objective was to assist the PRG in its drive to create a strong and viable agricultural sector.

The government was quick to adopt the recommendations of the FAO team. In addition to the team's emphasis on institutional restructuring of the Ministry of Agriculture and improved training at the level of policy making, the government's strategy for correcting the malaise in agriculture emphasised the following: (i) the attainment of a more equitable distribution of land; (ii) improved training, education, housing, health and transport facilities for agricultural workers and farmers; (iii) greater provision of extension services including an effective co-ordination of such services; (iv) the introduction of modern technology; (v) the production of non-traditional export crops in addition to the traditional ones; (vi) the provision of increased credit to farmers, especially funds from the state banks; and (vii) the establishment of commercially viable and efficient state corporations in this sector.

This was not empty rhetoric. Indeed, some of the government's most radical initiatives were undertaken in this sector. The development of the state and cooperative sectors in this pivotal area of the economy was comparatively phenomenal. Among the most notable initiatives were the Grenada State Farms Corporation (GFC), Grenada Agro-industries Ltd (GAI), Marketing and National Importing Board (MNIB), National Fisheries Corporation (NFC), Livestock Production and Genetic Centre (LPGC), the Forestry Development Corporation (FDC) and the National Agricultural and Cooperative Development Agency (NACDA).

The development of state farms

The Grenada State Farms Corporation (GFC) was doubtless one of the most important arms of the State's involvement in agriculture. The amount of land under its control, the geographical spread of the farms, as well as the wide-ranging power of the GFC were such that it was in a position to influence the future of the island's agriculture.

Established in late 1980 (People's Law No. 6l), the Corporation sought to manage, develop and operate the estates and farms which the PRG had inherited from the Gairy administration. These were acquired from Gairy's opponents in the 1970s. But as was characteristic of 'Gairyism', the farms and estates (together with their physical facilities) degenerated to very low levels as a result of neglect, poor organization, and corruption. Marketing arrangements were ad hoc, often organized by the workers who worked on the farms rather than by the produce officer in the Ministry of Agriculture to whom this task was assigned. As political supporters of Gairy, the workers on the farms were allotted small parcels of land on the same estates for their own farming. One consequence of this arrangement (coupled with limited supervision) was that the workers concentrated on their own private farming to the detriment of the state farms. The net result of these constraints was poor worker productivity, low output, and persistent deficits on most of the farms. According to a report from the Caribbean Development Bank only three of 23 farms made a profit in 1980 (Caribbean Development Bank, 1982a, p. 4). Another source noted that EC$4 million was spent on these estates in 1978. Yet the revenue generated was under EC$250,000, an operating loss of some EC$3.75 million (Government of Grenada, 1982b, p. 110). The GFC thus began its operations in early 1981 with a view to integrating the inherited farms into the national development strategy for the economy and reversing these losses.

The law which established the GFC empowered the organization not only to hold property, but to sue, contract services, trade in agricultural goods and services, borrow funds, sell shares in the Corporation or property, as well as to establish agencies and offices. Five critical functions were assigned to the GFC, viz: (i) maintain, manage and control the farms of the Corporation; (ii) develop on a commercial basis all farms under GFC; (iii) stimulate and undertake agricultural development on Grenada Farms and to participate in agricultural development projects as are approved by the Minister of Agriculture; (iv) stimulate development among small farmers in close proximity to Grenada Farms (eg, by supplying inputs to small farmers); and (v) perform any other function consistent with agricultural development as the Minister may, from time to time, direct (Government of Grenada, 1982i). Although provision was made in the law for discharging its functions and obligations, the Grenada Farms were required to be managed on strict commercial lines. Hence the principal source of funds was expected to be derived from the sale of farm produce. Indeed, closer examination of the functions of the GFC (especially one and two) suggests that it was meant to serve as a model organization. It would demonstrate to the farming community, especially small producers, that a farm is a business unit and as such efficiency was critical to its survival and success.[5]

The farms were aptly sited for initiating new farming techniques, erosion control, irrigation, fertility maintenance, and new products for export and domestic consumption. They were distributed throughout the island, with the heaviest concentration in the east and south. Despite the possible 'demonstration effect' which this distribution was expected to create, it certainly raised major problems for efficient management of the state farms. This constraint was further compounded by the poor quality of the staff which were appointed for the purpose. The supervisors and managers were described as 'farm hands promoted over the years, had little formal

91

educational training, and no agricultural training' (Inter-American Institution for Co-operation in Agriculture, 1981, p. 5). Another independent source lamented in early 1983:

> At present, there is no policy regarding the management of human resources, no standardised recruitment process, no overall training programme, no compensation policy based on job descriptions and job evaluation, no performance appraisal system, no coherent employee benefits programme, no system for dealing with industrial relations, and most serious of all, no system of personnel record-keeping (Green, 1983, pp. 24-25).

These organizational weaknesses contributed enormously to the poor financial performance of the GFC (discussed later in this chapter). Yet the government was determined to increase the amount of land under its control from the 4,000 acres (roughly nine per cent of the total agricultural acreage) which originally constituted the GFC.

As was noted earlier, the 1981 Agricultural Census revealed that substantial acreage of some of the island's best agricultural land was either unutilized or underutilized. To correct this anomaly the PRG enacted a *Land Development and Utilization Law* (People's Law no. 21, 1981). This law gave the government power to compulsorily lease for a period of ten years any estate over 100 acres declared by the Land Development and Utilization Commission to be 'idle'. This Commission was assured of full state protection in the execution of its duties: 'No action, suit, prosecution or other proceedings shall be brought or instituted personally against any member of the Commission in respect of any act done bona fide in pursuance or execution or intended execution of this law' (Government of Grenada, 1982i, p. 114). Of course, it was the government who determined whether or not the act of the Commission was 'bona fide'.

Under this law the Commission had power to demand detailed information from owners or occupiers of land such as: (i) the size and boundary of the land under its ownership or control; (ii) the proportion of the land in use and the manner of its use; (iii) the form of land tenure; (iv) encumbrances (if any) relating to the land; and (v) details of any registration number, volume, folio, or other information in relation to the land or persons with legal claims on the land. After this information was obtained the next stage was to carry out an inspection of the land; aimed at determining its condition, type of activities undertaken, and ascertaining what crops were most suitable to be cultivated on it.[6] Once the Commission collected data on the land the owner could not lease or dispose of the land without the approval of the Commission. The owner of unutilized or underutilized land could (in some cases) avoid compulsory acquisition - i.e. by submitting an acceptable development plan for the land. If this plan was rejected by the Commission a period of three weeks was allowed for him to submit an appeal against the Commission's decision (i.e., in the event of an acquisition).

As a result of a significant amendment to the law in December 1982 the period for an appeal was reduced to seven days after the service of the Commission's notice. The Land Utilization Law thus shifted into a higher gear. The full text of the amendment read:

> Where any land shall have been declared to be idle land under the provisions of Section five whether or not the Idle Land Order made in respect thereof shall have become effective or been published in the Gazette and the Minister in his discretion considers that for any of the purposes of increasing production, providing employment or otherwise serving the national interest the Crown should obtain a lease of such land without delay the Minister (i.e. Minister of Agriculture) may make an order (hereinafter called an "Immediate Leasing Order") in respect of such land (Government of Grenada, 1982i, pp. 242-43).

As a result of the Land Utilization Law the government was able to increase the amount of land under its control by as much as 9,000 acres by July 1983. Added to the 4,000 acres under the GFC, this means that the state controlled almost 30 per cent of the total agricultural land in the island after a mere four years in office. Reportedly, the acquisitions which came in the wake of the Land Utilization Law was only phase one of the operation. Phase two was meant to target estates between 50 and 100 acres.[7]   According to some critics the law was primarily geared against non-supporters of the government.[8] The small size of Grenada made it easy to determine the social and political background of every landowner of note. In this sense the PRG was guilty of some of the very crimes which Gairy had previously committed.[9]

Expressing its suspicion and disapproval of the PRG's Land Utilization Law the 1982 World Bank team noted:

> The question that first must be answered is why is the land idle. Land is idle either because it is marginal in economic terms, or because the owner has no means of working the land, or because he is not interested in cultivating it. Leasing the land compulsorily from owners might prove productive only in the latter case. In the other two cases, changing control over the land will not address the fundamental issue. Incentives and/or stronger support to the farmer would be required (World Bank, 1982a, p. 12).

Although there are some obvious grains of truth in this remark it missed the point that in many cases the reason for unutilization or underutilization of land in Grenada was not merely lack of financial resources to develop it. As demonstrated in Chapter One the inequitable distribution of land in Grenada and elsewhere in the Caribbean was largely due to historical factors. Indeed, the owners of much of the land acquired by the PRG were not even resident in the island any longer. Sizeable tracts were either left uncultivated, rented to private farmers, or left under the supervision of friends and relatives. It was their absence which facilitated the PRG's relatively easy acquisition of this land. It was therefore economically rational for the government to bring the idle land into cultivation, especially given the widespread unemployment of young people in the country.

Promotion of cooperatives

One of the government's response to youth unemployment was to establish cooperatives in the productive sphere of the economy, particularly in agriculture. Although the state had considerable land under its control, that land was earmarked for its own purposes. The dominant means of acquiring land for cooperatives was from the private sector.

The National Cooperative Development Agency (NACDA) was set up to assist this process (People's Law number 18, 1980). As specified by the law, NACDA had three objectives: (i) to coordinate the activities relating to the establishment and development of cooperatives; (ii) provide the services necessary to enhance this development; and (iii) to advise on matters relating to cooperative principles and management. The slogan of the organization **'Idle Hands plus Idle Lands = End to Unemployment'** spoke for itself. First, the unemployed person or group identified land that they were willing to bring under production. Through technicians attached to NACDA, a 'feasibility study' was conducted to determine whether the land was capable of fulfilling the intended purpose. If it was, the government would negotiate with the owner to see if it was possible to obtain freehold or leasehold purchase of the land. Once it was procured (on whatever arrangement) it was then given to the particular cooperative on a leasehold basis. To finance the new cooperatives a revolving loan of EC$1 million was granted to NACDA[10] by the state-owned National Commercial Bank on concessionary terms.

Like the GFC and other productive state enterprises the enterprises under NACDA were expected to operate along strict commercial lines. To this end losses sustained by new enterprises were only absorbed by NACDA in the first year of its operation. Further loans to cooperatives by NACDA were made contingent on their financial performance. Some cooperatives were fortunate to receive funds directly from international aid donors. Provisions were also made for a cooperative to obtain a second loan for diversification or expansion purposes. But this was only allowed after nine months of successful operation.

In commenting on the significance of the cooperatives Coard had this to say:

> NACDA is changing the idea that the old colonial-type estate is the only model for agriculture, and showing our people how they can produce together, sit down, organize, plant and reap their own harvests. In doing this, it has brought the youth back to the land in a significant way, sending down the average age of our agricultural worker from 62 to 51 years. If we go on like this, after next year it will be 40, and the year after, 29! Comrades, our agriculture is becoming young again! And all that young muscle and brain power, working together, is what will cause real and solid economic construction (Government of Grenada, 1982e, pp. 41-42).

Performance of state and cooperative farms

That NACDA was a new model of agricultural development in the Grenadian context is indisputable. So too was GFC - conceived, as it were, as the leading vehicle for transforming Grenada's agriculture. But novelty has its price and this was to account for the disappointing performance of both the state farms and cooperatives - a disappointment which even the PRG conceded.

With respect to the GFC, its account recorded a deficit of EC$640,525 in 1981. This operating deficit increased to EC$1.4 million in 1982. Although output for 1982 was targeted at EC$2.83 million, only a pitiful 37 per cent of the target was attained. In outlining the reasons for this dismal performance the PRG noted the following: (i) Poor organization and management, and no systematic practice of record-keeping or accounting[11]; (ii) primitive farming practices; (iii) multi-cropping activities; and low worker productivity which not only resulted from factors (i) and (ii), but also from farmers' advanced age, poor nutrition, lack of education, as well as the continued practice of private farming during the time they should be working on state farms[12]; and (iv) weak linkages between the GFC and other allied state enterprises, most notably the MNIB and GAI (Government of Grenada, 1983e, pp. 50-51).

These problems were not peculiar to GFC. They afflicted NACDA even more. Although young and energetic the members of the cooperatives had no experience in the activities in which they were engaged. Neither did they

95

understand the principles behind cooperative forms of ownership. Referring to the slow growth and progress of cooperative enterprises in the island Coard remarked: '...our youths are more interested in working with government than in joining co-ops. This came out in our unemployment survey of April 1982' (Government of Grenada, 1983e, p. 31). The majority of these enterprises operated at a loss like their GFC counterpart. For this reason NACDA was unable to recover most of the loans made to the enterprises. The monthly recovery rate in agriculture (with the exception of Tivoli Ford and Vegetable Service Society) as of the third quarter of 1982 was an abysmal 7.7 per cent. It was even worse in the manufacturing, construction and service sectors, where the recovery rates were zero per cent.[13]

Despite their poor performance the cooperatives had a vital role to play in the new society that the PRG were constructing. Apart from helping to grapple with the bottlenecks in the agricultural sector the cooperatives were devised to foster socialist and collectivist forms of consciousness among their members. In the words of Prime Minister Bishop the new enterprises were meant 'to kill individualism' (cited in Sandford and Vigilante, 1984, p. 23). This explains why the PRG was so alarmed at the sluggish rate of growth in the development of cooperative enterprises. The state farms were also conceived in terms of the long term commitment of the government to socialism: 'In a petty-bourgeois society such as Russia was in 1917, the transition from capitalism to socialism can only be effected by moving away from small-scale individual peasant farming through the development of state farming and socialized cooperative farming'.[14]

Arising from the party's intense deliberations on the future of the country's agriculture was the conclusion that 'the development and modernization of agriculture hold the key to winning the peasantry to socialism and the transformation of the countryside along socialist lines'. Priority tasks for 'the years ahead' would be: (i) to make the GFC the leading vehicle for beginning to lay the basis for the socialist transformation of agriculture; (ii) to win the peasantry gradually to socialism by building the alliance of the working class and the peasantry through a programme of concessions and by building and strengthening the Productive Farms Union[15]; and (iii) to establish joint venture companies with large estate owners who are willing to increase production, but are constrained by financial problems.[16] Party members were urged to study this 'Resolution on Agriculture' closely with a view to implementing its conclusions when the time was opportune. The party also held extraordinary discussions on the prospect of a compulsory national service and labour army in Grenada. The Committee which met to consider this matter was advised to draw insights from the Cuban experience. It was also urged to study carefully 'the present political trend in Grenada, the particularities of our society, the possibilities of implementation of the National Service and the Labour Army' as well as the possible 'political and economic consequences'. The conclusion from the study was that 'the first and best time to introduce the idea of National Service and Labour Army should be at the fifth (5th) Anniversary in which the Commander-in-Chief would spell out the gains of the revolution and explain the necessity for defending these gains against the permanent enemy, imperialism'.[17] The purpose of this plan was apparently to create a large and permanent workforce for the state farms.

In the interim the government began to intensify its efforts to bring about efficiency and increased output in the agricultural sector, especially on the farms managed by the GFC. One urgent problem in this regard was the lack of finance to further develop and rehabilitate the farms. In 1982 the government successfully procured a loan of EC$5.4 million from the Caribbean Development Bank. The loan was meant to develop 1,903 acres of land over a five-year period. A part of the funds was also earmarked for augmenting and upgrading the equipment, machinery and infrastructure serving the farms. The agricultural development programme was to entail the replanting of tree crops where their deterioration was severe, improvement of drainage and general field sanitation measures, general maintenance, as well as the cultivation of 9 hectares of avocados and cloves, 12 hectares of vegetables and the establishment of a sheep enterprise on 46 hectares of land.

The project was approved on the grounds that it was expected to lead to substantial increases in agricultural production, foreign exchange earnings and in land and labour productivity. The foreign exchange potential of the project was seen as very promising given the wide assortment of crops that the GFC was involved in; some were geared towards generating foreign exchange and others towards retaining hard earned foreign currencies. In fact, the financial rate of return of the project was calculated at 25.7 per cent after taxes. To minimize the risks in this venture attention was placed on the vital question of management and training. This was particularly important - not only because of the poor track record of the Grenadian authorities in this area; but also because the project covered a diverse number of enterprises ranging from vegetables, tree crops, to animal production. Each of these enterprises required special managerial skills.

An administrative nucleus was thus established in Grenville, staffed with workers with skills in different areas of management, accounting, clerical duties, and agricultural science. Other workers were also trained on an ongoing basis, both inside and outside Grenada, in pest and disease management and vegetables and tree crop production.[18] A tight communication network (mainly radio sets) was also put in place to facilitate contact between estates, as well as between the estates and the main office

97

building. Hitherto, this was a daunting problem for the GFC given the wide dispersion of the farms over the island.

Emulation

For its part the government sought to raise worker productivity by introducing the novel practice of emulation campaigns. In an address made in October 1981, 'Emulation is the Seed that Brings the Fruit of Excellence', the Prime Minister explained the meaning and importance of the concept. The address was delivered on the first of what was to become an annual event - National Emulation Night (for Outstanding Students and Educators).

But emulation was to be promoted not only in the schools but in every organization and institution in the island (both private and public). Managers in workplaces were urged to award prizes to outstanding individuals and groups. For instance, a special prize was to be awarded to the 'manager of the year' and 'worker of the year' in every enterprise. The trade unionists were called upon to collaborate with managers to form production committees in every workplace. To achieve the goal of increased production and efficiency Disciplinary, Education and Emulation Committees were to be set up alongside the Production Committees. 'The Emulation Committee would set production targets and devise and organise brotherly and sisterly competition among the workers to make sure they are met, as well as publicly recognising and saluting the achievements of exemplary workers and producers' (Government of Grenada, 1982f, p. 29). These committees were expected to be particularly effective in the state sector. But elsewhere opposition was expected from some segments of private capital and those trade unions that were outside the control of the government.[19] One reason for opposition was the government's insistence that workers should be allowed to play an active role in the decision-making process at the workplace. They also advocated the institution of profit-sharing schemes to give workers a stake in the enterprises and thus induce them to work harder.

On the state enterprises various forms of moral and material incentives were provided to outstanding workers. These included media coverage (so important to poor, downtrodden people), agricultural implements, books, gift tokens, bus passes, trips overseas, holiday, and cash awards. In 1981 a worker known as 'Coonyahr' was made 'worker of the year' for his invention of a beetle trap which was effective in removing a particularly destructive pest on one of the government farms. So much attention was (deliberately) focused on Coonyahr for his invention that since then he has been widely known on the island as 'the Hero of Production'.[20] Apart from initiative and creativity, the emulation criteria used on the state farms included attendance and punctuality, treatment of equipment and other facilities, completion of work assignments on time, willingness to cooperate, participation, and attendance in all activities organised by the state - e.g. socialism classes and voluntary work in the community.

The emulation scheme on the state farms brought workers together each month to discuss the problems on the particular farm, examine critically production targets, and to suggest ways of improving agricultural productivity. On every state farm, a 'worker of the month' was to be chosen by the workers themselves. Workers were also to share in the profits that they helped to generate. With this profit-sharing scheme, one third of all profits was to be distributed among workers, one third was to go back to the state and the other third ploughed back into the farm for its continued expansion (Bishop, 1982a, p. 170). Other benefits and incentives included improved working conditions, provision of adequate toilet, canteen, health and sanitation facilities, sick leave, a pension plan, and the policy of equal pay for equal work for female farm workers. This policy of equal pay was to be generalized to the entire agricultural sector.[21] This was part of a wider drive aimed at rural development. Through these measures it was hoped that agricultural productivity would increase substantially, thus enabling the government to achieve its economic and social goals, as well as meeting its loan obligations to the Caribbean Development Bank.

Other state sector enterprises in agriculture

Marketing and National Importing Board and GAI Limited

To rationalise the operation of the state farms and NACDA, efforts were made to establish close linkages with the Marketing and National Importing Board and Grenada Agro-industries Limited. Although the MNIB pre-dates the PRG[22] it was not until 1979 that it began to play a major role in the Grenadian economy. As originally established the main functions of the MNIB were to market agricultural produce not already marketed by another statutory body. This included the purchasing and reselling of products; establishing and operating outlets for purchasing, delivery and grading; trading in food-stuffs for livestock, seeds, fertilizers, farming implements, etc., and establishing and operating storage facilities. Besides, the Board was empowered to be the sole purchaser, handler, processor, seller and exporter of any commodity the government saw fit. This latter clause was amended by the PRG to enable it to monopolize the importation of certain specified commodities (agricultural and/or non-agricultural).

The main objectives of the MNIB for the economy were: (i) to promote import substitution (by reducing food imports, developing linkages with agro-industries, increase export earnings by promoting greater outputs of existing products and developing new ones, developing an efficient marketing system geared towards providing marketing information and intelligence, and secure guaranteed markets for produce); (ii) increase national income through greater export activities; and (iii) increase output, income and living standards of the farming sector. Among the groups targeted were farmers and Grenadian consumers. For the former, the Board sought to provide secure markets (locally and externally) at fairly stable prices and to increase their output and income by keeping them informed on market trends, prospects and the corresponding direction of farm investment. The consuming public were to benefit from improved produce quality and price as well as securing regular supplies of produce (Vahcic, 1983, pp. 64-65). The objectives of the Board thus reflected commercial and social ends - many of the latter were outside the ends pursued by the private sector.

By 1983 it was clear that the MNIB had already begun to attain many of the proclaimed goals. The Board bought as many as 78 products from farmers. In principle it was committed to buying any marketable product which was offered by farmers. A total of 1.3 million pounds (weight) was bought in 1982. This was some 75 per cent higher than the quantity bought in 1981.[23] According to the Census Report one out of every eight farmers in Grenada traded with the Board. This suggests that farmers continued to market their produce by the traditional sources. One reason for this was that the Board lacked adequate transporting facilities to compete with long-established hucksters who either had their own vehicles or had permanent transport arrangements with vehicle owners. Small farmers were obliged to transport their produce themselves to the MNIB depots - many of which were located at considerable distance from their farms.[24]

The MNIB was perhaps more successful in changing the mix of Grenada's exports. An excellent example is the production of aubergines. A market was sought and successfully found in the UK. Over 70,000 pounds were traded during the second half of 1981. This contrasted sharply with the 15,000 pounds which were exported for the whole of 1980.[25] Trading links were also established with a number of non-traditional countries including socialist countries. This was aided by the establishment of a Shipping Division to MNIB in 1982. In that same year the Board purchased a motor ship 'the Albatross'. The aim was to reduce the delays in meeting overseas orders. Before the acquisition of this ship the Board had to rely on existing shipping lines often paying out large sums of money to them.

The MNIB also served as the principal distribution outlet for the produce of Grenada Agro-industries Limited. GAI operated a factory at True Blue and a food processing laboratory at Tanteen, St George's. The laboratory processed and packaged local spices for both the local retail and export trade. It was also engaged in processing selected fruits and vegetables into canned juices and nectars as well as bottled jams, jellies and chutneys. A state-owned Fish Processing plant was also established at True Blue. This plant specialized in the processing of frozen and salted fish products, principally for the domestic market. In the first six months of its operation the GAI produced an impressive 51,072 units of mango nectars, 17,693 units of tamarind nectars, 4,272 of paw-paw, 12,318 units of guava-banana, 14,147 units of nutmeg jellies, 12,798 units of hot sauces, 4,379 units of chutney, 2,768 units of spicy sauce and 2,301 boxes of guava cheese. Total sales recorded for the enterprise during its first six months stood at EC$298,726 (Government of Grenada, 1982b, p. 67). To boost the sales of the enterprise the PRG popularized the slogan 'buy local and eat local'.

Many of the products produced by GAI were of an exceptional quality. Several products from the enterprise even won medals at International Trade Fairs. Nutmeg jam, for instance, won a gold medal in 1981 at the Bulgarian International Trade Fair (Government of Grenada, 1982b, p. 67).

But the problems of GAI were overwhelming. These included: (i) inadequate storage space for raw materials (many of which were easily perished); (ii) irregularity, inconsistency and inadequacy (both quantity and quality) of raw materials from farmers; (iii) transportation bottlenecks which led to late deliveries of raw materials from farmers to factory; (iv) improper knowledge of the processing technology in some cases; (v) exorbitant costs for tins and bottles - many of which were too large for their contents,[26] (vi) technical problems such as frequent breakdown of machines and unavailability of spare parts,[27] and (vii) poor marketing and managerial problems. The managerial problem was particularly severe since it meant that this often produced long delays in solving the other problems which the enterprise encountered. As for marketing, Coard struck home directly when he noted: 'Making a product is one thing, but getting it sold is another. Although our products were sold far and wide, a lot more could have been done by the MNIB to market them abroad' (Government of Grenada, 1983e, p. 57).[28] Many of the products of GAI ended up no further than on the shelves of MNIB or in their store rooms, thereby producing huge increases in the Board's storage costs.

Referring to the managerial and marketing weaknesses, government scientist, Dr Radix had this to say: 'Every product requires its own marketing specialist. You can't employ people with rudimentary experience in razor blade marketing to market perishable goods. Besides you can't over-price your product to make up for other inefficiencies in production and distribution' (Author's interview with Dr Radix in May 1987).

The unrealistic pricing of the enterprise's products contributed in large

101

measure to the stockpiling at the MNIB. Besides it must be remembered that these products had to compete with cheaper, more attractively presented and better known imported products which bedecked the shelves of shops and supermarkets all over Grenada.[29] As for fish-processing, performance was particularly abysmal. This was largely due to the structural weaknesses of the National Fisheries Company (NFC)[30] which was responsible for supplying raw materials to the plant. These problems were so severe that the government was obliged to close down the NFC in early 1983 - less than two years after its establishment. Of the eight boats in the fishing fleet (all donated by the Cubans) only one functioned properly. Lack of spare parts and fishing apparatus meant the loss of many boat days. Inexperienced fish-crew and weak management further compounded the problems (Government of Grenada, 1983e, pp. 53-54).

Given the managerial weaknesses of the MNIB, one wonders to what extent the Board was able to distribute local produce to domestic consumers cheaper than its competitors. Sales revenue, reportedly, increased from EC$6.5 million in 1981 to EC$12.2 million in 1982 - and 'this enables MNIB to make a profit of over EC$0.5 million which were not wasted but put into productive use by the state sector'(Government of Grenada, 1983e, p. 62). This remark confirms the importance of the profit motive to the Board. In the absence of data on the profit margins of other competing marketing agents, it is impossible to determine whether prices charged to consumers by the Board were cheaper than those charged by their competitors. For the producer, however, the existence of the MNIB and the guaranteed market which it provided meant that (at least) they were able to obtain better prices for their produce from private traders. They at least had the option of comparing these prices with that offered by the MNIB. On the import side of the Board's operations, according to the available information, the prices charged to the consuming public were significantly reduced. This was largely due to the fact that the Board bought products in bulk and often from cheaper sources. In 1982 MNIB imported 2,270 metric tonnes of fertilizer. The price per 110 pounds bag was EC$6.00 less than what the Board previously sold at.[31]

The Livestock Production and Genetic Centre

Apart from its involvement in crop production and agro-industries the state also expanded its operations in the venture of livestock production. Again this was related to the government's long term aim of achieving greater self-sufficiency in food supply, hence reducing dependence on imported supplies of meat, milk, and other related products. The importance of a viable livestock industry in Grenada can be appreciated from the fact that in 1980 alone a total of 2.02 million kilograms of meat products valued at EC$ 6.3 million was imported into Grenada. This represents a definite upward trend over the years and a tremendous drain on scarce foreign exchange resources (Government of Grenada, *Economic and Social Survey: Agriculture*, n.d., p. 7).

The government thus established The Livestock Production and Genetic Centre (LPGC) in 1980 at Mt Harman, in the south of the island, for the breeding of top quality pigs, goats, sheep, and certain categories of poultry (layers, ducks, and turkey). Plans were also made to develop other ancillary products such as energy from biogas plants, fertilizer and feed (from rejects from crop production and other wastes) and algae. Through the use of advanced methods of super-ovulation and artificial insemination production was expected to increase rapidly.

And it seemed as though LPGC was set to achieve its aims. In 1981 its output stood at EC$37,600. This rose sharply to EC$181,100 in 1982 (Government of Grenada, 1983e, p. 52). Although the figure for 1982 was just over half the targeted sum of EC$353,000 it was still impressive since the assumptions on which the target was based were broken. These included the timely procurement of finance to buy the stock as well as the delivery of the full stock of breeders ordered. With respect to the former there was a delay of some six months. As for the latter only half the required stock was delivered. The importance the government placed on the development of a livestock industry is amply demonstrated in the manner in which it acquired the land for the LPGC project. The land was owned by the state, but it was previously rented to small farmers for the growing of sugarcane. Although it was providing a livelihood for these farmers and their families (and despite the importance of this strata to the class alliance which the model of non-capitalist development required) the state did not hesitate to repossess the land.[32]

It is difficult to deny the soundness of the objectives and intent of the state enterprises discussed so far. To a considerable extent many of the problems cited could be regarded as inevitable in the early stages of an enterprise. It should also be borne in mind that the Grenadian state had virtually no experience or tradition in productive activities. To the credit of the PRG, they recognized the existence of the problems and had already begun to introduce corrective measures. From their failures in direct production they were also made aware, with greater conviction, that farmers outside the state sector could not be ignored - least of all the small peasants who (numerically) dominated the agrarian sector. As such a number of direct steps were taken to assist them and their families.

The Productive Farmers' Union

The problems highlighted in *The 1981 Agricultural Census* (credit, poor infrastructure, underprovision of extension services, pests and disease, praedial larceny and labour shortage) were to constitute the basis of government policies for the rest of the farming sector. The Productive Farmers Union (PFU) became the leading organization representing the interests of small farmers with functions similar to those of NACDA.

PFU was established in 1980 with 1,200 small farmers. Its main office was set up in Grenville, but plans were made to establish similar offices throughout the agricultural centres of the island. The organization supplied fertilizer and agricultural implements to small farmers at concessionary rates but its main function was to provide loans to its members. These were allocated on the basis of production plans rather than the standard criteria used by commercial banks. Through this loan system farmers were encouraged to grow crops prioritised by the State, such as crops for GAI, vegetable produce and food crops for export.

The government's dominance of the banking sector put this organization in good stead to undertake this function. The National Commercial Bank (NCB) and the Grenada Development Bank (GDB) were to play a catalytic role in this new thrust of agricultural promotion. Referring to the NCB (established in 1979 in the wake of the withdrawal of the Canadian Imperial Bank of Commerce) Coard pointed out that the bank 'has had tremendous impact in forcing the foreign banks to pay better interest to the people, to lend money at lower interest rates and other factors of this sort' (Government of Grenada, 1982b, p. 42). Boasting the label 'the People's Bank' NCB was reputed to lend more for productive purposes than any other commercial bank operating in Grenada. An estimated 69 per cent of all loans made for agricultural purposes between 1979 and 1981 was made by the NCB (Government of Grenada, 1982e, p. 28). The acquisition of Grenada Bank of Commerce, in 1983 (formerly the Royal Bank of Canada) placed the government in an even stronger position to marry the resources mobilized by commercial banks to its developmental priorities. Additionally, the GDB (formerly the Grenada Agricultural and Industrial Development Corporation) was overhauled for this purpose.

People's Law No. 33, 1980, empowered GDB to provide financial advice and to provide or assist in procuring managerial, technical, and administrative services for development programmes in the country. It was also responsible for appointing relevant staff members, subject to the approval of the Minister of Finance. One of the revolutionary government's first moves was to appoint a new Board of Directors to replace the previous Board which had virtually no experience in agriculture, commerce and industry. By hand-picking members of the Board (in much the same way as Gairy did) the PRG ensured that its policies would be executed without opposition. The government also took steps to fill strategic posts which were vacant in the organization, often for very considerable periods of time. This could be regarded as one indication of the weakness of the GDB. For the greater part of 1980 the organization had no confirmed manager. Managerial functions were thus performed by the Project Officer assigned to GDB by the Caribbean Development Bank. An accountant was subsequently appointed to the post (Caribbean Development Bank, 1980a, p. 10).

In 1980 there were also vacancies for two technical officers with background in agriculture, one debt collector, and one industrial specialist. The PRG tried to fill these posts, but were never able to find suitably qualified personnel on account of the dearth of skilled manpower in the island. To alleviate the problem the Caribbean Development Bank provided consultants from time to time on a short term basis as well as organized crash courses for GDB's staff. The manpower shortage was certainly debilitating in its effects. But this debilitation was more pronounced in the industrial sector. Compared to the GDB's Farm Improvement Scheme (FIS), funds earmarked for Small Industry Credit (SIC) and Agricultural and Industrial Credit (AIC) schemes were grossly underutilized.

Towards the end of 1980 the PRG instructed the GDB to use the undisbursed funds to finance projects under the FIS. Measures were also put in place to alleviate the problem of poor debt recovery and bad debts. According to a CDB source, at the end of 1979 arrears of principal on sub-loans amounted to EC$1.2 million, 'of which recovery of EC$0.78 million or 31 per cent of GDB's total loan portfolio appeared extremely doubtful' (Grenada Development Bank, 1980a, p. 13).

This alarming situation was partly the result of the organizational weaknesses of the GDB and legacies from the Gairy regime. As one source put it 'The development of the Grenada Development Bank which existed before but which was in a state of total bankruptcy with most of the money having been stolen by the Gairy regime in a very vulgar way, with money moving from one bank to another and half of it disappearing in between' (Government of Grenada, 1982b, p. 42). Reportedly, some of the loans advanced before 1979 were not understood in strict business terms but were interpreted by recipients as patronage for their loyalty to Gairy's party (Author's interview with officers at the GDB in June 1987). As a result of the Bank's inability to manage its resources properly, the CDB (the GDB's main creditor) was reluctant to grant further credit to that institution. After one year under the PRG, however, the CDB adopted a more favourable attitude to loan requests from the GDB. In commenting on the new wind of change set in motion by the PRG, the CDB wrote 'GDB has gone through a rebirth and the organization is now functioning more efficiently. Proper administrative systems have been implemented and accounting systems and loan procedures have been introduced and streamlined. Security requirements for loans have also been tightened' (Caribbean Development Bank, 1980a, p. 10).

Loans from the CDB now began to surge upwards. In 1980 alone a record sum of EC$1 million was loaned to the GDB on concessionary terms.[33] Plans were also made by the CDB to augment the GDB's resources as the organization strengthened further. There was also a sharp rise in the rate of disbursement of funds. For 1977 and 1978 disbursements averaged EC$200,000 annually. Yet by the end of 1979 a total of EC$700,000 was disbursed (Caribbean Development Bank, 1980a, p. 16). This suggests the credit bottleneck which farmers typically faced was at last beginning to be alleviated.

Inroads were also made into the poor roads over which farmers had to transport their produce.[34] One estimate put the amount of produce lost (through bruising) in the process of transportation at 30 per cent.[35] To improve farmer's incomes feeder and farm roads were constructed. Through the CDB EC$6 million was raised for the rehabilitation of feeder roads in 1981. Another 25 miles of roads was also constructed in 1982 (Government of Grenada, 1983e, p. 159). With the help of the PFU small farmers were also mobilized to provide voluntary labour to assist with road construction and repairs. The PRG also began the Eastern Main Road Project - a road which was designed to connect St George's to St Andrews. Some 40 per cent of the island's export agriculture was transported along this route (Government of Grenada, 1982b, p. 97). Apart from benefiting farmers the provision of improved roads was also seen as a measure which could assist the Grenada Forestry Development Corporation to achieve its objectives. These centred on the cultivation of trees and production of wood, especially for the manufacturing of furniture aimed at overseas markets.[36] Improved roads also meant that less time would be lost in travelling, and reduced expenditure on vehicle repairs.

Strict measures were also introduced to deal with the age-old problem of praedial larceny[37]. As highlighted in the 1981 Census Report this was a formidable disincentive to further investment in agriculture. Indeed, it was also one reason why commercial banks were generally reluctant to accommodate loan requests from farmers. The problem was widely discussed throughout the country, especially in the mass organizations. At a mass organization Conference Workshop in February 1983 it was suggested that purchasing institutions should ensure that goods offered for sale were made by bona fide sellers. Government should equip these institutions with information on the size of farmer's holdings, the type of crops they were

106

involved in, and their average output. If the quantity of goods offered for sale was substantially higher than the average output, an investigation should be undertaken. It was also recommended that the police should raise their presence in rural areas, and that thieves should be made to do hard compulsory labour on the farms from which they stole (Government of Grenada, 1982f, p. 3).

On the basis of these recommendations the PRG began to take decisive action to deal with the problem. The presence of police officers was visible at distribution outlets. It was hoped that their presence alone would help to deter would-be traders in stolen goods. A law was also drafted and widely discussed for punishing offenders. The punishment was to include exorbitant fines and imprisonment for long periods (up to two years) under conditions of hard labour. Plans were also made to introduce a comprehensive 'identification card' system which should be presented by sellers to anyone with authority to request it. These measures may appear draconian, but they were simply a reflection of the importance the PRG attached to agriculture.

Greater attention was also paid to the provision of extension services and other technical assistance to farmers, especially in the area of disease management. With the help of the Canadian government a Cocoa Rehabilitation Programme was introduced. The Canadian International Development Agency (CIDA) provided EC$2.5 million for this project in cash and materials. The coca plants were sold to farmers at reduced price. Under the aegis of the Cocoa Rehabilitation Project, thousands of disease-ridden plants were replanted.[38] Without a complete replanting, the yields from the plants would have continued to decline on account of the deadly beetles, thrips, 'witches broom' and other pests. A sum of US$105,000 was also obtained from the Food and Agricultural Organization to help the government in its fight against another destructive disease known as 'Moko'. This disease was particularly destructive to the island's faltering banana industry. Efforts were made to establish membership with as many international organizations as possible in order to procure further technical assistance in agriculture.

But the government was prepared to use this assistance to complement its own efforts rather than relying on outside help totally. To this end, the PRG re-established the Mirabeau Farm Training School which was closed under the Gairy regime. The facilities of the school were expanded to cater for 150 students per year instead of the previous 50. Emphasis at the school was on the training of extension officers. Research was also undertaken on the control of pests and diseases. An agricultural training school was also opened at La Sagesse in the parish of St Davids. The school provided residential courses to young school-leavers in the areas of soil management, vegetable crop husbandry, irrigation and farm management. The government's aim was to provide more technical services to farmers. Although the extension officers played a positive role,[39] their work was severely handicapped by transportation problems. Very few possessed their own vehicle, yet they were required to travel all over the country to cater for an average of 200 farmers per extension officer (Commonwealth Secretariat, 1982, p. 6). Shortage of funds meant that the government was never able to undertake the suggestion made in the Secretariat's document to provide small 90 cc motor cycles for as many extension workers as possible.

Education policies

Nevertheless, other, more affordable services, which were also critical to the raising of agricultural productivity and output, were undertaken with great enthusiasm. Pride of place went to education. The government was convinced that recurrent problems such as weak management, poor organization, bad record-keeping and accounting, low worker productivity and the constant use of primitive technology were products of the country's educational system. This was no less true of the agricultural sector. As one government source put it:

> Many agricultural workers, foremen and managers are comrades who have not been able to gain much education. Long ago we used to think that you didn't need education if you were going to work with your hands. Why bother to keep a girl or boy in school so long when it is land they are going to work? But today, when we are trying to bring our country into the twentieth century, it is becoming clear to us that education is necessary not only for "office work" but for every kind of work. A worker can do better work if he/she is educated: better carpentry, better road-building, better cultivation. Modern methods of agriculture demand educated workers (Government of Grenada, 1983e, p. 47).

The education system, like every other facet of Grenadian society, was seen as a colonial relic, designed to serve the purposes of the Colonial Power. Children of workers who were fortunate to attend school received elementary and ad hoc exposure to reading, writing and arithmetic - the so-called '3 R's'. Learning by rote, under the constant threat and use of the whip, became the norm for disseminating this basic knowledge. Thought, reasoning and critical reflection on the value of the educational content were discouraged. English nursery rhymes, poetry, kindergarten songs, and events (e.g. 'London Bridge is Falling Down', 'The Cow Jumped over the Moon', and the Reform of Wilberforce) thus took precedence over local events and imagery.[40]

Shortages of textbooks, learning aids, teachers and dilapiadated school buildings were perennial problems. So too was absenteeism and drop outs as many poor families were obliged to send their children to work to supplement the family income. But those at the apex of the society had no such problems. Their children were normally schooled and trained in the 'Mother Country'. They were also the recipients of the scholarships which were administered by the Mother Country. Gairy too was known to encourage this practice.

Bold steps were taken by the PRG to move the education system onto a different path. Education policies were now based on the principles that: (i) education is everybody's right, not a privilege for a select few; (ii) education must be a continuous and lifelong process; and (iii) education must be a principal factor in the creation of the new society (Bishop, 1982a, p. 234). Since functional illiteracy was still rampant[41] in Grenada, the Centre for Popular Education (CPE) was established in 1980 with the goal of eradicating illiteracy among the population.[42] Grenadians who were previously denied an education were eagerly encouraged to register with the Centre and volunteer teachers were sought.

Volunteers were reminded by the Prime Minister that:

> To teach a brother or sister to read and write is a deeply rewarding task, it is a revolutionary duty for those who know to voluntarily place their knowledge at the service of those who do not. By undertaking this task with the discipline, consistency and enthusiasm that it requires, we will succeed. We will succeed not only in teaching our fellow countryman to read and write, but through that process volunteer teachers will also learn a great deal themselves and will help to build a deeper spirit of unity, understanding and collective endeavour (Bishop, 1982a, p. 165).

Posters such as 'Each one, teach one' and 'If you know, teach! If you don't, learn' were displayed on walls all over the country.

For more formal training the PRG relied on trained teachers rather than mere volunteers. For this purpose, the National In-Service Teacher Education Programme (NISTEP) was created to train teachers en masse. NISTEP was to replace the former Teacher's College which typically trained only 25 teachers per year.[43] Each year 500 teachers underwent a three-year in-service programme organised in three centres. The teachers visited the centres one day per week as well as for part of the vacation periods to study Language Arts, Mathematics and Education Methods during the first two years; and Science, Social Studies, Agricultural Science and Health Education during the third. The other four days a week were spent in the classroom where they participated in teaching activities under the guidance of NISTEP tutors and their fellow trained teachers. NISTEP was also made responsible for the transformation what was regarded as an irrelevant school curriculum.[44] The aim was to refocus the curriculum to make it relevant to the needs of the society. As Bishop (1982a) put it:

> We need a curriculum to practically aid our liberation, not keep us dependent on outside powers that will do nothing but exploit us. Remember comrades, that the origin of culture itself is the land, the soil, the way we produce and feed ourselves, the way we survive and grow. We need a school curriculum that points directly to those necessities, for if we do not start that process at school, our new generation will grow up ignorant and incapable of developing their greatest asset - the rich and fertile soil of our land (p. 239-40).

This was a far cry from the days when agriculture was greeted with contempt (given its close historical relationship with West Indian slavery). Not only were agricultural chores lauded but through NISTEP even barefoot peasant farmers could participate as teachers in the schools. This was what the Community School Day Programme (CSDP) was about. People from all walks of life in the community who had a skill were encouraged to teach students on the day when their teachers were studying at the NISTEP centres. The children of peasants and other low income earners became the principal beneficiaries of other state initiatives in education such as the provision of free milk and lunch, uniforms and free secondary education for all.[45] For the first time children from humble backgrounds were given the opportunity to study at universities, providing they satisfied the university matriculation requirements. This was due to the government's efforts to obtain scholarships and training assistance from overseas countries, as well as the financial contributions to the University of the West Indies which were restored after they had been ceased by Gairy. Grenadians could now be found studying in Cuba, Kenya, Hungary and other Eastern Bloc countries, as well as at the regional university.

According to the Prime Minister's 1981 address 'Education is Production Too' things had reached the stage where more university opportunities were available than there were qualified Grenadians available to fill them (Bishop, 1982a, p. 235). Bishop was correct, as revealed by a worrying correspondence in 1983 by Richard Jacobs, the then Grenadian Ambassador to the Soviet Union. This correspondence noted that up to March 1983 Grenada received 80 university or technical scholarships from the Soviet Union alone; yet, complained Jacobs:

> We have accepted 18 of which two of our students have given up the course. Of the remaining 16 at least eight do not have the minimum

requirements for entry to the level of education they expected to receive upon leaving Grenada ... It is much better to ask for five scholarships and fill four of them than to ask for 40 and send only four people. This gives the impression ... that our students prefer not to study in the USSR. It introduces a certain question mark and works in a negative way on state to state relations.[46]

Many of these scholarship holders were being trained in agronomy. The policy of incorporating agriculture into the school curriculum also represented an important step in the direction of encouraging young people into agriculture. Ultimately it was hoped that the influx of youths into this critical sector would alleviate the labour shortages which constantly dogged farmers as revealed in the 1981 Agricultural Census report. But apart from its vocational focus, the PRG's education policies had overt political goals. The year 1983 was thus dubbed 'The Year of Political and Academic Education'. In the party's view:

> Without education, no genuine people's democracy can be built since real democracy always assumes the informed, conscious and educated participation of the people. Without education, there can be no real worker participation, no substantial increase in production and productivity, no individual and collective growth, no true dignity, no genuine independence. As a nation we will in 1983 be striving collectively and individually to learn more about ourselves and our condition so that together we can forge ahead to a confident future (Coard, 1985, pp. 20-21).

The political content of the education programme was geared towards raising the ideological and cultural levels of the population. Through socialism classes educators were expected to promote the ideas of Marxism/Leninism among their pupils until they developed a deep class consciousness. Indeed, the lack of this type of consciousness was seen as the principal cause of retreat on the non-capitalist path as evidenced by countries such as Egypt and Ghana.

Health policies

Recognizing too that health and production go hand in hand the government also directed its attention and resources to this area: 'Like education, expenditure on health is really an investment because a healthy population is better able to cope with the problems of building the country' (Government of Grenada, 1983e, p. 14). Appropriately enough, l4.5 per cent (EC$9.8

million) of recurrent expenditure was spent on hospitals, health clinics, and public health programmes in 1982. In his 1980 speech 'Health for All - A Right of the Caribbean Masses' the Prime Minister outlined the state of the health service which his party inherited. He also articulated clearly the philosophical foundations which would guide health policies in the new Grenada (Bishop, 1982a, pp. 150-156).

Preventative medicine was to be promoted and emphasized as opposed to curative. The former was considered to be more economical than the latter which required expensive equipment and scarce foreign exchange to import drugs of all kinds. The importance of a clean environment and the observance of hygienic practices were thus popularized through films and lectures organized by public health technicians. The mass organizations were also active in organizing clean-up campaigns in the community.

Through the Grenada Food and Nutrition Council (GFNC) Grenadians were tutored into proper nutritional habits.[47] As a result of overseas assistance (especially from Cuba) medical services and facilities were dramatically improved. The incomes of private medical practitioners received a blow as it was now forbidden for them to see private patients either at or during their working hours at the government hospitals. Besides, free medical care was now provided for everybody by the government. More beds, drugs and other hospital supplies were provided.[48] Hospitals were repaired and new facilities established. In December 1979, for instance, an Eye Clinic was opened in St George's. By October 1980 each parish in the country was equipped with a dental clinic for the first time. Yet before the revolution there was only one such clinic in the whole island. This was based in the capital, St George's.

Other rural services

Plans were also formulated (and modest efforts made) to endow the country-side with services similar to those obtained in the urban areas. Again, this was designed to make the rural areas attractive to young people. Chief among these services were electricity, improved transportation and pipeborne water in every house. But for such services to be cost-effective in the long run attention would have to be paid first to the adequacy of existing housing facilities. According to the latest survey[49] on housing (done in 1970): 'severe overcrowding existed in buildings that were in a serious state of disrepair and the majority of the households were without the essential services of pipe-borne water, sewerage facilities and electricity'. Significantly (and as was to be expected) most of these were concentrated in the countryside.

The survey noted further that many of these 'houses' were make-shift dwellings (72 per cent were made from wood, 63 per cent constructed over

20 years ago, 36 per cent had pipe-borne water, 44 per cent had electricity and 66 per cent only had access to outside (pit) toilets). The PRG's response to this deplorable situation was two-fold: provision of low cost housing units which were sold to Grenadians at concessionary rates, and the introduction of a National Housing Repair Programme in 1979. The latter programme began with the provision of EC$7 million designed to grant loans to persons desirous of carrying out housing repairs. Up to EC$1,000 worth of materials could be obtained with modest repayments at only EC$17 per month interest free. Persons with income under EC$150 per month were only required to repay two-thirds of the cost over a ten-year period on an interest free basis. Again, the community was encouraged to volunteer their labour to help other Grenadians with their repair work.[50] By 1981 as many as 16,000 people obtained benefits from this programme (Government of Grenada, 1982e, p. 18). Reflecting on the importance of the project an agricultural worker, Connyhar had this to say: 'We didn't believe it when they tell us about repairing our houses, but when we see the materials come I repair my roof and one long side. Now I don't hear people saying again that Gairy union was good' (Government of Grenada, 1982c, p. 64).

As a result of these social advances, and the PRG's deliberate policy of making them available in the countryside, the farming community was better able to raise output and agricultural productivity - if only because they now lost less time travelling to the urban areas for many of these services. Besides, the provision of farm roads and feeder roads, extension services, credit, market (through the MNIB and GAI) and education were vital pre-requisites for greater productivity. So too were the benefits and incentives to workers provided by Acts such as the *Rent Control Law*, *Workmen's Compensation Act*, *Maternity Leave Law*, *Trade Union (Recognition) Act*, and the repeal of the 'anti-worker' laws enacted under Gairy.[51] Without these provisions for farmers and their families, the gloomy scenario depicted by Coard was inevitable: low worker productivity = low profits = low wages = labour shortage = collapse of agriculture (Government of grenada, 1983e, p. 48).

Overview of agricultural performance (1979-1983)

Despite the initiatives which the revolutionary government undertook in this vital sector (see Appendix 4:A:1), agriculture performed dismally throughout the period. The depression was particularly noticeable in the performance of Grenada's traditional export crops. This is set out in table 4:2.[52] As the table indicates, both output and prices fluctuated sharply around a downward trend. Cocoa and nutmeg - the country's two key exports - recorded falling prices

Table 4:2
Grenada: value, volume and unit value of agricultural exports
(Value expressed in US$ million, volume in millions of pounds
and unit values in US$ per pound)

Item	1979	1980	1981	1982	1983
Banana:					
value	3.74	4.11	3.71	3.39	3.24
volume	31.03	27.46	22.41	21.17	19.53
unit value	0.12	0.15	0.17	0.16	0.17
Cocoa:					
value	10.03	6.76	7.06	4.62	4.06
volume	5.34	4.11	5.90	4.62	4.92
unit value	1.88	1.64	1.20	1.00	0.83
Nutmet:					
value	4.60	3.16	3.02	3.02	3.25
volume	5.07	3.35	3.79	4.50	5.34
unit value	0.91	0.94	0.80	0.67	0.61
Mace:					
value	0.89	0.68	0.63	0.93	0.76
volume	0.74	0.55	0.46	0.72	0.75
unit value	1.20	1.24	1.37	1.29	1.02
Fresh Fruits:					
value	0.36	0.28	0.49	1.67	4.14
volume	1.43	0.85	1.73	5.69	15.17
unit value	0.25	0.33	0.28	0.29	0.27

Source: Ministry of Finance, Central Statistical Office, Grenada. (See also International Monetary Fund, 1984, p. 59).

for every year of the revolution. In the case of cocoa, prices plummeted from US$1.88 per pound in 1979 to US$0.83 in 1983. Nutmeg prices fell less dramatically, from US$0.91 per pound in 1979 to US$0.6l in 1983. All in all, total foreign exchange from bananas, cocoa, nutmeg and mace fell from

US$19.26 million in 1979 to US$11.31 million in 1983.

Although the price of bananas was fairly stable for the most part total earnings from banana exports fell progressively. Unlike the other crops, the main problem faced by the banana industry was not markets but natural disasters. Between 1979 and mid-1981 there were five such disasters - 2 hurricanes, 2 sets of flood rain and heavy winds. In bemoaning these losses and the unprecedented incidence of disasters, Coard affirmed that they: 'raise certain questions as to whether certain people are not tampering with the weather situation in the Eastern Caribbean .... Every time millions of our dollars have been spent since the revolution in fixing to the best of our ability, our roads, bridges, and sea defence walls, another disaster would come and rip up all the roads again, make rivers out of them' (Government of Grenada, 1982b, p. 33).

In the case of nutmegs, increased output from farmers ended up no further than the processing stations.[53] Apart from shrinking demand for nutmegs, aggravated by the recession in the world economy, the stockpiling - some seven million pounds up to 1983 - was largely a consequence of the PRG's attempt to secure better prices for the product by eliminating middlemen and selling directly to users. Missions were sent overseas in search of new markets, but they often returned empty-handed. In September 1983, for instance, the manager of the Grenada Nutmeg Cooperative Association, a representative of the MNIB, and Grenada's Ambassador to Venezuela, travelled to the South American countries of Argentina, Brazil, Colombia and Venezuela to solicit business. But lack of shipping facilities and the debt problems of these countries forced the team to explore other possibilities: 'contacts were established, but the prospects of increasing sales to Argentina and of initiating sales to the other countries are still hampered by the lack of suitable shipping connections and the serious foreign exchange problems of the countries concerned, particularly Brazil, which have forced restrictions on imports, especially of non-essential items such as spices' (Grenada Cooperative Nutmeg Association, 1983, p. 18).

In desperation the PRG turned to the Soviet Union and accepted an unsatisfactory trade agreement in 1982. This involved supplying 500 metric tons of nutmeg a year for the next five years on barter terms.[54] Although this arrangement had the potential to eliminate the stockpiles, what the PRG needed was hard foreign currency to finance its development programmes - some of which were highly import dependent (e.g. the airport). In the meanwhile Grenada ended up losing its traditional nutmeg buyers. Even in the aftermath of the US-led invasion in October 1983 the new government which replaced the PRG had problems persuading the Netherlands to resume business with Grenada. By this time the Authorities had also lost the contract with the Soviet Union as diplomatic relations with Russia were instantly

115

severed following the invasion. Referring to the five-year contract with the Soviet Union Rex Dull, economist from the US Department of Agriculture's Foreign Agricultural Service, had this to say: 'They were purchasing to help Grenada. Their consumption is actually insignificant... They were taking the nutmeg off Grenada's hand for political reasons, and to gain political foothold in that country'.[55]

Although obtaining less revenue from the industry, the Grenada Nutmeg Cooperative Association, which was responsible for marketing the product overseas, was obliged to draw down on its reserves to keep the industry afloat and to mitigate the declining fortunes of farmers.[56] The amount transferred in 1979 was EC$1.4 million. For 1980, 1981, 1982 and 1983 the figures were EC$1.8 million, EC$2.6 million, EC$1 million, and EC$1.4 million, respectively (Grenada Co-operative Nutmeg Association, select years). The situation was similar for the other traditional crops. The difficult economic situation also forced the other Marketing Boards to deplete their reserves and even to incur deficits (IMFa, 1984, pp. 4-5).

Doubtless the PRG blamed the crisis on 'the system of imperialism'. In articulating the government's position Whiteman put it like this: 'Because of a system of imperialism ... we are losing EC$160 million a year ... We can't continue to ask farmers and workers to produce more bananas when they are only getting five cents of the banana dollar - we are getting EC$40 million annually for this instead of EC$200 million for exports - because prices of exports do not directly relate to spiralling costs of fertilizer and other inputs'.[57]

Again they turned to the Eastern Block countries to forge new trading arrangements to supplement and ultimately supplant the 'exploitative West'. But another shock awaited the PRG. Despite their desperation they did not hesitate to reject an offer from the former German Democratic Republic (GDR) to buy Grenadian bananas at a price which was less than a quarter of what they obtained from the United Kingdom and the EEC (Payne et al., p. 114). In vain did the PRG try to obtain better terms from the former GDR. The trade agreement was regarded by the GDR as 'solemn'. Grenada's ambassador to the Soviet Union, Richard Jacobs, warned that any revision of the arrangement would damage 'state to state relations' not only with the GDR but with the entire Socialist Community: 'My own view is that once the agreement is signed at that level (Heads of Government), there is no going back and even if it is disadvantageous to us we just have to implement it. It is indecent to be seen as wanting to revise an agreement arrived at by the two Heads of Government' (United States Department and Department of Defence, Document entitled *Grenada's relations with the USSR*, p. 6).

In the case of containing imports and stimulating the production of non-traditional agricultural crops, however, the results were more encouraging. Food imports as a percentage of total imports exhibited a consistently downward trend for the period 1979-1983. These were 30.6 per cent, 28.9 per cent, 28.2 per cent, and 27.5 per cent, respectively (Government of Grenada, 1983e, p. 25). This was largely a result of the government's import control policies and its education policies which encouraged Grenadians to 'buy local and eat local'. Although structural transformation is a long-term development, by definition, steps were made to change the composition of Grenada's agricultural output. Mention has already been made of the introduction and promotion of new crops, particularly fruits and vegetables. Foreign exchange earnings from non-traditional agriculture reached EC$4.5 million in 1982 as against the EC$1.4 million for 1981 (Government of Grenada, 1983e, p. 28). Much of this was exported to Trinidad and Tobago where a buoyant market existed for them. So important was this trade to the then buoyant oil republic that by 1982 Trinidad had become Grenada's second largest trading partner, preceded only by Britain. In that year as much as 31 per cent of Grenada's exports was absorbed on the Trinidadian market. Export of fruits and vegetables to Trinidad escalated from 1 million pounds (at a value of EC$0.6 million) to 14 million pounds (EC$10 million) in 1983 (IMF, 1984a, p. 5).

Concluding remarks

In conclusion, it must be stressed that despite the faltering performance of agriculture under the PRG it would not be correct to blame the government entirely for this state of affairs. According to Joefield-Napier (1985) '... the failure of the export sector was partly due to the half-hearted attempts that were made to introduce major policy initiatives' (p. 24). Joefield-Napier refused to say what these 'major policy initiatives' should have been. If by this he meant greater expenditure on agricultural infrastructure and traditional export crops this would not have made any significant inroads into the problems encountered by the PRG in this area. As we have seen, natural disaster, market shortage and declining prices in the wake of the world recession were the government's main trouble-spots. And as Thomson (1987) demonstrates, these problems were also the lot of Grenada's neighbours. Under these circumstances it was judicious for the government to do what it did - i.e. emphasise vegetable production and other non-traditional exports rather than traditional crops.

Some analysts have also attributed the depression in Grenada's agriculture to the government's land acquisition policies (for example, World Bank, 1984; and Sandford and Vigilante, 1984). As the World Bank team put it: 'The future of agriculture in Grenada is closely related to the outcome of the

State Farms issue. Previous administrations acquired small land holdings and supposedly neglected estates in the national interest but sometimes without mutually agreed, or even fair, compensation' (p. 36). This was less true of the PRG than it was for the Gairy regime. The former was determined to bring all idle land under cultivation to boost output. The state's direct involvement in agricultural production was a symbol of its deep commitment to increase agricultural output and agrarian transformation. Even Ambursley (1983), a staunch critic of the PRG, conceded that the regime's land acquisition policies: 'clearly (did) not amount to an expropriation and contains a number of provisions that can be used by landowners to prevent the acquisition of their property' (p. 209). Subject to its limited resources, the government offered incentives and various forms of technical and infrastructural assistance to farmers in the hope that they would boost their output. For success in this sphere (economic) was of critical importance to the path of non-capitalist development.

Notes

1. B. Coard, 'National Reconstruction and Development in the Grenadian Revolutionary Process', Speech made at the First International Conference in Solidarity with Grenada at St George's, 23-25 November, 1981, in Government of Grenada, 1982b, p. 45.

2. A more detailed discussion of this theme can be found in Brierly (1974).

3. Farmers were asked to identify (up to two) from the following list the most acute problems for them - praedial larceny, planting material, marketing, extension help, labour, water, roads, diseases, and credit.

4. The findings of the Census were put into sharper focus by an aerial survey which was carried out by the Ministry of Agriculture in 1982. The photographs from the survey indicated how land was utilized in the country.

5. For a discussion of the case for developing a class of 'business farmers' in the Caribbean, see Mandle (1985b).

6. The Commission could still declare the land to be 'idle' if it was fully cultivated by 'unsuitable' crops. To avoid a lease the owner would have to comply with the crops recommended by the Commission. If false information was given to the Commission the individual could be fined up to EC$500 or imprisoned (with or without hard labour) for up to one year (see Government of Grenada, 1982i, p. 111).

7. See Sandford and Vigilante (1984), pp. 79-80. The authors base this claim on documents which were confiscated by the US in the wake of the political crisis of October 1983 (document captioned 'Ideas Concerning Land Reform, GS 002600, undated as well as notes from 'SG', 12 October, 1080). See also 'Minutes of the NJM Central Committee Plenary', (13-19 July 1983), in Seabury and McDougall 1984, p. 273.

8. Author's interview with personnel at the Caribbean Development Bank and in Grenada (May-June, 1987).

9. It must be recalled that before 1979 The New Jewel Movement had thrived on Gairy's contemptible practice of confiscating land from

those who were deemed to be disloyal to his regime. Indeed, they were at the forefront of those who denounced this policy.

10. Up to the third quarter of 1982 the agricultural sector received as much as 67 per cent (i.e. EC$30,221) of the total amount of funds disbursed by NACDA (see Government of Grenada, 1983a, p. 4).

11. As an example of the severity of this problem Coard pointed out that the GFC was not even able to provide the Ministry of Planning with basic information about itself to enable the Ministry to make plans for 1983. In the end the Ministry had to send its own staff to take stock on all the farms 'managed' by the GFC. His dismay at this pathetic state of affairs is evident in his remark 'If you do not know how many trees you have, if you do not know where you are, you cannot say where you are going' (see Government of Grenada, 1983, p. 51).

12. Most of these workers worked for only three to four hours per day. Yet they were paid for a full day's work - albeit at the pitiful sum of EC$8.50 per day (see Green, 1983, p. 29).

13. See Government of grenada (1983a), p. 4. It may also be noted that the cooperatives did not succeed in making a significant dent on the unemployment problem. Up to mid-1983, they employed a mere 0.4 per cent of the total labour force, i.e. 45 workers in agriculture, 39 in manufacturing, 40 in construction, and 32 in services (ibid., pp. 4-5).

14. (Grenada Document), 'Notes from 'SG'' (dated 10 October, 1980, 22 October, 1982, and 25 November, 1982). See also, Government of Grenada (1983e) for further information on the limitations of small scale agriculture, even when the ultimate goal is not construction of socialism.

15. PFU denotes Productive Farmers Union. It was conceived as a mass organization which would be active in the small farming community.

16. See (Grenada Document 111-10), 'Central Committee Resolution on Agriculture', (January, 1983) in Seabury and McDougall (1984), pp. 119-120.

17. See (Grenada Document, 111-9), 'National Service and Labour Army,' in Seabury and McDougall (1984), pp. 114-118.

18. Plans were also made for GFC workers to participate in the Mardi Gras Programme which was funded by the UNDP. This programme provided training to Grenadians in soil and water conservation techniques.

19. Of the eight trade unions in the island, three were outside the control of the government - the Public Worker's Union, the Grenada Union of Teachers and the Technical and Allied Workers' Union. These were to pose a major threat to the PRG, given their militant demands for substantial wage increases.

20. The trap was made from local breadfruit wood. The beetles were attracted to the gum from the wood.

21. See Government of Grenada (1982c), pp. 56-62 for a further exposition on the state's attempts to improve the conditions of agricultural workers. The report was compiled by Fitzroy Bain, President of the Agricultural and General Workers' Union, which represented this category of workers. Mention should also be made of the National Insurance Scheme which was introduced by the PRG in April 1983. The Scheme provided various forms of benefits (including sickness, invalidity and maternity, retirement and survivors' pensions, old age and funeral grants) to its members - many of whom were employees in state enterprises.

22. The MNIB is a statutory organization, and was first established in 1973 under Gairy's Administration.

23. See Government of Grenada (1983e). See also the 1981 *Agricultural Census Report* for the distribution of produce by district and for Grenada as a whole among the MNIB and other marketing outlets. According to the data 7.92 per cent of non-agricultural produce was marketed by the MNIB, 21.2 per cent by traffickers, 29.5 per cent by central markets, and 41.2 per cent by makeshift outlets in the village.

24. This call for more MNIB depots was one of the most frequent recommendations made at the Zonal Councils on the Economy: 'MNIB should establish contacts in all villages to co-ordinate the availability of crops in the different villages in order to prevent the problems faced by farmers in carrying produce to MNIB and those not accepted' (see Government of Grenada, 1983b, p. 2).

25. As a result of structural and seasonal factors, Grenada was never able to produce a regular and reliable supply of this product despite the guaranteed market for it. This did not augur well for the procurement and development of future trading contracts.

26. For example, it was common for four ounces of jam to be bottled in 16oz containers. Cans, bottles, and packaging materials accounted for as much as 50 per cent of the cost of production of GAI's products. These were mainly imported from Trinidad (author's interviews with Dr Radix and Dr Marcelle, chemists, at the Produce Laboratory, Ministry of Agriculture, June 1987).

27. Production was sometimes hampered for long periods since, in some instances, parts had to be specially designed for these machines - many of which were out-dated. The machines originated in the Eastern Bloc Countries (author's interviews, see footnote 26 above).

28. See Government of Grenada (1983e), p. 57. It should also be noted that Grenadians travelling overseas, especially hoteliers, and other prominent visitors to the island were also relied on to promote these products abroad. Many were urged to bring back boxes of nectars, juices, etc. with them as a means of showing solidarity with the revolution. Like the MNIB, many Grenadian embassies overseas held 'stockpiles' (author's interviews with Grenadians at the Ministry of Agriculture, June 1987).

29. The Coffee Processing Plant and Grenada Sugar Factory mirrored many of the problems encountered by GAI (see Government of Grenada, 1983e, pp. 57-58). Referring to the problems of the former Coard, noted 'supplies of raw coffee are limited. We have to rely on importing beans from abroad. Our own farms need to produce more ... we have not yet made enough headway with selling this product abroad' (ibid., p. 57).

30. The target of the company in 1982 was EC$947,900 worth of fish catchment. Only EC$175,200 was attained - a figure which was insufficient to meet its own expenses for 1982, let along providing revenue to the government.

31. See also Government of Grenada (1982e), pp. 30-31 for data on the import of rice, sugar, and cement.

32. See project document 'On the Utilization of the Mt Hartman Valley for Integrated Animal - Vegetal Production with Self-sufficiency in Energy', (Ministry of Agriculture, Grenada, 1982). Interestingly the key technicians for the implementation of the project were all non-Grenadians. Again this reflects the seriousness of skilled manpower in small, underdeveloped countries like Grenada.

33. Interest was to be four per cent per annum. See (Caribbean Development Bank, 1980a, pp. 23-30) for other terms and conditions.

34. The road system in the island has remained unchanged since major construction ended in the 1930s. And this was despite the floods and hurricanes which hit the island over the years (see Caribbean Development Bank, 1980b).

35. See Government of Grenada (1983e), p. 159. This was also supported by the author's interview with staff at the CDB in May 1987.

36. Like the other State enterprises, this corporation had its problems. Apart from inaccessible roads it suffered from incomplete knowledge of forestry resources, lack of appropriate technology, and market intelligence.

37. During my interviews with farmers in Grenada in May 1987, the consensus was that this problem was incurable. As one group of farmers in Grenville put it 'It is in the nature of some people to reap what others sow since reaping is easier than sowing'.

38. The CIDA programme aimed to replant 20,000 cocoa trees over an eight-year period (see IMF, 1984a, p. 4).

39. For example, it was they who initiated the practice of field packing in the banana industry. This practice has been found to be very effective in improving the quality and yields of bananas. Unlike the other WINBAN territories which packed over 70 per cent of their bananas in the field, Grenadian farmers (by 1983) were only packing 28 per cent of their bananas in the field. This was a contributing factor to the greater fortunes of banana producers in St Lucia, St Vincent and Dominica (see Thompson, 1987, and IMF, 1984a).

40. See Searle (1983) for an interesting and thorough discussion of this point. Searle also discusses the 'cultural revolution' which the PRG sought to bring about.

41. As much as 45 per cent of the population was estimated by the government to be illiterate. These were mainly the people engaged in productive activities (see *Free West Indian*, 26 April 1980, p. 1).

42. See the Centre's Teaching Manual 'Education for True Liberation and Economic Independence' for more specific information on the aims and objectives of CPE, the teaching materials used, structure of CPE, and other details on the Centre.

43. Through NISTEP the problem of teacher shortage was expected to be eliminated in a matter of years. In 1977/78 only 39 per cent of the 752 primary school teachers in the island were formally trained. In 1978/79, the figure was 39 per cent (or 298). For 1979/80 it fell to 33 per cent. It fell even further in 1980/81, i.e. to 30 per cent or 235 teachers (see UNESCO, 1982, p. 9).

44. A Young Scientists' Club was to be set up in every school in the island. The aim was to expose children to scientific activities from an early age, 'to make science a part of their lives' (Government of Grenada, 1983e, p. 121).

45. Many schools were also repaired, several built, and more furniture provided. As much as 22.5 per cent of Grenada's recurrent expenditure was earmarked for education in 1982. The figure in 1981 was 21.3 per cent. Note, total recurrent expenditure in 1982 was EC$67.6 million, a six per cent increase over the 1981 figure (see Government of Grenada, 1983e, p. 14).

46. Embassy of Grenada in the USSR, from W. Richard Jacobs, captioned 'Grenada's Relations with the USSR', (Un-numbered Grenada Document, March 1983).

47. See Commonwealth Secretariat (1982) for background information on the GFNC, especially its functions and objectives. The latter are discussed in chapter one of the document.

48. According to Prime Minister Bishop 'The hospitals in Grenada prior to the revolution were regarded as extensions of the funeral agencies.

You literally went there to die. Even the most basic items ... bandages, aspirins, sheets, X-ray machines were never working' (*The Nation*, Barbados, 14 November 1979, p.16).

49.   A more recent survey was conducted at the end of 1980 but the author was unable to locate it. However, as *Housing in Grenada* (a government document) noted the housing situation was likely to have deteriorated further by 1979 since unemployment was notoriously high during the 1970s, most Grenadians could not afford bank loans, high cost of building materials, and limited activity in the construction sector. The document cited data from a 1977 UN study which put housing requirements for the next 14 years at 1,047. The UN study further noted that few, if any houses, were constructed between 1977 and 1979.

50.   The repayment from beneficiaries under the scheme were planned to be ploughed back into the project so that it would continue to improve the country's housing problem. The programme was initially funded by the local commercial banks, and EC$250,000 from a grant received from OPEC. Funds were also sought to provide loans to farmers so that they could build adequate houses on their own land and in the vicinity of their farms (hence they would spend less time to travel to work).

51.   *The Maternity Leave Law* was an important advance for women. For the first time employers were legally compelled to retain the jobs of female employees until the expiry of their maternity leave. They were also obliged to pay them a full salary for their three-months leave. Violation of these terms could in imprisonment of up to one year, or a fine of EC$2,000 (see Government of Grenada, 1982c).

52.   See also Government of Grenada (1983e), pp. 25-28; and World Bank (1984), pp. 10-15.

53.   According to Errol Berkely, Grenadian agricultural economist based at the Caribbean Development Bank, output of traditional agricultural produce was doubtless greater than what is depicted in table 4:2, since the figures in the table only measure output marketed by organised marketing outlets, e.g the MNIB and the Nutmeg Board. It is difficult to measure the 'unorganised' trade with hucksters and other produce transported by boats to the vibrant market in Trinidad. Mr Berkeley also made the insightful remark that since prices for some of these

125

produce had dropped so sharply, there was not much incentive for farmers to market all their produce given the costs of harvesting, transportation, and the uncertainty of markets. The data in the table must therefore be interpreted with caution (author's interview with Mr Berkeley in May 1987).

54. This was a major initiative to eliminate the middlemen who previously reaped enormous profits from Grenada's nutmeg industry. Referring to the background to this trade agreement with the Soviet Union, Coard had this to say: '...what we discovered in the first year of the revolution when the Soviet Trade Delegation visited Grenada is that the exact quantity of nutmegs which the Soviet Union buys from Holland every year happens, by sheer coincidence, to be the exact quantity of nutmegs which Grenada sells Holland every year. Holland has no nutmegs tress, I might add - it's the wrong climate. So we are just having the middlemen in fact making money out of us' (Coard, 1985, p. 39).

55. See *The New York Times*, Sunday 22 January 1984, 'Nutmeg Diplomacy in Grenada: The Aftermath of Invasion'. See also the *Trinidad Express*, Thursday 22 October 1981 'Revolutionary Policies have backfired'. In words similar to Dull's, the article noted 'The snag was that the nutmeg is a luxury item which the Soviet Union does not need. When pressed, they agreed to buy nutmegs from Grenada but on condition that Grenada took Soviet goods in exchange'.

56. The Commodity Boards operate an internal 'price stabilization programme'. When the price of the traditional exports is high, the Boards which market the farmers' produce retain a part of the proceeds to form a 'Reserve Fund' to cushion price decreases. To protect the farmers' income the PRG re-organised the membership of the Commodity Boards. Instead of the members previously handpicked by Gairy, it now nominated members who were committed to advancing the interests of small farmers.

57. *Trinidad Express*, 3 March 1981, 'Grenada Underpaid on Export Markets'. Whiteman was making reference to the banana industry in particular. But the charge was general as evidenced by similar remarks made in various government documents.

5 Transformation of the tourist industry

Despite its relatively strong foothold in the agricultural sector, the main emphasis of the PRG's economic policies centred initially on the development of tourism. Tourism to Grenada was like oil to the Middle East countries. This chapter discusses the main initiatives pursued in this sector, with emphasis on the construction of the controversial international airport and the policy of 'New Tourism'. The performance of the tourist industry during the years of the revolution is also critically appraised. The discussion is set in the context of academic discussion of the role of tourism in development.

Tourism as a vehicle for development

Few, if any, would disagree with the proposition that tourism can play an important role in economic and social development. This is particularly true for small, underdeveloped economies such as those in the Caribbean. Apart from the physical handicaps of (small) size - especially a narrow and limited configuration of resources - these countries suffer from the usual problems associated with the export of primary products. These include adverse terms-of-trade conditions and unstable markets (which imply that foreign exchange receipts are also uncertain).

Tourism, on the other hand, is characterised by fairly stable and predictable prices, which are largely determined by the host nation. Additionally, the tourist product is more income-elastic than raw material exports.[1] By complementing other exports, tourism can also play a useful role in the diversification of the export base of underdeveloped countries and hence help to stabilize foreign exchange earnings. Apart from generating desperately needed foreign exchange, tourism has the potential to provide jobs and tax revenues to the host country. It is also worth noting that trade in physical, tangible merchandise is more vulnerable to protectionist policies than the tourist trade, especially visitors from the Western bloc.

For the Caribbean region one of the best known studies on how tourism can contribute to development is the *Zinder Report* (1969). Although the data on which this Report is premised is outdated, the Report remains influential in the region. The multiplier effect of tourist expenditure in the Eastern Caribbean was estimated at 2.3. That the size of the multiplier was the same for the eight Eastern Caribbean territories examined in the study was enough reason to be suspicious of the accuracy of the estimate. One becomes even more suspicious when the authors record that tax revenue in each of the islands was exactly 15 per cent of the estimated total contribution of tourism to national income. Wages, too, were exactly 25 per cent of the total impact on national income in each of the territories (Zinder et al., pp. 38-39).

The authors argued that the multiplier and its attendant benefits would have been substantially higher were it not for the structural constraints of the economics under consideration (i.e. limited diversification and a heavy import orientation). In their view multiplier models 'normally generate multipliers ranging from 3.2 and 8, depending on the types of economies (ibid., p. 35). The crudeness of this remark and their 'multiplier model' has not escaped the attention of critics (Levitt and Gulati; 1970; Bryden and Faber; 1971). As Bryden and Faber put it: 'the Zinder tourist multiplier bears very little relation as it is used here to any multiplier employed by Samuelson or any other competent economist (Bryden and Faber, 1971, p. 67).

The critics demonstrated that Zinder's multiplier was, in fact, 'a measure of dollars changing hands' which is not the same thing as an income multiplier'. This is the error of double counting or what Bryden and Faber termed 'multiplying the tourist multiplier' (ibid., p. 69). Besides, the authors of the Report failed to allow for import leakages in the tourist sector. The extent to which the Zinder Report exaggerated the tourist multiplier can be judged from the estimates provided by the critics. Using the same data Levitt and Gulati arrived at a figure of .84. In a similar fashion, Bryden and Faber obtained an income multiplier of between 0.6 and 0.76 ('depending on the precise assumption adopted regarding the effect on cost structures'). In commenting on their multiplier Bryden and Faber noted: 'We would not wish to imbue with spurious accuracy any estimate of a coefficient so vague conceptually even if it is founded on more rigorous data than that presented by Zinder. What can be asserted strongly, however, is that the relevant tourist multiplier is extremely unlikely to be as high as 1.00 in most of the Eastern Caribbean Islands, and is certainly nowhere near the value claimed for it by the Zinder Report' (ibid., p. 69).

Doubts have also been raised about the extent to which tourism can serve as a significant generator of employment.[2] Although stressing the importance of tourism in this regard, the Zinder Report made no attempt to estimate the number of jobs attributable to this sector. This probably had to do with the unavailability of reliable data and methodological problems. The conclusion from Marshall's study on 'Tourism and Employment in Barbados'[3] is worth reproducing in this regard:

> Although our results are necessarily tentative given the quality of the data, our general conclusion must be that tourism's performance as a significant employer of labour in Barbados is disappointing. Not only has the sector only recently achieved our rather generous definition of significance, but that level was sustained for only a short time, and has since declined. Employee/room ratios are similar to those in the more developed islands in the Caribbean like Jamaica and Puerto Rico, and within that context luxury hotels in Barbados seem to perform creditably. But given the very high cost of job creation in tourism in Barbados, and in the Caribbean as well, if the Bahamas is any indication, we must query whether we in the Caribbean can afford such an expensive employment generating exercise (Marshall, 1978, p. 44).

Mention must also be made of the sociological, socio-cultural, and environmental costs of large-scale tourism.[4] Again this is another important omission from Zinder's study. In reaction to Zinder's recommendation that a better cost:benefit return can be obtained by going after the higher spending tourists, Bryden and Faber scathingly asserted that this proposition 'appears to ignore completely the social consequences of consciously aiming for visitors who would spend in under ten days in Barbados and in under five days in most of the Leeward and Windward Islands an amount greater than the average share of the GDP of a local inhabitant for a full year' (Bryden and Faber, p. 73). This may well be a contributing factor to the resentment and indifference from the local population towards visitors (which the Zinder Report observed but attributed to a 'lack of understanding about what tourism is, or what it would do to help the islands'). Another suggestion is that the resentment 'may well be .... that they (the natives) see themselves being relegated to second place after the tourists' (Abdullah, 1974, p. 10).

According to Doxey (1975)[5] the initial impact may be characterised by euphoria from the natives rather than resentment. Varying degrees of irritation set in as tourist numbers increase and contact between natives and visitors increase (see table 5:1). It is also believed that the degree of irritation will be dependent in part on the type of tourism promoted. Cohen (1974) and Mathieson and Wall (1979) distinguish between four types of tourists, viz, (i) the organised/institutionalised mass tourist; (ii) the individual mass tourist;

129

Table 5:1
Index of tourist irritation

1. The level of euphoria

People are enthusiastic and thrilled by tourist development. They welcome the stranger and there is a mutual feeling of satisfaction. There are opportunities for locals and money flows in along with the tourist.

2. The level of apathy

As the industry expands people begin to take the tourist for granted. He rapidly becomes a target for profit-taking and contact on the personal plane begins to become more formal.

3. The level of irritation

This will begin when the industry is nearing the saturation point or is allowed to pass a level at which the locals cannot handle the numbers without expansion of facilities.

4. The level of antagonism

The irritations have become more overt. People now see the tourist as the harbinger of all that is bad. 'Taxes have gone up because of the tourists'. 'They have no respect for property'. 'They have corrupted our youth'. 'They are bent on destroying all that is fine in our town'. 'Mutual politeness has now given way to antagonism and the tourist is 'ripped off'.

5. The final level

All this while people have forgotten that what they cherished in the first place was what drew the tourists, but in the wild scramble to develop they overlooked this and allowed the environment to change. What they now must learn to live with is the fact that their eco-system will never be the same again. They might still be able to draw tourists but of a very different type from those they so happily welcomed in early years. If the destination is large enough to cope with mass tourism it will continue to thrive.

Source: Cited in A. Mathieson and G. Wall, *Tourism: Economic, Physical and Social Impacts*, (Longman, London and New York, 1982), p. 138.

(iii) the explorer; and (iv) the drifter. It has been suggested that host resentment is likely to be higher with mass tourism (category one) since this type of tourism creates physical enclaves of wealth and privilege in the midst of squalor and material deprivation.[6] Besides, the impersonality of contact between hosts and tourists may lead to mutual suspicion and distorted views about each other. The conspicuous spending habits of the mass tourist may also create false impressions on the part of natives and these may incite crime and even prostitution.

As yet there is no hard, empirical evidence to substantiate many of the sociological and socio-cultural impacts attributable to tourism. Although the arguments adduced are largely impressionistic, they can be used as a basis for a more rigorous investigation geared towards deepening our understanding of the many issues posed by tourism as a locomotive for development. The benefits of such studies to tourism planners cannot be over-emphasised. The foregoing survey of some of the principal issues involved in tourism is a useful backdrop against which we can examine the PRG's tourist strategy. High social costs, coupled with a minute multiplier effect, and various possible environmental problems,[7] caution us to consider a whole host of factors before committing scarce resources to large scale tourism development.

The PRG and 'New Tourism'

Had Grenada been better endowed with natural resources (especially valuable minerals) the revolutionary government would probably not have assigned so prominent a role to tourism. Perhaps this sector would not even have figured in the government's economic strategy at all, given the multitude of problems associated with it, and the threats which a further opening of the society posed for a revolution which was still in its formative years. But the sheer paucity of resources in Grenada made it imperative for the government to promote tourism. It was Jean Holder, Executive Director of the Caribbean Tourism Research Centre, who made the famous remark 'tourism is to the Caribbean what oil is to the Middle East' (Holder, 1983, p. 46).

But the PRG were not prepared to create an overdependence on tourism. As we have already noted, diversification was one of the watchwords of the revolution. Bishop summed up the dilemma faced by his government as follows:

> In terms of the development of the economy comrades, over the next 10-15 years, as we see it, the next five years - emphasis will undoubtedly be tourism. That is not to say that we like tourism, that

is because we have no choice. Tourism is the sector that has the greatest potential for giving us the profits to invest in the areas we really want to invest in - agriculture, agro-industries, fisheries, and non-agro industrialization generally. That is really where we will like to go, but those cannot produce the money at this time, while tourism can (*Line of March*, p. 30).

The industry was thus seen as a major generator of foreign exchange, especially in the short run. To maximise this critical benefit, and at the same time to alleviate undesirable socio-economic, socio-cultural, and environmental consequences, the revolutionary government sought to promote a policy of 'New Tourism'. This was conceived as the antithesis of the traditional variety of tourism. The essential features of the 'old tourism' were articulated in an address made by the Prime Minister in December 1979 on 'The Socio-cultural and Environmental Impact of Tourism in the Caribbean'.

> The major problem with the 'old tourism' is that it grew up in an imperialist age and is therefore beset with all the worst features of imperialism. As such, tourism was never intended as a means of developing the national economy and society. Rather it was a means of increasing dependence on the metropole and of providing development for the few, and underdevelopment for the vast, vast majority of the people of our islands (Bishop, 1982a, p. 68).

To demonstrate this thesis Bishop went on to examine the pattern of ownership, control, and organization of the tourist sector. This sector was developed along the same lines as sugar, bauxite, bananas, oil and other primary exports of the Caribbean periphery. For the most part they were all owned by multinational corporations. (Names like Hilton, Holiday Inn and Inter Continental are well known to people living in the Caribbean). These foreign complexes were typically set up under the aegis of a wide range of concessions and privileges by the state. Among these were tax holidays, duty free imports, access to land space, and freedom to repatriate profits generated internally. As Bishop noted: 'In some cases ... they even claimed our beaches for their exclusive use' (ibid., p. 69).

The traditional tourism plant was also developed as an economic enclave with virtually no linkages with the rest of the domestic economy. Items consumed within the industry originated from abroad, as were construction materials, decor for the hotels, and skilled manpower. The tourist enclaves were also places of privilege, glamour, and affluence witnessed the 'sturdy buildings with water and sewerage and electricity and good food, and not too far down the road were local villages and dwellings where conditions were just the opposite'(ibid., p. 69. Under the sub-heading 'Racism and Black Self-

Image', Bishop went on to point out the domination of the industry by white visitors. This, for him, was dangerous given the historical background of the new nation-states in the Caribbean where race, colour and class were so closely intertwined. Since 'blackness' was equated with 'inferiority' and 'whiteness' with 'superiority' he was of the view that the old tourism was 'very damaging to a growing black confidence in self' (ibid., p. 69). He noted further: 'To make matters worse, the metropolitan visitors brought with them some of the worst aspects of their culture - inflation, consumerism, drug abuse, homosexuality, prostitution, gambling. Because of their 'high' social position in the West Indies context, there was a great danger of them being regarded as a 'reference group' which locals, particularly the young, imitate' (ibid., p. 70). Because substantial aspects of the tourist product[8] can be offered by more than one destination 'regional separatism' may result from the old tourism instead of 'reginal cohesion'. In Bishop's terminology 'each island (attempts) to promote its own "sun, sea, and sand" at the expense of everybody else's' (Bishop, ibid., p. 70).

The new tourism philosophy aimed to invert all the features which were associated with 'old tourism'. One of its ideals was to view tourism 'not merely as a business but as an instrument of world peace and understanding where peoples from all over the world can meet in an atmosphere of mutual respect and develop closer understanding of their different cultures' (Bishop, ibid., p. 71). New tourism would also seek to sever the historical relationship between tourism, class and colour. As such, efforts would be made to consciously encourage non-white visitors from the Caribbean and the wider Third World, to complement other tourists - especially during the off-season period when hotels typically operate with considerable excess capacity.[9]

To increase the tourist multiplier, New Tourism would seek to establish linkages with other sectors of the economy, particularly agriculture, agro-processing, manufacturing and handicrafts. Indigenous culture would also be promoted - dance, music, poetry and other linguistic expressions - instead of local culture 'being determined by some preconceived notion of what the tourist might expect' (Bishop, p. 72). Plans were made to target special interest groups who may be interested to observe the island's culture in action as well as to get a first hand experience of the process of change that was under way in Grenada. For example, overseas-based teachers may wish 'to come and see what is happening in the Centre for Popular Education programme or in the National In-Service Teacher Education programme' (Government of Grenada, 1982f, pp. 91-92).

There was no place in this type of tourism for socially deleterious practices like gambling, drugs, and prostitution. Offenders would feel the full weight of the law: 'take prostitution, if you catch local prostitutes - lock them up and rehabilitate them. If you catch foreign prostitutes coming in - deport them. So we will have to develop a very careful set of rules and guidelines to ensure that tourism doesn't get out of hand' (*Line of March*, p. 31).

Doubts have been raised about whether there was any substance to this philosophy of new tourism (Ambursley, 1983; and Mandle, 1985a). At best it would have to be a long-term goal given the objective requirements of the economy, especially for foreign exchange to finance the country's escalating import bill and its investment plan. Even then, accommodation problems would remain since most of the island's accommodation facilities were privately owned. Private sector participation in this area of the economy was planned to increase, not diminish, since the state lacked the material resources to develop the sector on its own steam. This meant that the more affluent, traditional variety of tourist would be favoured with its attendant sociological and socio-cultural problems. It also had direct implications for the distribution of benefits from tourist development between those who owned and controlled hotels and those who merely supplied casual labour.[10]

A less daunting task for the government was the physical planning of tourist plants,[11] tourist attractions,[12] and general infrastructure. These were welcome by the private sector since they posed no major threat to their existence and continued prosperity. To the contrary, some of these initiatives (e.g. airports, improvements of public utilities) facilitated their quest for profits.

The international airport project

The decision to build an international airport at the phenomenal cost of US$71 million (EC$237 million) was a clear indication of the importance which the PRG placed on the development of tourism. The government was convinced that Grenada had excellent untapped tourist potential. Deputy Prime Minister, Bernard Coard, went further. At the Aid Donors Conference in Brussels he told delegates: 'It is an established fact that Grenada possesses the greatest potential for tourism development in the Caribbean today' (Government of Grenada, 1981c, p. 4).

This claim was substantiated by other independent bodies. A 1976 World Bank Tourist Sector Review had this to say:

> Grenada is one of the most attractive islands in the Caribbean. Its excellent beaches are backed by spectacular mountain scenery, rich with lush vegetation. Its harbour at St George's, the capital, is rated the prettiest in the islands and serves both as a port-of-call for cruise ships as well as a centre for yachting in the Grenadines. The climate is warm with a pleasant seabreeze throughout the year. In short,

Grenada fulfils most people's image of a tropical paradise (cited in Government of Grenada, 1981c, p. 5).

Another study, The 1980 European Tourism Demand Study, evaluated 26 Caribbean countries and placed Grenada in the number one position on the basis of climate, beaches, and natural attractions. But the study concluded on a grim note. Grenada was designated a 'touristically disadvantaged destination' on account of 'accessibility problems' (cited in Hudson, 1983, p. 52). The airport at the time (Pearls Airport) suffered from a number of deficiencies. These included (i) a runway which was too small to accommodate large, wide-bellied jets; (ii) impossibility of night and instrument landings given the encirclement of the site by steep hills; and (iii) and dimensions which did not conform to the standards recommended by the International Civil Aviation Organization (ICAO).

The impossibility of night landing facilities, especially, had grave implications for the promotion of tourism in Grenada. For unless the flights arrived in Grenada before nightfall visitors would be obliged to overnight in the neighbouring islands of Trinidad or Barbados. Some visitors ended up making the connecting island their destination, especially when hoteliers insisted on a minimum booking for three nights. Not only was this extra expenditure onerous for the visitor but visitors (especially long distance travellers) were further inconvenienced by making connecting flights, claiming and reclaiming baggage, clearing customs, checking in, and overnighting elsewhere. According to one source some 50 per cent of annual visitors to Grenada overnight in other islands at approximately US$85 per visitor causing a loss of US$1.3 million to Grenada (Government of Grenada, 1981c, p. 5). The future of the industry in Grenada was threatened further because tour operators and travel agents, reportedly, stopped selling Grenada as a tourist destination on account of the difficulties of securing confirmed bookings for their clients between Barbados and Grenada. And since some of these countries have laws to protect consumers, claims could be made on travel agents.

As far as the Grenadian authorities were concerned the solution to these problems lay in the construction of a new international airport. This was not a lone voice crying in the wilderness. Long before the PRG committed itself to this project the 'airport problem' was studied in numerous quarters[13] and several of the studies and reports urged that 'construction should be started as soon as conveniently possible' (Government of Grenada, 1981c, p, 11). A notable feature of these studies is that they invariably ended on an inconclusive note, thus necessitating further studies. The latest study, undertaken by the World Bank in 1976, also identified Point Salines as the most appropriate site for the construction of an international airport. It concluded that 'the existing runway at Pearls acted and would continue to act as a constraint on the development of air transport and tourism growth' (Hudson, 1983, p. 54). But before action could begin the team recommended that a further study should be done to ascertain the technical, economic and financial feasibility of an airport at Point Salines. This chorus was joined by a later team from the OAS Secretariat in 1977 which concluded:

> After reviewing all of the technical studies that have been undertaken in relation to the 'airport problem' and alternative forms of transportation ..., and mindful that the economic and financial cost of resolving the airport dilemma over the long term constitutes the second largest investment in the proposed Investment Program of Grenada, the OAS Secretariat suggests undertaking additional limited or comprehensive feasibility studies as are necessary to reconcile existing technical discrepancies of an economic, social and engineering nature. The most appropriate vehicle might be a comparative cost benefit analysis of the two proposed future airport alternatives to review in depth the various areas of discrepancy. Subsequent to this study, the airport might be financed by a consortium of financial agencies which may include the Venezuelan Investment Fund, the Canadian Investment Fund (CIDA financed the Barbadian airport), the World Bank, the Inter-American Development Bank, or German financial institutions, on terms most favourable to Grenada (OAS Secretariat, 1977, pp. 31-32).

The OAS Secretariat in its recommendation for further study was adding insult to injury. When the administration of the island's affairs fell to the PRG in 1979 they were determined to search for funds and commence this all-important project - a project which had been the dream of Grenadian leaders since 1955. Admittedly, this drive to start such a mammoth project was a fundamental departure from the promise made in the 1973 manifesto. When questioned about this retreat, former Cabinet Minister Kenrick Radix gave the following reasons: (i) People are entitled to change their ideas, especially since the world, itself, is in constant flux; (ii) the party too had been transformed since 1973; (iii) the need for funds for the eventual transformation of the country became more real once the NJM came into power in 1979; and (iv) the longer you wait to carry out such a project the more expensive it would be in monetary terms.[14] Tourism Minister, Lyden Ramdhanny, also noted: 'Investors have told us they will pour not a bucket of concrete for any hotel construction until Grenada gets an international airport' (cited in *Barbados Advocate*, 10 April 1983).

Aspects of these sentiments were dramatically echoed by Bernard Coard at the Conference in Brussels:

History has recorded that at particular moments countries are forced to decide on the most important project that they need to undertake in order to achieve further economic development and then go all out to attain that objective. For some countries it has been the development of railroads, for others devastated by World War I, it was immediate and total electrification of the country so that the industrialization process could proceed apace. For yet others it has been a seaport to realize their commercial potential, for others it is access to the sea. For Grenada, we believe with all humility, that it is an international airport, so that we can realize our tourism potential. This is our firm position (Government of Grenada, 1981c, p. 4).

In another passage of the same conference address Coard also spoke about the phenomenal escalation in the cost of the airport since the first study was done in 1955:

If the entrepreneurs of the more studies and yet more studies growing industry in the world want to ask for more studies to be done for another two or three years, by the time we got along to build this international airport, I would humbly suggest this US$71 million could easily become a US$150 million and perhaps then, there would need to be a study to determine whether that was a suitable figure or whether that was not too high a price (Government of Grenada, 191c, p. 19).

Work eventually began at the new Point Salines site, only a few miles away from the island's main tourist resorts, in January 1980 with the arrival of construction equipments from Cuba. In all, the Castro government agreed to provide more than half the cost of the project, i.e. US$40 million in the form of manpower and machinery.[15] The remainder of the funds was to be raised by the Grenadian government, whether by internal sources or external. This was no easy task for a small, poor, underdeveloped country like Grenada, especially given the numerous other commitments and demands on the PRG's paltry resources. Apart from Cubans and Grenadians, outside interests were to benefit enormously from the project. These included the Florida-based companies, Layne Dredging and Norwich Engineering, Metex (a Finnish Company), and Plessey (a British company).

The master plan adopted for the airport was essentially an updated version of the one produced by Scott Wilson Kirkpatrick and Partners and Economist Intelligence Unit in 1969. But with Grenada's most important tourism partners (Europe and North America) moving increasingly to wide-bodied, long-haul jets of the B747, DC10 and L1011 variety, the government now decided to construct the entire runway of 9,000 feet at once. A further 800 feet was added later. The length of the runway was to be a major bone of contention with the United States. The fact that the airport was virtually a gift from the Cubans added further to these fears. The United States was convinced that the airport would be first and foremost a military asset to the Eastern block. As expressed by Sandford and Vigilante (1984), in a work with a strong pro-US bias, the airport: 'would extend the reach of Cuban jetfighters throughout the region, and provide an important refuelling station for Cuban transport aircraft on their way to resupply Cuban forces in Angola' (Sanford and Vigilante, 1984, p. 90).

The length of the runway was hardly any basis on which to rest this allegation. According to two survivors of the PRG[16] the economics of airport construction loomed high in the minds of their decision-makers. The OAS economic secretariat in their 'Economic Study of Grenada' had pointed out in 1977 that: 'original airport planners in Grenada failed to foresee that within some 30 years of initial construction, Pearl's airport would be inadequate in relation to aeronautical and technical innovation'. They went on to advise: 'Owing to the large economic, financial, and social costs of airports, present planners of the future Grenada airport would be well advised to develop an air access strategy to last at least for the next half century' (OAS Secretariat, op. cit., p. 26). Further advice came in 1978 Circular Reports from the International Civil Aviation Organization:

> Caribbean traffic growth and changes in aircraft technology require the continued expansion of existing facilities and raise the problem of financing such development. In general terms it can be said that the absence of at least one runway of not less than 3,000m (9,800 feet) in a country restricts the operation of long-haul international services with modern equipment and is a potential limiting factor on the development of a pattern that fully meets the transport requirements of a country (OAS Secretariat, p. 6).

It should be stated further that a runway of 9,800 feet was not unusual by Caribbean standards (Government of Grenada, 1981c, p. 30). Indeed the PRG was of the view that there was a direct relationship between a country's airport size and the amount of tourist business it would be able to attract. Thus countries like Grenada, St Vincent and Dominica (without an international airport) tend to fare less well than their more fortunate counterparts in Barbados and Puerto Rico, for example. This correlation between airport size and tourist numbers is open to question. However, it is a clear testimony of the importance which the regime assigned to an international airport.[17] Their projection of tourist arrivals once this project was completed in 1984 is also revealing.

With the completion of the project, it was projected that Grenada's share of Caribbean tourism would move from the 1981 figure of 0.4 per cent to at least 1.0 per cent by 1990 (see table 5:2 for the projections for the entire period). It was projected that a total of 1,225 rooms at a cost of EC$149.9 million would be required to facilitate the 'pessimistic projections'. The figures for the 'optimistic projections' was 1,814 rooms at a cost of EC$232.1 million (see, also, table 5:2 for the cash flow projections for the project). Major spin-offs were expected to flow from these developments, not least of which was employment generation for both skilled and unskilled workers.

Table 5:2
Visitor arrivals (stay-over) and cash flow projections (1981-1990)

Year	Optimistic projections	Pessimistic projections	% of Caribbean total	Loss/surplus (US$ m)
1981	34,800	32,200	0.4	(9.2)
1982	36,400	34,000	0.4	(7.5)
1983	57,600	52,000	0.6	(3.6)
1984	60,600	54,600	0.6	(2.2)
1985	84,800	74,400	0.8	0.5
1986	88,800	76,800	0.8	2.5
1987	117,000	99,000	1.0	7.2
1988	122,000	102,000	1.0	11.2
1989	129,000	105,000	1.0	16.3
1990	135,000	108,000	1.0	22.36

( ) denotes loss

Source: Government of Grenada (1981c), p. 8.

Recognising that the 'airport dilemma' was only one part of the 'air access problem' Coard assured his listeners that the other part, 'the airline problem', would be solved once the airport was constructed. The regional carrier, Leeward Island Air Transportation (LIAT) is well-known for its inefficiency. Late arrivals and departures, loss of baggage, and failure to obtain seats even when advanced bookings are made, were regular occurrences. For this reason LIAT is derisively (but appropriately) dubbed by Grenadians as 'Leave Island Any Time'.[18] The poor assessment of the service provided by LIAT can be gleaned from the remarks made by visitors in the survey carried out by the

Caribbean Tourism Research Council (CTRC) in 1982. Two such remarks read as follows: 'Our luggage arrived two days after us, so we had no clothes to put on. If the luggage is not going with the passenger, it should get to the person on the arrival of the next plane to your destination'. 'We suggest that LIAT airline is a great obstacle to more people enjoying your beautiful country' (CTRC, 1982, p. 8).

To cope with the increased number of visitors projected by Coard, it was clear that LIAT would have had to be substantially supplemented or even supplanted by other airlines capable of providing adequate and reliable service to Grenada. According to Coard's presentation at the Conference, investors from the United States, Canada, and the United Kingdom were already approaching his government on the subject of landing rights when the international airport was completed. Just how correct this information was, we do not know. Doubts have been raised about whether the United States would actually establish an aviation agreement with Grenada: 'With the completion of the airport, it is certain that the United States would resist coming to an air treaty until it had extracted major concessions from Grenada. In effect, the airport/tourist strategy would have strengthened the American bargaining position in its efforts to influence Grenadian policy, especially foreign policy' (Mandle, 1985a, p. 29). Without this vital bilateral agreement visitors from the US bound for Grenada would have continued to experience difficulties in Barbados and Trinidad.

This was not the only area for doubt. Were Coard's projections for visitor arrivals attainable? Would the private sector be willing to commit their capital to the expansion and development of tourism facilities on the scale required? Obviously, no firm answer can be provided to these questions since the regime collapsed before the completion of the airport in 1984. With respect to the first question, our response is likely to be in the negative if the trends in Grenada's tourism sector, during the revolutionary and post-revolutionary periods, is anything to base a judgement on.[19] And since members of the private sector generally felt they were under siege (especially given the government's strong propensity to apply 'revolutionary manners' to those perceived as 'non-collaborators'), the answer to the second question cannot be affirmative either, at least so long as the revolutionary government continued with its 'repressive' practices. (The extent to which the PRG was able to harness the support of the business class is discussed in detail in chapter six below). With much justification, therefore, we can say there was a fundamental flaw inherent in the development strategy of the PRG-dominated as it was by one single project. This was to cost the government dearly in both economic and political terms.

The World Bank's position on the issue was that Grenada did not require an airport with such an extensive runway. 'The present air-access problem would be solved adequately by the first phase of the airport - a 5,200 ft. runway with night landing facilities' (World Bank, 1982a, p. 16). The various arguments adduced by the PRG for a more sophisticated facility were casually dismissed. The World Bank report noted further:

> In order to justify the massive investment in the airport, the number of tourists to Grenada would have to increase substantially, well beyond the capacity of facilities to accommodate them. This implies that airlines or charter organizations will schedule the island, and that the required accommodation, infrastructure and service became available. However, it is doubtful that airlines will stop in Grenada with the frequency necessary. The economics of the airline industry today suggest that Grenada is likely to continue to be served by feeder aircraft from neighbouring islands, as shown by the recent reduction in direct flights to St Lucia by BWIA. Also, there are, as yet, no agreements with charter organizations to schedule Grenada. The present government marketing strategy of targeting special interest groups such as bird watchers and divers is not likely to increase substantially the number of visitors to Grenada. Lastly, the resources allocated to the Department of Tourism are inadequate. The Department is understaffed and underfunded, the budget for 1981, for instance, amounted to less than 1 per cent of 1980 tourism earnings (World Bank, ibid., p. 16).

The Report concluded its section on tourism by stressing that the need for the government to rethink its tourist strategy.

Apart from inviting severe opposition (and even outright economic aggression) from the United States, the demands of the project created an enormous cash-flow problem which brought the economy to a virtual collapse by mid-1983. Not only were funds diverted from social welfare programmes and capital projects, but to keep the airport project going the government was obliged to introduce measures which incurred the displeasure of the private sector. These included onerous taxes and the introduction of a law which made it mandatory for commercial banks to deposit 20 per cent of their funds with the government.[20] Despite these initiatives the liquidity situation in the economy remained tight. As a matter of last resort the government turned to the International Monetary Fund in August 1983 for 'assistance'. This move in itself was a serious threat to the viability and survivability of the revolution since the country's economic policies would in effect be dictated by the one who 'pays the piper'. The PRG knew this only too well. The experience of Michael Manley of the People's National Party (PNP) of Jamaica with the Fund was still fresh in their mind. But apart from resorting to even more draconian measures, they had no real alternative.

141

At the Brussels conference Coard admitted the enormous physical strain which this project placed on them: 'each single Minister of the Government of Grenada including the Prime Minister (spent) 80 per cent of (their) time travelling throughout the world and spending sleepless nights over the past two years in order to raise (the remaining) US$30 million (Government of Grenada, 1981c, p. 4). And despite his persuasive and well prepared address he left Brussels disappointed, having only succeeded in raising a paltry US$2.2 million from the European Economic Community (EEC). This was a clear triumph for US propaganda against the regime[21]. To the US the project was first and foremost a military asset for the Eastern bloc countries.

Although Moscow was covertly approached for a loan of EC$15 million they did not consider it prudent to participate in this politically-sensitive project. Thus the request was brushed aside. The aid boom that the regime experienced in its first two years was not to be repeated during its remaining years. Of the EC$38.7 million spent on the airport in 1981 only EC$0.8 million originated from local sources. Grants to the tune of EC$27.1 million came from Algeria, Syria and Cuba while a loan of EC$10.8 million was procured from Libya (Government of Grenada, 1982e, pp. 21-22).

Promotion of handicrafts

A less controversial tourist-related initiative was the promotion of the handicraft sector. Insights into the way handicraft was perceived, as well as the structure and functioning of the sector before 1979, can be gained from the following remark from the newly-appointed OAS Handicraft Development Consultant, Barrington Brown:

> Craft appears to be accepted as a poor cousin or merely a means of existence. In most cases it was observed that handicraft was geared as a supplement to income only. The unawareness and misunderstanding of the value of handicraft in its various contributions to national growth, e.g. economic return, foreign exchange earner/ export, cultural statement, employment possibilities, import substitution, demonstrated the need to educate the producers, vendors, buyers, and potential buyers in matters relating to the value of the handicraft industry (Brown, 1979, p. 14).

Craft items were lacking in imaginative designs, displayed signs of poor craftsmanship, carried prices which bore no relationship to their quality, and were marketed in an ad hoc manner. Partly as a result of these weaknesses it was also believed that Grenadians, especially the young, were showing 'a rapidly decreasing interest in the craft' (Brown, ibid., p. 28). The state of the industry would probably have been worse had it not been for the existence of the Handicraft Development Centre. Established in 1966, the Centre trained approximately 20 persons per year (mainly in light handicrafts and jewellery). Training sessions were also held once per week for persons who already had some knowledge of craft. This number was estimated to be 3,000, of which the majority were aged between 26 and 35 and were women. Given the lack of an organised market, craft producers tended to produce three days per week and spent the rest of the week trying to sell their products. The training offered at the Centre left much to be desired since those delivering the training were themselves poorly trained. There were no accountant clerks, quality control supervisor, and product design officer.

In response to these problems the PRG set up the Grenada National Institute of Handicrafts (GNIH) in 1979. This organization was made responsible for (i) research, development, and prototype production; (ii) training and developing handicraft technology; (iii) purchasing of raw materials; (iv) quality control and pricing; (v) marketing and promotion of craft items at home and abroad; and (vi) financial assistance against confirmed orders of craft items from producers. At the national level the Institute sought to achieve increased production for the benefit of domestic and overseas consumers (especially tourists), generate employment (through the utilization of the island's raw materials), and promote indigenous culture in the spirit of the Caribs and Arawaks[22] - Grenada's first craftsmen. Appropriately, the Institute's motto read 'Helping the Hand to Build the Land'. The employment potential of the sector can be gauged from the diverse range of raw materials at its disposal. These include woodcraft, strawcraft, sculpturing, needlecraft, leathercraft, stonecraft, and jewellery craft (see table 5:3). The Institute's emphasis on indigenous raw materials placed it on a different footing from its competitors in the private sector - Tikal, Noah's Arcade, Gran Bazaar, Amados, and Spice Isle Perfume Shop - which utilized considerable quantities of imported raw materials and even stocked large quantities of imported handicraft.

To rationalise the operation of the Institute plans were made to forge links with the Grenada Tourist Board. The Board was urged to include craft items in its catalogue, brochures, posters and other printed material. It was also encouraged to stage exhibitions on Grenadian handicrafts during its overseas promotional campaigns. These measures were intended to rationalize the international marketing budget for handicrafts.

The performance of Grencraft, the marketing arm of the GNIH, mirrored the successes and failures of the PRG's efforts in the handicraft sector. Grencraft began its operations in September, 1981. Although the bottomline of its balance sheet failed to show a profit there can be no doubt that the organization had begun the process of achieving its stated objectives - if only

Table 5:3
The distribution of craft materials in Grenada
and their possible product lines

Materials	Raw Materials Product Line
Wood	Carvings, trinkets, furniture, boxes, trays, bowls, spoons, mortar and pestle
Wicker	Trays, lamp shades, furniture, baskets, bags
Coconut Shell	Jewellery, ash trays, cups, coin banks, lamp shades
Banana Bark	Hats, table mats, floor mats
Leather	Clutch purse, handbags, sandals, pouches, cases, chokers
Cotton thread	Crochet, embroidery, strong art, fixings
Kush-kush	Mats, hats, rugs, bags
Corn Trash	Hats, bags, dolls
Coconut Bone	Flex bangles, planters, frames, wall hangings
Sea shells	Vases, boxes, figurines, decorations
Gourds	Ash trays, penholders, cups, lamp shades
Bone	Jewellery: pendants, rings, brooches
Black coral	Jewellery: pendants, bangles, rings, brooches
Gru-gru (seed)	Rings
Turtle shell	Brooches, bracelets, ear-rings
Cow hooves, horns	Jewellery, pendants, brooches, ear-rings
Pandanus	Bags, floor mats, chair seats, hats, slippers, bags, table mats, etc.
Sisal	Mats, bags, chair seats, rope, hats, slippers, bags, mats, etc.

Adapted from B. Brown (1979), p. 38.

because for the first time craft producers were assured of a ready market. Time previously spent in the pursuit of markets for their produce (estimated to be as much as 50 per cent in some cases) could now be devoted to production. Not only was the cultural awareness of craft heightened but for the first time the developmental potential of the sector was recognised, promoted, and formalised in government policies.

With time, the government would have no doubt weathered the major problems plaguing the sector. Moreover, the lack of adequate finance was at the root of these problems. Grencraft operated without a marketing officer and with limited working capital for the first six months of 1982. The resultant problems were: (i) the notable absence of a long term (or even medium-term) marketing strategy for the organization;[23] (ii) promotional campaign was negligible; (iii) a low priority to public relations effort; (iv) difficulties experienced in securing new or improved designs into production for market testing and retail; (v) lack of trained sales personnel; (vi) uninitiated buyers are given a free hand to purchase items without supervision, resulting in the purchasing of significant quantities of substandard goods; (vii) failure to implement a stock control system; (viii) arbitrary marketing intelligence; (ix) the proposed two year moratorium period of the organization was prematurely terminated, leaving it to fend for itself and without working capital (Brown, 1982, pp. 1-2).

Financial difficulties also created severe transportation problems. As late as 1982 Grencraft did not own a single vehicle. It was obliged to hire a small van on a monthly basis to collect products, raw materials, and make deliveries. The meagreness of its income meant that it was hardly able to meet even this basic monthly fee. Aid was sought from friendly organizations to alleviate this problem. Similarly, the organization was not able to provide qualified staff personnel in the accounts department. Its first accounts clerk was not appointed until March 1982. It was around the same time that a marketing officer was appointed for the first time; thanks to loans from the state-owned National Commercial Bank, and the Marketing and National Importing Board.

Soon after taking up posts the impact of these personnel began to be felt. Exhibitions were hosted in Grenada, other Caribbean islands and North America. Plans were also made to mount exhibitions in various European countries, so long as funds could be provided.Grencraft received it first major overseas promotion in June, 1982. Between 14-22 June, a mini-trade exhibition was staged in three central Trinidadian towns (Port-of-Spain, San Fernando and Fyzabad). Although the emphasis was not on sales, an impressive quantity of craft items was bought - amounting to some EC$20,000. In his Report, the Handicraft Adviser commented: 'The two day experience in Port-of-Spain surpassed all our expectations and the inclusion of a cultural presentation assisted in boosting sales considerably' (Brown, 1982, p. 11). Plans were thus made to supply craft items on the Trinidadian market on a regular basis, especially during the carnival period when the island abounds with tourists. Another exhibition held in St Vincent from 27-30 August generated EC$4,334 in sales. The theft of significant quantities of the exhibits testified to the general acceptance of the product (Brown, 1982, p. 12).

The exhibition was also mounted in several important North American tourism centres. At the Eastern Hotel and Tourist Association Convention held in November 1982 in New York, the major focus was on Grenada. The Convention was attended by travel writers and representatives from various parts of the United States and the Eastern Caribbean. The presentation included a display of craft items from Grencraft, slides, posters, and handout material on the GNIH, as well as brochures and catalogues highlighting Grenadian products. From New York the team went to Washington, California and Toronto. The team finally returned to Grenada on 4 December. The products were generally well received. At the exhibition held in Trinidad, for instance, visitors voiced the following remarks: 'Exhibition too short, have never seen Spice Isle products anywhere in Trinidad, I cannot believe these things are made in Grenada, should have brought more goods, you will see me at Carnival, when are you coming again'? (Brown, 1982, p. 52).

This keen interest in Grenadian handicrafts led the Handicraft Adviser to make a wide-ranging list of recommendations in his Report. These were geared primarily towards improving product design and use of materials, diversification of the product line, greater promotion of craft items overseas, training of craftspersons in design, adaptation, and other aspects of handicraft production for export, and follow-up activities to the 1982 exhibitions. The government was equally keen to implement these recommendations. Thus in 1982 when the Adviser applied for a grant of US$49,095 to train 35 students 'to be full-fledged producers for Grencraft' the government enthusiastically approved the project. The importance of the sector to the new society envisaged by the PRG can be gauged from its comments on this occasion:

> for too long has our culture (of which our craft is but one aspect) been left unattended to survive in the barest sense possible. By orienting the programme primarily towards young people - otherwise unemployed and rural based - this training will assist Grenada at several different levels: development and upgrading of an indigenous culture form, provision of employment, (and) provision of supplies for an existing market. The benefits, therefore, far outweigh the costs, given especially that the trainees would also from the start, be

involved in production (cited in Brown, 1982, p. 37).

And given the outstanding contribution of the consultant, Barrington Brown, to the development of Grenadian handicrafts the Prime Minister remarked further: 'It is however strongly recommended that to ensure the practical success of the programme the services of the present OAS Consultant be retained, at least for the duration of the training programme'.[24]

In a certain sense it can be argued that the government's efforts in the handicraft sector was concrete evidence of the 'New Tourism' in action. The emphasis on indigenous sources of raw materials, catenating the various sectors of the economy, and elevating things quintessentially 'Grenadian' went far beyond mere rhetoric - as witnessed by the government's plans for the food sector of the tourist industry.

Tourism/agriculture linkages

A survey was carried out in 1983 to investigate the pattern of consumption in the tourist sector.[25] The main objective was to determine the possible linkages that could be established between tourism and agriculture. A sample of ten per cent (representing roughly 58 rooms) of the tourist sector - comprising 2 full-service hotels, 2 apartment hotels, a guest house and 1 restaurant - was examined. On average the restaurant served 150 meals per day during the peak season and 20 per day during the low season. A high proportion (estimated at 50 per cent) of the island's accommodation belong to the self-catering variety.

Based on this sample it was estimated that annual food costs of the tourist sector amounted to just over EC$4.25 million. It was further estimated that local production accounted for 66 per cent in terms of weight and 52 per cent in terms of value. So far as the estimates of the different categories of consumption items were concerned meat absorbed the greatest proportion of the total food costs (i.e. EC$1.3 million from the EC$4.25 million). This was followed by seafood (EC$0.8 million), dairy products (EC$0.54 million), vegetables (EC$0.52 million), and fruits (EC$0.5 million). Interestingly, the highest level of leakages by value occurred in meats (86 per cent imported). Miscellaneous goods, especially oils and fats, accounted for 73 per cent while dairy goods and fruits (particularly canned juice) amounted to 65 per cent and 63 per cent, respectively. In fact, some items under the various categories were wholly imported, for example, milk, butter and cheese in the case of dairy products.

The Report also presented data on the sources of supply of consumption items and the attendant problems. As much as 83 per cent of the respondents obtained their meat supplies from local supermarkets. The bulk of the sea-food used in the sector was supplied directly by Grenadian fishermen, although some frozen fish was bought from the supermarkets. The main problems with supply seemed to have been lack of reliability and poor quality (CTRC, 1983, p. 19). From the survey it was also found that the main factors determining the preparation of menus in the tourist sector were: cost of food, availability of supply, storage facilities, customer demand, chefs' specialities and the quest to serve something distinctly Grenadian. This last factor figured prominently on the list; it was cited by all respondents. Just over eight in ten (83 per cent) identified cost of food as a major determinant. The figure fell to 67 per cent for the factor 'availability', while only 33 per cent selected the option 'chef's specialities' as a determinant of menu preparation (CTRC, ibid., p. 20).

Another notable feature of the study was the well-thought-out model which it provided for integrating the two sectors, tourism and agriculture. The Report made the self-evident, but very important, remark that 'the programme to increase the amount of local foods and beverages by tourists must be seen as a set of interrelationships between a wide span of institutions and practices' (CTRC, p. 1). Ten groups, with well defined roles and functions, were identified - viz, (i) hotel and restaurant personnel (managers, chefs, purchasers, waiters/ waitresses); (ii) wholesalers; (iii) retailers; (iv) market researchers; (v) training institutes; (vi) agricultural extension workers; (vii) promotion agencies; (viii) tourists; (ix) farmers; and (x) financial institutions. It was stressed that these entities should work together to ensure that the following conditions are satisfied: (i) indigenous dishes are available on menus in tourist establishments; (ii) the dishes must be well prepared and presented; (iii) local foods must be comprehensively and successfully promoted; (iv) local foods must be adequate in both quantity and quality; (v) local foods must be effectively distributed; (vi) local foods must be price competitive vis-a-vis imported foods; (vii) local foods must be conveniently packaged; (viii) new products and new ways of preparing existing products must be continuously developed; (ix) information on markets, food supplies and technologies must be regular, adequate, timely, and comprehensively used (CTRC, pp. 11-12).

Not only must the agricultural sector be dynamic and flexible but the farming community must understand how information from market research may be meaningfully utilized and must be prepared to organise their farms on strict business lines so that it could respond to the demands from the tourist sector. Similarly, financial institutions were urged to display flexibility in repayments schedules and in extensions of credit. Problems such as the vagaries of the weather, praedial larceny, destruction caused by pests, and declining incomes due to inaccurate forecasting of demand, should all be dealt with on terms which recognise the developmental needs of the society.

Failures in any of the links within the system would ultimately lead to a reduction in the volume of local produce consumed in the tourist sector. Similarly, consumption (of local goods) would lag behind expectations if development programmes are implemented on a piecemeal basis and if they failed to be directed at the system as a whole. One can get some insight into the state of the food sector of Grenada's tourist industry from the comments made by visitors in the 1982 CTRC survey (see Appendix 5:A:1). The comments reflect both constraints and opportunities for integrating sections of the agricultural sector into tourism.

Although the Grenadian agricultural sector, marketing and distributional mechanisms were not yet sufficiently developed to perform the role assigned to it, it is clear from the study that the plan to integrate the two sectors was well thought out in both conceptual and empirical terms. And no pretence was made in the study that the required changes (structural, institutional, and attitudinal) could be achieved overnight as some critics of the development strategy of the PRG seem to expect. Mandle, for instance, argues: 'If the airport had opened in 1984 as scheduled and if tourist arrivals had increased as expected, it is clear that the domestic food sector would not have proved immediately competent to meet the growing needs of the arriving guests' (Mandle, 1985a, p. 41). The blame for this state of affairs cannot be justifiably placed at the door of the PRG, given the myriad problems they inherited in the agricultural sector and the various initiatives they took in agriculture. Arguably, the revolutionary government took agriculture much more seriously than past leaders in Grenada and the wider Caribbean region. As for the latter, a well-known Agricultural Adviser (Ronald Baynes, Barclays Bank International Limited, Barbados) had this to say:

> It is most unfortunate that few Caribbean territories have evolved workable official policies which actively encourage agricultural expansion. In fact, in some islands, it is difficult to understand the official perception of the role of the agricultural sector relative to the other sectors. In one particular territory where agriculture contributes better than 80 per cent to its Gross Domestic Product, a recent survey showed that the national purse allocates something in the order of two to three per cent of the annual appropriation to agricultural services in that country (Baynes, 1977, pp. 175-76).

The PRG would have doubtless spearheaded more changes in the agricultural sector had it not been for the financial burden of the international airport. But, then again, even this project was linked to agriculture, albeit secondary to tourism. It is equally difficult to deny that tremendous scope existed for creating linkages between the two sectors. Indeed, the CTRC study revealed that already the food sector of the tourist industry was utilizing a fair amount of local produce. According to Jane Belfon, Director of Tourism under the PRG, the success story of the local restaurant "*Mamas*" was a clear testimony of the soundness of the government's plans for the sector.[26] This restaurant is owned and managed by a Grenadian, Mrs Inslay Wardally, known universally in her restaurant as Mama. In the words of the Tourism Director 'this restaurant serves local dishes without apology to the visitor's origin. Yet they keep on coming back for more whenever they are in Grenada' (author's interview with Jane Belfon in May 1987). Not only is the food completely local but all the decor and furniture originate in Grenada, especially products from Grencraft. The range of food offered and the culinary skills of Mama were fittingly captured by an American tourist in the *New York Times*:

> stewed callaloo (a kind of spinach), breadfruit salad, stewed manicou (opossum with a rich, gamy taste), stewed tattou (armadillo, mildly reminiscent of venison), baked barracuda (a fish), lobster salad, curried breadnut and lambie (conch), baked plantains and yams, and rice and red beans in coconut sauce. The soup was creamed breadfruit, with a taste like fresh squash, but on other days it can be made from callaloo or pumpkin - or ochre leaf or yam leaf or young cocoa leaf. Sometimes Mama serves a crayfish in the soup, explaining, "We, the people of Grenada, chew off the head of the crayfish and suck out the juices (*New York Times*, 5 February 1984).

Another restaurant, *La Belle Creole* at Blue Horizon Hotel, received popular acclaim with tourists. Like Mama's this restaurant specialises in local foods. However, La Belle Creole adds a continental tinge to its local dishes. For instance, callaloo quiche is one of their most successful specialities. Given the importance of the Blue Horizon Hotel in the overall tourist sector there is good reason to believe that the practice of emphasising local dishes could catch on. With its 36 fully equipped suites this hotel is second to Ramada Renaissance (the former Holiday Inn) in terms of room facilities (*Visitors Guide*, 1987). In terms of occupancy level, Blue Horizon is the island's most successful hotel, consistently attracting an occupancy rate of 80 to 90 per cent[27]. Its success has been attributed to the personal and aggressive marketing style of the proprietor.

According to a well-informed source in the tourist sector, the drive to serve local foods and beverages was least developed in the state owned hotels[28]. This is not surprising given the numerous weaknesses of the Grenada Resorts Corporation (GRC), the company which was formed to manage the various hotels and other tourist-related properties acquired by the state. These included the Hibiscus Inn, Apple Inn, Horse Shoe Bay, Seascape Inn, Carifta

Cottages, and Camp Carriacou. Since its commencement in 1979 the GRC has never been able to make a profit. The loss for 1982 amounted to EC$230,000. Unpaid loans to the National Commercial Bank stood at EC$650,000 at the end of 1983 (Government of Grenada, 1983e, p. 65). Coard cited four reasons for GRC's dismal performance: (i) overstaffing (as much as twice as many workers to each room when compared with private sector hotels; (ii) managerial weaknesses; (iii) inexperience of the workers; and (iv) cash flow problems resulting in part from late payments and non-payments of bills by government ministries (Government of Grenada, 1983e, p. 65). On a macro level performance of the tourist sector for the period was perhaps even more disappointing.

Overview of tourism performance

The 4½ years tenure of the PRG was a bleak period for the island's tourist industry. The trend in visitor arrivals and cruise ship calls is set out in table 5:4. To facilitate easy comparisons data are also provided for the immediate pre-1979 and the post-1983 periods. From an impressive figure of 32,2000 stay-over visitors in 1979, the number of stay-over visitors progressively declined until it reached a low of 23,200 in 1982. At the same time cruise passengers fell from 145,600 (in 1980), 77,600 (1981), 62,100 (1982), and finally to 50,200 (1983) (see table 5:4).[29] Even when viewed in terms of monthly arrivals, to make allowance for the seasonality of the trade, the picture shows no marked improvement. Thus for the peak months in Grenada's tourism (January and March - the period for the winter traffic - and August, the month for carnival celebrations and new medical students) the figures failed to peak. For January 1980, 1981 and 1982 the figures were 3,225, 3,050 and 2,437, respectively. For March 1980, 1981, 1982, the numbers stood at 3,210, 2,415, and 2,617, respectively while for August for the same three years the figures were 2,956, 2,776, and 3,762, respectively.[30]

An analysis of the figures reveal that the decline was most pronounced in the US segment of the market. From a high of 9,100 stay-over visitors in 1979 the figures plummeted to 6,800 (1980), 5,100 (1981), 5,000 (1982), and 5,300 in 1983.[31] Interestingly (though not surprising) they show a sharp increase after 1983. Thus for 1984, 1985, and 1986 the figures were 8,400, 8,900 and 11,100, respectively (see table 5:4). On the brighter side, visitors from the Caribbean segment of the trade recorded an upward trend, especially since 1980. In 1985 the grand total of 21,300 was reached (see table 5:4). Though important to the Grenadian economy, this rising traffic from the Caribbean could not compensate for the decline in visitors from the traditional sources since the pattern of their expenditures varies considerably.

151

Table 5:4

Tourist arrivals and cruise ship data, 1976-1986

Year	No. of stay-over visitors ('000's)	Cruise ship calls	Cruise passengers ('000's)	Yacht calls
1976	24.5	187	106.9	1436
1977	28.6	184	108.5	1609
1778	32.3	188	116.3	2079
1979	32.2	200	138.7	926
1980	30.1	236	145.6	1865
1981	25.0	131	77.6	1376
1982	23.2	103	62.1	1602
1983	32.4	80	50.2	1445
1984	39.5	65	34.2	1343
1985	52.0	173	90.7	2726
1986	57.3	223	113.9	2135

Source: Department of Tourism, *Annual Statistical Overview* (St George's, Grenada).

For the economic well-being of the host society it is not numbers per se which is important but the length of their stay as well as the amount of money they spend during that period.

A visitor expenditure and motivational survey conducted by the CTRC in 1982 found that: (i) Non-Caribbean visitors (i.e. those from the traditional markets) spend an average of nine nights per visit compared to 3.6 for Caribbean visitors; (ii) Non-Caribbean visitors typically stay in hotels and guest-houses while regional visitors stay with friends and relatives.[32] The former spend an average of US$901 per party per trip (i.e. US$60 per person per night) while the latter spends an average of US$329 (i.e. US$20 per person per night); and (iii) The average size of the visiting party is 1.7 to 1.8 for extra-regional visitors compared to 1.32 for regional visitors (CTRC, 1982).

The dislocation of the tourist industry in revolutionary Grenada had a disastrous impact on the Grenadian economy. This is not surprising given the importance of that sector to the nation's well-being. It is estimated that tourism contributes as much as 50 per cent of the country's foreign exchange earnings and, additionally, has important spill-over effects on employment (especially in the hotel and restaurant sector), tax revenues and the retail trade.[33] According to CTRC source: 'The Hotel and Restaurant sector accounted for just about half of the tourist sector's contribution. The sector employed 1,738 persons. Visitor spending was estimated ... to be US$12.4 million in 1981 as compared to US$18.6 million for domestic exports and US$19.0 million for total imports. Most of the US$12.4 million spent was attributed to tourists arriving by air' (CTRC, 1983, p. 4).[34]

Estimates provided by the PRG were consistent with the CTRC figures. Thus in their 1982 'Revised Economic Memorandum on Grenada', the PRG wrote: 'Even in decline, tourism contributed about 49 per cent of Grenada's total foreign exchange earnings in 1981. In 1980, foreign exchange earnings were 18.5 per cent higher than total domestic merchandise exports. Performance of tourism in 1981 was lower than in 1980, and foreign exchange earnings declined by US$2.0 million' (Government of Grenada, 1982g, p. 12).

A close examination of the figures for tourist arrivals for the entire Caribbean reveals that Grenada's decline was particularly dramatic (Smith, 1988, chapter six). Among the eight countries belonging to the Organization of Eastern Caribbean states (OECS), Grenada fared worst. Only two countries in this group, St Lucia and St Vincent exhibited a marked decline, and even then the decline was not as sharp as Grenada's. Besides the overall impact of declining numbers would be less severe in these two territories since they were in control of a larger share of the tourist trade. Between 1980 and 1982, for instance, St Lucia had a cumulative total of 218,500 visitors (stay-over) compared to 78,300 for Grenada. In the case of St Vincent the figure was 132,200 - just under twice Grenada's share.[35]

The decline in Grenada's share of the tourist trade attests to the fickleness and unreliability of the tourist industry as a vehicle of development. Again, they cast doubts on the viability of the PRG's development strategy. An international airport, no matter how well-endowed to provide comfort to travellers, by itself does not necessarily mean that more visitors will be attracted to that particular destination. The 'image' of the destination is perhaps the single most important factor that tourists take into consideration when making their holiday arrangements. The quest for holidays (especially somewhere in the tropics) amongst people living in industrialised economies has come to be almost inseparable from their culture. Although many are still too poor to materialise their wish, others still travel to distant lands overseas even in recessionary periods. In a period of recession these holidays are likely to be financed largely from past savings or credit arrangements. There can be no doubt that the revolutionary process which was under way in Grenada and the adverse publicity which it attracted from unfriendly countries, most notably the US, was at the root of this decline. Even conservative institutions such as the International Monetary Fund and the World Bank admit the severity of this factor although they take great care in pointing out other contributory factors, like the world recession and the deterioration of Grenada's tourism plant.

The fickleness of the tourist industry and the importance of 'image' to tourists can be gauged from the aforementioned Visitor Survey carried out in 1982 when the Grenada revolution was in full swing. When asked if there was anything that they particularly liked or disliked about their visit to Grenada a number of interesting remarks were made. These encompassed customs and immigration procedures, taxi services and ground transportation, hotels, restaurants, people, things to do, and even the revolution, although they were not asked specifically to comment on it. Although responses were mixed they were generally unfavourable.[36]

Under the category 'Revolution', for instance, the following remarks were made: (i) 'As a socialist and member of the New Democratic Party in Canada, I was inspired by revolutionary Grenada, and will encourage everyone to come and see it for themselves'; (ii) 'The people were very friendly and helpful. Our only recommendation would be to use another word for revolution, because revolution has a negative connotation to tourists'; (iii) 'Too much militaries'; (iv) 'Disliked over-emphasis on the revolution'; (v) 'Long Live the revolution'; (vi) 'There is a sense of purpose and unlaziness which is hard to find in other countries. Long live the PRG'; (vii) 'Tremendously impressed with political initiatives and the consciousness of the people'; (viii) 'We disliked soldiers coming into the restaurants with large guns hanging over their shoulders'; (ix) 'When there are military manoeuvres it is best to tell the hotels to inform the guests so that they would know what to expect'; and (x) 'Disliked all the bad talk about the US on radio and in the press, which makes the US visitors uncomfortable' (CTRC, 1982, pp. 8-9).

With respect to 'Customs and Immigration Procedures', visitors noted the following: (i) 'Welcoming at the airport, the entry is intimidating, long waiting period to clear immigration and customs'; (ii) 'Grenada is the only island we have ever had to open our baggage every time we come'; (iii) 'The people are kind and quick to help strangers, but some immigration officers could be harsh at times'; (iv) 'I disliked the intimidating immigration personnel at the airport'; (v) 'I disliked seeing the armed personnel at the airport'; (vi) 'Airport, immigration and customs, etc. leave a lot to be desired due to lack of facilities'; (vii) 'Airport and entry procedures enough to make you wish to return to Barbados straight away'; (viii) 'Immigration men took too long, and the men at the customs made me feel like a smuggler. The young boys handling the baggage at the customs were pushy'; (ix) and 'Quicker entry process, more friendly attitudes of inspecting groups and better entry facilities' (CTRC, 1982).

The plummeting of tourist numbers must have come as a surprise to the PRG given the amount of resources invested in this area during their brief tenure. The paradox of the situation is that Gairy did virtually nothing to promote tourism yet Grenada under him experienced a relatively prosperous trade for the most part. The only notable exception was the period after the disturbances of 1974 when the whole island rose in anger against him.[37]

Nevertheless, the PRG's efforts in this area have been acknowledged and applauded by no less a body than the private sector organization, Grenada Hotel Association (GHA):

> Government for the first time in the history of Grenada provided EC$1,100,000 budget (up from EC$700,000) in spite of the reduction in available rooms on the island.[38] This is highly commendable. Most of the promotions (overseas)... were sponsored by the Ministry of Tourism. Other areas well worthy of commendation are: (i) the opening of a Tourism Office in Toronto; (ii) the creation of a Tourism Council, which has replaced the Tourist Board. The council is an advisory body to government on all aspects of tourism; (iii) the hosting of an OAS team in May/June, whose mission it was to recommend a plan of action for the development of tourist attraction and sites; (iv) on-going seminars for taxi drivers, vendors and other tourist personnel (Grenada Hotel Association, 1982, p. 4; emphasis added).

The promotion tours which the President alluded to in his 1982 Report were as follows: (i) World Travel Market - England, December 1981; (ii) Market place 1982 - Jamaica, January 1982; (iii) International Tourism Exchange - Berlin, February/March 1982; (iv) Caribbean Tourism Association North East Travel Trade Show - New York, March 1982; (v) Grenada Canadian Promotion across Canada - April/May 1982; (vi) Trinidad Promotion - May 1982; (vii) Grenada Canadian Promotion in September and October 1982; (viii) Caribbean Tourism Association North East Fall Travel Trade Show and Grenada Presentation, New York - October/November 1982; and (ix) Trade Shows in Brussels and London - November/December 1982 (Grenada Hotel Association, 1982, p. 2). In the words of the GHA President, Mr Royston Hopkin: 'In spite of a significant decline in stay-over visitors to our island during the past year, member hotels of our Association have participated in more promotional tours than ever before in the history of our Association' (GHA, 1982, p. 1). [39]

Other unprecedented initiatives included the restructuring of the country's tourist organization to include a Ministry of Tourism with its own Minister of Tourism. For the first time a full time Director of Tourism was appointed.

The Director, Jane Belfon, was potentially a tremendous asset to the industry given her wealth of experience in this area, including service overseas.[40] But her presence made no appreciable difference to the depression in Grenada's tourism. Neither did the Banderanti Commuter Aircraft which the government purchased for US$1.5 million to mitigate the air access problem. The establishment of a Grenada Interline Desk at the Grantley Adams International Airport in Barbados was also an important innovation, albeit one which, again, failed to generate the anticipated benefits. Whatever it did, the writing was now on the wall. The image of the country in western circles had been brought into disrepute, and, with it, the tourist industry in which the PRG had placed so much hope. Moreover, the United States, Grenada's arch enemy, would ensure that the island's image continue to slip disastrously in the marketplace. According to evidence compiled by the revolutionary government the United States International communications Agency (USICA) was guilty of waging a massive propaganda campaign against the Grenada revolutionary process:

> Only three weeks ago (i.e. beginning of July, 1981) in New York, in Brooklyn and Manhattan, the third survey since the revolution was done by our comrades in New York. This survey took the form once again of getting people to contact different travel agencies and tour operators in the New York area inquiring about holiday trips to Grenada. Twelve of the 18 agencies approached made it clear that Grenada was not a safe place to visit, that Grenada (as they put it) was a Soviet and Cuban proxy, and went out of their way to try to stop these tourists from coming to our country. When pressed, several of them admitted that this information was given to them by the State Department (Bishop, 1982b, p. 212).

Bishop also asserted that USICA was guilty of encouraging Caribbean journalists to report unfavourably on the revolution. Just how active the media was is evident from the amount of space major newspapers devoted to Grenada. In June 1981 alone a total of 144 articles were published in nine regional newspapers on the revolution. Another 103 articles were published by the same newspapers during the period 15-30 September 1981 - an average of 6.5 articles per day. The tone of these articles was malicious for the most part. *The Daily Gleaner* of Jamaica was particularly scathing in its attacks. The frequency of its adverse front-page articles made it known in Grenada as the *El Mercurio* of the Caribbean. The electronic media was also active. January 1981 saw the screening of the infamous CBS documentary 'Attack on the Americas', followed by 'The Prisoner and the Police State' in May of the same year (Government of Grenada, 1982b, p. 120 and p. 137).

To counter such allegations the government issued a personal invitation to foreigners under the slogan 'don't listen to propaganda, come and see for yourself'. The nature of what was reported in the foreign media is evident from the following text:

> Those who claim that we have cut down the forests in Grand Etang and have now pitched the roads where the forests used to be and have missiles aimed at neighbouring islands, let them go to Grand Etang and when they return home report what they saw. Those who claim that there is a naval base in Carriacou, let them travel to Carriacou - it is only 10 minutes by plane - and if they find any naval base we would like to see it ourselves. Those who publish photographs that show barbed wire blocking off our beaches, we invite them to go to all of our beaches and if they find one with barbed wire tell us, we want to see it. Those who ask "what are the Cubans doing here" those who ask "why do we need an army", those who say "why do we have a militia", those who say "why are we always talking about destabilization", those who feel that they must come here and question us about how much arms we have and where the arms come from and what we need the arms for, let us give them the answer that the free people of Grenada have been giving. Let us give them the answer that whenever Gairy or mercenaries or any other counter-revolutionary elements land on our beaches they will discover the size of our army, how many guns we have, where the guns come from, and whether we can use the guns (Bishop, 1982b, p. 120).

This 'propaganda destabilization', as the PRG termed it, was a major setback for the PRG on the economic front. The revolution was still in the formative phase and (apart from the tourist sector) there was no other sector in the economy with the capacity to generate much-needed foreign exchange in the short term (and the PRG had already committed the lion's share of its scarce resources to the development of tourism). The counter-attack from the PRG in the Grenada media did not help the situation. The anti-United States pronouncements were often interspersed with slogans such as 'Every tourist is a potential destabilizer'.[41] The Grenadian staff in the overseas tourism departments complained in vain that the government's rhetoric was severely undermining their efforts to sell Grenada to would-be visitors. They were constantly told to ignore what was being said at home on *Radio Free Grenada*.[42] The government's counter-attack was to prove to be doubly counterproductive since it infuriated large segments of the private sector. A Report on the industry tendered to the government in June 1981 by the Grenada Chamber of Commerce and the Grenada Hotel Association advised the PRG to 'abandon counterproductive political rhetoric' (cited in *Barbados Advocate*, 17 June 1981). The Report states further 'we cannot complain of adverse publicity and bad press reports overseas when our own media do more damage to the industry than any other'. The direction of the government's foreign policy also came under sharp attack. Reference was made to Grenada's voting pattern in the United Nations on the Soviet Union invasion of Afghanistan and its open friendship with communist countries - countries which add very little to the well-being of Grenada's tourism. The strategic role of the US in Grenadian tourism and the influence which the US wields in the West was also highlighted. Hence the two private sector bodies stressed 'the people and their representative governments in our market cannot be separated. A rhetorical attack on such governments is taken by the people to be an attack on the nation. People will not often spend discretionary income on their enemies' (*Barbados Advocate*, 17 June 1981).

The findings of a survey on vendor trade, conducted in January 1981, was also brought to the government's attention by the Grenada Chamber of Commerce and the Grenada Hotel Association. According to this survey the number of vendors engaged in the sector fell from 160 in 1979 to 80 in 1980. When asked 'what do you think are the causes for the fall in the tourist trade?', 20 per cent expressed the view that 'the CIA (werc) keeping people away', 30 per cent said 'Maybe they are afraid to come to Grenada', and 50 per cent reportedly said 'The tourists are staying away because the Cubans are here'.[43]

Under these circumstances where hoteliers were experiencing declining fortunes - a situation which they attributed fundamentally to the image of the country - it is unlikely that the private sector would have responded to the government's call for increased investment in tourist plants to meet the requirements of the new airport.[44] The downward trend in Grenadian tourism (we could even say dislocation) suggests quite clearly that the new airport would not provide any magic answers to Grenada's development problems. Neither could more aircrafts, better staffing at the local tourist board, increased public utilities, more and better hotels, or even increased promotional campaigns overseas. The real cause of the country's unattractiveness was its anti-imperialist, pro-Soviet stance and the adverse publicity which it has consequently attracted in western circles. This image is hard to reverse once acquired - witness the Jamaican experience in the 1970s under Michael Manley.[45] As Jamaica's subsequent experience shows (and later Grenada under Herbert Blaize) a return to the model of dependent capitalism was a vital prerequisite to the improvement of the tourist climate in both of these cases.

Notes

1. See Mathieson and Wall (1982), especially chapter three for a detailed discussion of the economic impacts of tourism, and the superiority of the tourist product *vis-à-vis* other export products in underdeveloped economics.

2. Two good examples, especially from the perspective of the Commonwealth Caribbean are Bryden (1975); and Marshall (1978).

3. Marshall examined significance with respect to employment in tourism as a proportion of the total work force, employment in relation to the amount of capital required to produce these jobs, and employment in relation to employee/room ratios.

4. Studies on the non-economic dimensions of tourism have received very little attention compared to those which deal with the 'economic impact' of the sector. Among the factors which contribute to this gap are: (i) the difficulties in subjecting non-economic consequences and costs to rigorous, quantifiable analyses; (ii) the relative lack of widely accepted methodologies for measuring non-economic costs; (iii) the relative absence of this type of data (unlike data on tourist expenditures, tax revenues and the like which are normally collected by government departments); and (iv) the bias of many of the agencies which seek to promote tourism - concerned as they are with the 'positive' side of tourism.

5. See Doxey (1975). Doxey's framework is based on evidence drawn from the experience of Barbados and Niagra-on-the-Lake in Ontario, Canada. The change depicted in the framework is assumed to be uni-directional (see Mathieson and Wall, 1982, pp. 137-138).

6. It is usually mass, institutionalised tourism which analysts have in mind when they charge that tourism is nothing more than a new form of colonialism and imperialism. As in the past, the tourist typically comes from developed countries, and the economic and social relationships from the past persist without any major alteration.

7. The environmental impact may include the following: air, water, thermic and soil pollution, destruction of landscape, damage to plans and animal life (see Economist Intelligence Unit, 1979, p. 87).

8.   According to Medlik and Middleton (1975) the tourist product is a composite phenomenon which 'covers the complete experience from the time he leaves home to the time he returns to it. In other words, the product is not an airline seat, or a hotel bed, or relaxation on a sunny beach, but rather an amalgamam of many components or a package' (see Medlik and Middleton, 1975, p. 132). Medlik's and Middleton's definition captures the fickleness of the product. The attractions of the destination, the way the country is subjectively perceived by the tourist, the facilities on offer (accommodation, entertainment, recreation, and catering), and accessibility of the destination are all part and parcel of the product. The variations in any of these could affect the flow of visitors to the particular destination.

9.   It must be noted that the statements embodied in the 1973 manifesto were more forceful and unequivocal in their call for a new type of tourist 'who would love to come here but cannot afford the present nonsensical prices. But once in power the government realised that though low-spending tourists were important, it was more essential to procure as much economic benefits as possible from the industry. Non-affluent tourist were thus reduced to a 'complementary role' - to be mainly targeted in the off season.

10.   The basic challenge for the PRG was to develop the maximum linkages between tourism and other sectors of the economy, generate an equitable distribution of benefits from tourism, and ensure that tourism develop in a way which was compatible with the local culture and goals of the revolution. This was a rather formidable challenge - indeed, one which was perhaps unattainable even in the long-term.

11.   For details of these, see OAS/PRG Document 'Physical Tourism Development Plan Zone 1, Grenada', (1983). Zone 1 referred to the south western part of the island, with major focus placed on the Grand Anse area. As stated in the document the terms of reference was to assess the physical potential for tourism-growth in all of zone 1, and to identify appropriate areas for the location of tourist facilities and where possible, support services, make recommendations on infrastructure requirements to support growth, make recommendations to help realise integrated and harmonious land use, appropriate building density, height, setback and maximum size in tourist facilities and make provisions for the integrated use of natural and man-made resources by Grenadians and tourists (p. 1). The team

recommended in part that hotels should not be more than two storeys high, and must not exceed 150 rooms. Natural ventilation must also be considered during construction to economise on the use of energy.

12.   Attempts were also made 'to stimulate much fuller use of Grenada's rich, scenic, historic, and cultural heritage for national development in a way which will preserve it for future generations' (see Hudson, 1983).

13.   A sample of the various studies on the problem include:
(i) *Airfields for Grenada and St Vincent*, by Scott Wilson Kirkpatrick and Partners, (1955); 9ii) *Grenada Pearls Airport and the Proposed New Airport at Point Saline*, a report by B.B. Jupp, (1967); (iii) *Grenada Airport, Economic and Technical Feasibility Study*, vols. I and II, by the Economist Intelligence Unit and Scott Wilson and Kirkpatrick, United Kingdom; (iv) *A Civil Aviation Authority Study on the Feasibility of Conducting Night Operation at Pearls Airport*, Grenada and at Arros Vale Air- port, St Vincent, prepared by the Ministry of Overseas Development, and; (v) *World Bank Airport*, November 1976 (see OAS Secretariat, 1977, for details on the studies).

14.   Interview conducted by the author with former Minister for Legal Affairs, Agro-Industries and Fisheries, Kenrick Radix, in June 1987.

15.   The motive(s) for such a generous assistance from a country which is still trying to come to grips with its own economic woes remains a moot point. Was Cuba acting on behalf of the Soviet Union as some have argued? There is still no firm evidence to support this claim.

16.   Author's interview with Messrs Randix and Ramdhanny in June 1987.

17.   Incidentally Coard was not alone in this belief. According to Mr Byam, a CBD based economist who was assigned to Dominica for two years, the Prime Minister of Dominica, Eugenia Charles, sees Dominica's salvation as resting on an international airport. However, recognising the emotiveness of the term 'international airport' she uses the euphemism 'international site' when discussing the need for such a project with potential aid donors (author's interview with Mr Byam in May 1987).

18. Interestingly another regional airline, British West Indian Airways (BWIA) is better known in the West Indies as 'But Will It Arrive?'.

19. So long as this downward trend continued the government would not have been able to repay the funds borrowed to finance the project, at least not in the short term as they had anticipated. As depicted in table 5:2 a profit was expected from the venture by 1985. This was expected to reach the grand figure of EC$22.36 million by 1990.

20. Insurance Companies in the island were also obliged to purchase airport bonds with 10 per cent of their premium income. In return they would be paid an interest of six per cent per annum, tax free (see Government of Grenada, 1982f, 1982, p. 128).

21. Referring to this aggression from the United States Coard remarked: 'One comrade from Kuwait showed me an entire book of newspaper clippings in the Kuwait press dealing with our International Airport. That would give you an idea of the world-wide campaign, translated into several languages. The objective was to prevent us from getting the additional US$30 million required to complete the building of our International Airport'(Government of Grenada, 1982b, p. 37).

22. The sophistication of items produced by the Amerindians is evident from the impressive collection of their craft samples which are on display in Grenada's National Museum.

23. As stated candidly by PRG source 'Grencraft appeared to have been operating on a 'hand to mouth' basis and mainly concerned with shop and boat sales. So far as overseas marketing was concerned, Grencraft was ill-equipped to deal in competitive marketing situations - in need of very basic prerequisites such as standardised, realistic costing of goods, the compilation of a standard wholesale and retain price list, brochures, posters and updated and accurate catalogue's (Brown, 1979, p. 10).

24. See Brown (1979), p. 37. Note the Prime Minister's remark is further evidence of the objective problems (lack of skilled technical personnel in this particular case) which small, underdeveloped countries face in their quest for structural transformation and material betterment. In fact, although this particular project was approved it was never fully implemented due to financial constraints - another daunting problem faced by these countries.

25. See CTRC (1983). Although the survey was conducted by the Caribbean Tourism Research and Development Centre (CTRC), the PRG was instrumental in its organization. The study was funded by the USAID and CBD.

26. Author's interview with Jane Belfon in June 1987.

27. Author's interview with the owner/manager of Blue Horizon, Mr Arnold Hopkin, in June 1987.

28. Author's interview with the owner/manager of Blue Horizon, Mr Arnold Hopkin, in June 1987.

29. The number of cruise passengers would have been substantially less had it not been for the diversion of some cruise ships from Trinidad and Tobago, owing to an epidemic there in 1979 and 1980 (see Government of Grenada, 1982g, p. 11).

30. These figures were obtained from the Department of Tourism in Grenada.

31. According to Mr Arnold Hopkin, prominent hotel owner and manager in the island, a great deal of the tourists who came during this period were different from the conventional set. They were young professionals; social scientists for the most part, who were interested in analyzing the changes that were taking place in the society (Author's interview with Mr Hopkin, held in June 1987).

32. This is particularly true for Trinidadians (the largest group from the Caribbean visiting Grenada) who invariably have some relative in Grenada.

33. See Economic Commission for Latin America and the Caribbean (1984), p. 101 for further details.

34. See CTRC (1983), chapter five, p. 4. Note, air arrivals contributed some 90 per cent of foreign exchange earnings in the sector (Government of Grenada, 1982e, p. 11).

35. Although figures are not readily available on tourist arrivals in early post-revolutionary Cuba it is believed that Cuba's tourist industry was severely dislocated during the formative years of the revolution

(interview with officers at the CTRC, Barbados, in May 1987, including Mr Victor Kirton, chief statistical officer). Even today the largest influx of visitors come from the socialist countries. Jamaica, too, experienced a similar fate in the 1970s.

36.   See CTRC, 1982, (Appendix three), for the full range of comments.

37.   Again the response of tourists to the so-called Independence Crisis of 1974 demonstrates the fragility of the tourist industry.

38.   Under the PRG this budget was progressively increased. In 1980, for instance, it was EC$150,000 - a modest figure but yet substantial figure compared to the tourist budget under Gairy's administration. According to Jane Belfon, Director of Tourism under the PRG, Grenada almost lost its membership in all he tourist promoting institutions (regional and extra-regional) as a result of Gairy's failure to pay membership dues. In fact, the island was forced out of the World Tourism Association (WTA) for this reason. At the time of the interview with Jane Belfon (June 1987), Grenada was still outside the WTA. This was because the government could not afford to repay the huge arrears which have accumulated over the past 20 years.

39.   Grenada hotel Association, 1982, p. 1. In a similar vein an OAS consultant team in 1983 remarked 'The OAS has perhaps provided the greatest technical assistance in tourism to Grenada in the past few years...' (Government of Grenada, 1983d, p. 1). This can be taken as further evidence of the PRG's strong commitment to the development of tourism in Grenada.

40.   An American woman was also hired to promote Grenada in the US. Reportedly, this officer was paid a salary of US$6,000 per month, with all expenses paid' (cited in *Trinidad Express*, Thursday 22 October 1981).

41.   Author's interview with Beverley Steele, Resident Tutor of the Extra-mural Department, University of the West Indies, in June 1987. Tourists were sometimes questioned, and even physically assaulted by PRG supporters as they enthusiastically probed into whether or not the tourists were 'destabilizers'. This information was further confirmed by a private sector paper presented at a local conference in 1982. The document notes 'Grenada is ... perceived in yachting circles to be hostile to cruising as a few natural harbours are closed

to anchorage and there have been a few unfortunate incidents with security personnel' (Grenada Chamber of Industry and Commerce, 1982, p. 10). Besides, the government's constant plea to Grenadians to guard against an imminent invasion generated a real sense of fear, panic, and instability - thus helping to tarnish the country's image.

42. Authors' interview with Jane Belfon in June 1987.

43. Cited in *Trinidad Express*, Thursday 22 October 1981 - article captioned 'Revolutionary Policies have Backfired'.

44. Other problems which worried hoteliers include the frequent disruptions in water, electricity, and telephone supplies that have plagued tourism in recent times. According to the OAS Study 'periodically all of Grand Anse was without central power and frequently water was not available on the second floor of a main hotel' (Government of Grenada, 1983d, p. 19).

45. See Stephens and Stephens (1986). Referring to the crisis in Jamaica's tourism during this period they write: 'The concentration of the decline among US tourists shows clearly the effect of the adverse campaign concerning violence, political instability and presumed Cuban influence in Jamaica which was carried on by the US Press' (p. 128). They note further 'The alarmist articles, columns, and letters in the Gleaner had their counterpart in a series of extremely critical articles in the US and Canadian press. Some of these articles contained outright lies, in particular about Cuban influence in Jamaica' (p. 135).

6 The search for a patriotic national bourgeoisie

It was argued in chapter three that the revolutionary government opted for the mixed economy model - state sector dominant - in the hope that it could continue to draw on the skills, experience, material resources, and market connections of the private sector. The government's search for a patriotic national bourgeoisie and the reaction from the private sector was thus a crucial aspect of the revolutionary process, requiring an indepth analysis if the processes of socialist transformation are to be fully understood. This is the task of the present chapter. The chapter evaluates the development of the relationship between the PRG and the private sector. The consequences of the government's failure to develop an accommodation with the tiny, but influential, private sector are also discussed.

The development of an uneasy relationship

The government's first major meeting with the private sector took place on 24 May 1979, just over two months after the revolution. This was the occasion of the Annual General Meeting of the Grenada Chamber of Industry and Commerce (GCIC), at which Deputy Prime Minister and Minister of Finance, Bernard Coard, made an impassioned address about the role of the private sector in its development strategy.[1]

The address began with a statement on the importance of budgetary control and the legacies from the Gairy regime. Among the legacies were huge debts to regional and international organizations, and dilapidated infrastructure (roads, ports, bridges, water, telephone, hospitals, schools, etc.). Referring to the success of the tight budgetary control measures instituted by the revolutionary government since coming to power a triumphant Coard asserted: 'We have always insisted that we want to be judged by results, not rumours, not gossip, not propaganda, not malicious old talk. We are only asking you to judge us by results. That is all we are asking and these results like any standards must be impressive in just a short space of time to turn around the situation in terms of budgetary control' (Coard, 1979b, p. 2).

The Deputy Prime Minister went on to outline the main features of the government's development strategy, especially the role of private capital (both foreign and local) in the strategy. Here he made it patently clear, a point repeated on several subsequent occasions, that not all types of foreign investment would be welcome in Grenada. The foreign proposal must be 'mutually beneficial', and for it to benefit Grenada the following conditions must be satisfied: (i) It must be financed by funds originating from outside Grenada instead of competing with Grenadians for scarce resources as was the case in pre-revolutionary Grenada; (ii) it must be engaged in the sectors delineated by the Government. Proposals involving gambling, casinos and prostitution joints will not be permitted; (iii) it must bring in modern technology, which is both relevant to Grenada's needs and capable of being adapted to local circumstances. In other words there must be a transfer of technology; (iv) it must have a significant employment potential since unemployment is such a chronic problem in Grenada; (v) it must be capable of reducing the cost of living by producing goods efficiently and competitively *vis-à-vis* the price of similar imports; (vi) it must create opportunities for overseas markets - markets which are not previously accessible to Grenadian goods (Coard, ibid., pp. 6-7).

These six requirements were to provide the general guidelines for assessing proposals from foreign investors. Since a particular project cannot necessarily satisfy all of these requirements each proposal would be assessed on 'a case by case basis'. The proposal would be considered to be 'sound' if it satisfied one or more of the criteria laid down. What the government was doing here was to invert the old, discredited model of 'industrialization by invitation'. Foreign capital must be consonant with the needs of the host country: 'We do not believe like some people in some countries, and I shall not name any, in selling out a quarter or sixth - or a half or three quarters of their territories to foreigners with condition which say that the laws of the country do not apply to this area. The concept of creating a state within a state ... is alien to the government and people of Grenada' (ibid., p. 7).

Finally, Coard moved to the area of government policy with respect to the local private sector - a subject members of the GCIC listened to with interest. In elaborating on the significance of the mixed economy model he noted that, apart from its traditional functions, the government will now be engaged in productive and revenue earning ventures. Put bluntly, government will compete with the private sector for investment outlets. And if the private sector refused to invest in an area of the economy deemed to be strategically significant, then the government will take the initiative of investing in that sector. It was also stressed that the government: (i) will encourage and assist them (i.e. the private sector) "within reason"; (ii) will put an end to the forceable confiscation of private property without compensation; and (iii) will not allow unscrupulous members of the private sector to exploit workers and consumers. Neither will it tolerate parasitism within the labour force.

Developing point three further, Coard declared with incredible candour: 'All of us must work hard and honestly to develop the country. The private sector in our view is of critical importance in the government's development strategy, but government is not there to spoon-feed, change nappies, or mollycoddle the private sector. That must also be understood and I will be very frank with you' (ibid., p. 7).

Further, as if that was not enough, he affirmed that the government does not exist, as many believe, to eliminate all the risks from production - by giving monopoly privileges to businessmen, protected markets, tax concessions for 15 years or even for perpetuity, provide infrastructure, and even money from the treasury to get the business going 'What about the revenue of the country? What about further development of the country? To me that (i.e. expectations of the business sector) is unreasonable (ibid., p. 8). Appropriately enough, the first address ended with him urging that both the state and private sector should seek to be waste-conscious, generate as much employment as possible, increase productivity, improve the country's human resources, enhance the quality of life of workers and consumers alike and 'aim to make Grenada the kind of clean, peaceful and beautiful country, which we all know it is, and which we want to make it' (ibid., p. 8).

This was, perhaps, a too critical and trenchant note to begin on, although the counter view that it was important for the government to tell the private sector in clear and unmistakable terms what it was expecting of them is also relevant. Although direct and systematic opposition had not yet begun discontent soon came to the fore. It is worth noting at this point that the government enjoyed overwhelming support from the private sector during the early days of the revolution.[2] The statement issued by the then president of the Grenada Chamber of Industry and Commerce, Geoffrey Thompson, in the aftermath of the revolution is noteworthy:

> I do not anticipate any worrying changes in the methods and patterns of business or the direction of the government's foreign policy that would adversely affect the economy of the country. Certainly there will be changes, but I do not believe that in the medium and long-term they would be to the detriment of Grenada. ...This Chamber is

categorically opposed to any form of external intervention in our country's internal affairs and will mobilise all its resources against any threat to Grenada's sovereignty. At the same time we expect that our Caribbean neighbours and the world community will not encourage or participate in any action, economic or political, that would be inimical to the Grenadian people (*Barbados Advocate*, 19 March 1979).

The statement described the way the coup was executed as 'civilised'. It urged Grenadians and the private sector in particular to maintain high standards of business ethics, and to co-operate with the Government in all just and legal endeavours.

Much to the chagrin of the private sector, things did not quite develop in that way. It was not long before they felt under siege. One of the most worrying problems for the private sector was the growth and expansion of the state sector in productive activities. The government's 'encroachment' into the distribution trade was greeted with extreme resentment. This grievance (along with several others) was aired openly at a 1982 Conference co-sponsored by the GCIC on the subject of *Employment and Economic Growth*. The GCIC's Conference paper *Brief History of the Private Sector*' rejected the role of the government's MNIB on the grounds that the private sector: 'has a long history of capable and efficient management. Its performance over the years has been nothing short of commendable considering the constantly changing conditions under which it has had to operate. The commercial sector possesses the capacity to competently and competitively satisfy the needs of the society **now and in the future**' (ibid., p. 20. Emphasis added).

By giving itself monopoly privilege in the importation of five commodities the government was seen as marginalising the private sector in the name of the people: 'A concern of the private sector is that in the absence of competition profits generated through monopoly trading by Government can be used to subsidise prices of the other commodities which are imported in competition with the private sector and thus create unfair competition' (ibid., p. 20). Ignoring the welfare effects of the government's entry into this critical sector, they argued further that the MNIB was unnecessary, and unjustifiable since there was no increased economic activity for it to handle. It was their view that the further expansion of the MNIB would lead to the loss of jobs in the private sector, and these lost jobs would not be compensated for by new jobs in the MNIB.[3]

Yet they were fully aware of the government's intention to expand its involvement in this lucrative sector which they had monopolised for so long. The long list of commodities earmarked for bulk purchase by the government (published in their *Report on the National Economy for 1982 and the Budget - Plan for 1983 and Beyond*) added insult to injury.[4] All in all the list amounted to 99 items, comprising building materials, petroleum products, agricultural items, food stuffs, office supplies, packaging materials, industrial chemicals, spare parts for vehicles, equipment, asphalt products and animal feeds. In publicising the plan in 1982 the government argued that the aim was to save 'Grenada's tax payers (all of us) millions of dollars each year' (Government of Grenada, 1983e), p. 127).

But if the general public were convinced members of the business sector (especially those who previously handled these commodities)[5] were certainly unconvinced. Increasingly, they saw new government initiatives which sought to subordinate private sector activities to the state sector. This was fully consistent with the professed model of development (mixed economy schema with state sector dominant) which was never kept secret by the government.

Indeed, the plan to control the importation of an additional 99 commodities was part of a wider plan which would also embrace the control of the export trade. This pledge was made earlier in the party's 1973 manifesto. A government document 'On the possible Establishment of a State Trading Corporation for effecting Grenada's Trade with the Socialist Countries' revealed that the plan was to be fully implemented:

> With the growing disparity between our import bill and our export earnings - and consequently, with the growing unfavourable balance in our terms of trade - as a result of our entanglement in the world imperialist system the question of State direction and control of the country's foreign trade assumes increasing importance. This is so because it is becoming increasingly necessary to restructure and realign our foreign trade activity so as to bring them in line with our possibilities and our needs. (United State Department and Department of Defence, 1984, p. 121).

There was a notable departure from the plan as laid down in the government document. The government was to begin by taking over the control and direction of the export trade (given the small product range) since this would require fewer managerial and technical skills. In their deliberations about how to go about executing the new policy initiative a wide range of pragmatic questions were raised: (i) Who presently own/control these organizations?; (ii) What are the present arrangements for purchasing and marketing these commodities?; (iii) Where are the existing markets located and who are the agents/brokers?; (iv) What form should the intervention by the State take?; (v) What is likely to be the reaction and implications of those who now control these organizations?; (vi) What is likely to be the action of the workers in these organizations to state intervention and what steps can be taken to win or reinforce their support in participation?; (vii) What is likely to be the reaction of the farmers to state intervention?; (viii) How are the shipping Agents who presently handle these commodities likely to respond?; (ix) What benefits are farmers likely to gain from state intervention, and how can the state convince them of these benefits?; (x) What will be the gains to the revolution of a State Trading Corporation?; (xi) What are the disadvantages of taking this initiative, and how can they be minimised? (United State Department and Department of Defence, ibid., pp. 123-24).

Although posing the right questions it seemed as though the PRG were determined to implement their plan even if the answers to the questions indicated otherwise. Thus the *Report on the National Economy for 1982* noted 'concrete steps will be taken to import in bulk at least some of the items needed by the state enterprises, ministries, and institutions. In each following year the system will be operated more efficiently' (p. 126).

As for the managerial deficiencies of the state, these were only too wellknown to the private sector. Mention was often made of it in both public and private quarters. Their memorandum for the 1982 conference thus read:

> As Government has entered the commercial field in the name of the people, e.g. National Commercial Bank, Marketing and National Importing Board, National Fisheries, Agro-Industries, Grenada Resorts Corporation, etc. it would be useful and serve as a good guide to the private sector if the financial statements of these several enterprises could be published as in the case of the National Commercial Bank.[6] In so doing the private sector could monitor its own performance and take corrective action where necessary. Government is already in a position to monitor private sector performance through the financial statements made available to the Income Tax Department (GCIC, op. cit., p. 21).

This passage alluded to the generally poor financial performance of state enterprises which resulted in part from weak management. Even the PRG admitted they were particularly weak in this area. Thus in reviewing the consistent failure of state enterprises to attain their production targets and generate profits the government noted: 'such an underdeveloped society as ours had very few trained managers in the past. Now that we need dozens of managers and accountants to manage all the new projects, we find we are short of managers' (Government of Grenada, 1983e, pp. 37-38). Another passage in the same document stated further:

> it is a lack of ... **political consciousness** that causes some managers and Permanent Secretaries to refuse to attend the Management Training courses which the Government has been providing, at great

cost, through the In-Service Training Unit. Yet management is one of our weakest areas. Some Permanent Secretaries also block workers in their Ministries from attending middle management, supervisory and secretarial courses provided for them (ibid., p. 74).

Other aspects of the government's economic strategy and policies were also sharply criticised. With respect to tourism, for instance, the private sector sought to negate the government's philosophy of 'New Tourism'. To the private sector, traditional tourism was a more lucrative venture and as such it held the key to Grenada's development. Their thinking in this regard was clearly set out in the paper *Brief History of the Private Sector.* After reviewing the performance of the tourism sector over the past ten years they came to the conclusion that Grenada's tourist industry could be regarded as a sea of stagnation in an ocean of growth (GCIC, 1982, p. 2). The private sector urged the government to develop friendly relations with western governments, particularly the US and Canada. These countries were regarded as the hub of Caribbean tourism, and Grenada's in particular. It was estimated that the US market alone will contribute as much as 50 per cent of the total Caribbean tourist trade in the next six years (GCIC, p. 8). The private sector was also opposed to state ownership in tourism. It was recommended that the government should privatise the operations of the GRC[7] since 'in this way the government's limited managerial and financial resources can be better used elsewhere' (GCIC, p. 9). Any loss in revenue, it noted, would be compensated by lease rentals and corporate tax.

As for increased investment in new tourist plant (to complement the new airport) they called on government to grant 'more liberal incentives' to both local and foreign businessmen, arguing that whatever losses are incurred in granting such incentives will be far outweighed by benefits such as: (i) greater economic activity in the construction sector, hence more jobs, personal taxation and spending power; (ii) permanent job creation in hotel operations; (iii) more government revenue from tourist-related imports (e.g. food, furniture and decor for hotels), occupancy and airport taxes; (iv) increased activities and gains to personnel in the agricultural, handicraft and service sectors; and (v) an overall increase in foreign exchange earnings (GCIC, p. 8).

To invert 'new tourism' further the private sector urged the government to take steps to promote 'resident tourism'. This type of tourism, whereby foreigners establish their second homes in the tropics, was described by the private sector as 'the highest spending per capita type that can be attracted'. What is most striking about the alternative tourism strategy of the private sector was the overwhelming emphasis it placed on 'wealth generation'. The government's arguments about the sociological and cultural costs of traditional tourism were dismissed. Indeed, their strategy called for a re-direction of the island's foreign policies along traditional lines.[8]

Although a tiny minority of the private sector praised the government for some of the initiatives it took in the tourist sector (e.g., increasing the tourism budget, improving staff in the tourism department and infrastructural development) they did not hesitate to attribute the depression in the industry to the political stance of the government. Given the collapse of the tourist industry during the PRG years, the behaviour of the private sector was, perhaps, understandable. After all, it was they who felt the brunt of the effects of dwindling tourist arrivals since they continued to dominate ownership of hotels and restaurants in this sector. Declining tourist numbers also meant declining profits for those businesses involved in the distribution sector. Not only were they supplying less goods to the industry, but the suppression in the spending power of workers, vendors and others who derived income from tourism meant a further reduction in the demand for their goods and services.

Further discontent would certainly have resulted if the NJM had lasted long enough to implement in full their strategy of 'new tourism'. 'New tourism' would have meant 'new tourists' with limited purchasing power since many of them would be drawn from the Third World and the Eastern Bloc.[9] One suspects that some businessmen would have expressed their opposition by refusing to commit their capital to new tourist plants since the government's strategy meant declining and uncertain profits for them. The shortfall in their investment in this pivotal sector in the economy would have had to be absorbed by the state - with all the problems this implied for an already financially beleaguered government.

The private sector also had serious misgivings about certain aspects of government policies in the agricultural sector. Again they were of the view that this sector would perform better if left solely in the hands of private agents. The government's land acquisition policy was also resented. As they put it:

> Government has inherited large holdings of agricultural land which in itself presents a distortion of the optimum balance necessary between large and small holdings which ideally catered to optimum export and domestic production. The fragmentation of some of the larger estates has decisively upset the balance and decreased productivity. Return of ownership to private sector individuals/entities should be considered as personal (profit) motivation will make a difference to management efficiency and increased production (GCIC, p. 12).

The private sector's confidence in its own ability came out again in their views on cooperation in fisheries:

173

It is observed that scheduling and deployment of fleet vessels would appear to be inconsistent with established norms in the maximization of operations. Private sector endeavours in other parts of the Caribbean have met with minimal success when operated through **corporate** structures. This appears not to be the experience of individuals. It is suggested therefore that vessels could be leased/rented to individuals operating under a Cooperative umbrella .... This approach would encourage personal incentive and individual endeavour (GCIC, p. 35; emphasis in original).

The IMF and the World Bank closed ranks

The private sector's views received further support and elaboration from the International Monetary Fund and the World Bank; two international institutions which are wellknown for free market economic orthodoxy. Again the main sore spot was state involvement in the economy, particularly the role of the MNIB. The **preliminary** version of the 1982 World Bank Report[10] thus noted:

> The government through the MNIB is directly involved in marketing domestic agriculture products which may not be a useful activity for it. Firstly, MNIB's domestic marketing is not filling any gap. Most farmers (71 per cent) sell their products directly in central markets or in villages, while other growers (21 per cent) sell to 'hucksters' or trafficants. Only eight per cent of the farmers sell their products to the MNIB. Secondly, MNIB's domestic marketing activities subsidise several government institutions, while MNIB is in payment arrears to the state farms. The MNIB could perform a useful role by organising local production, helping match the characteristics of the products with consumer (including the tourist industry) preferences, helping farmers and hucksters to improve product handling, and helping develop external markets for domestic crops. But the actual marketing of products could be left to other economic agents (World Bank, 1982a, p. 15).

The Report went on to highlight the poor financial record of various public sector corporations, attributing their performance to weak management in the main.

Ignoring the 'people-orientated' nature of the government's development strategy the Report also questioned the wisdom of the rate of increase of the government's expenditure on social and productive activities: 'The goal of increasing public savings could also be supported by a prudent policy on public employment growth and future wage awards and increased productivity of public servants. The rate at which new social benefits such as those in education and health are introduced requires the attention of the government, as does the number of new public sector initiatives in areas which can be left to the private sector' (ibid., pp. 17-18).

Similar criticisms were levelled by the IMF. The Fund argued that the MNIB and state investment in economic activities had a negative impact on 'private sector confidence' and was the source of the deteriorating 'investment climate' in Grenada. It charged that the MNIB was operating under conditions of 'unfair competition' *vis-à-vis* local private importers. In fact a central feature of the IMF 'Agreement' which Grenada entered in August 1983 (discussed in chapter seven) was that the MNIB should relinquish its monopoly privileges during the period of the Extended Fund Facility (EFF) programme and hence compete with the private sector under conditions of 'fair competition'.[11]

A turn for the worse

Developments took a turn for the worse in 1982. With the persistent and ever increasing budget and trade deficits (see chapter seven), and the difficulties in raising new concessionary loans to finance the various state programmes, the government was increasingly obliged to resort to measures which further reduced their popularity with the private sector. The competition for commercial bank resources and government taxation polices were particularly resented.

Right up to September 1983 Grenada was a member of the Eastern Caribbean Currency Authority (ECCA).[12] This institution provided a common currency (the Eastern Caribbean dollar, pegged to the US$ at a rate of EC$2.70 for US$1 since July 1976) to serve the eight members states. But ECCA was not endowed with the power to pursue an active monetary policy in member countries. The level and structure of interest rates, credit allocation, and minimum liquidity requirements for commercial banks, were thus left to the banks themselves. But the governments in the respective territories sought to influence monetary developments by consultation with bank managers, the so-called 'moral suasion' phenomenon. In 1976 the Gairy government introduced a special deposit scheme which made it compulsory for commercial banks to hold five per cent of their total deposits (barring government deposits) in the form of treasury bills. This requirement was increased to 20 per cent in 1982 by the PRG, based on its belief that these funds were lying idle in the banking system. The excess funds were now channelled into investment. The PRG's domination of the banking system

175

placed them in an ideal position to regulate bank credit. Government borrowing from the state owned banks was particularly pronounced.

The private sector and their allies rejected the government's argument that there was 'excess liquidity' in the system. Although the bank resources would probably not have been demanded by the private sector, that was seen as being beside the point. Referring to the possible effects of a liquidity problem the GCIC argued: 'it will not only stifle growth of the private sector but cause serious problems in its day to day operations. The situation may have been further aggravated by Government borrowings (EC\$3 million) as provided for by Finance Borrowing Authorization Law 1982 (No. 26 of 1982) and the Loan (General Purposes) Law 1982 (No. 25 of 1982). If the private sector is unable to expand it cannot create further employment' (GCIC, p. 22).

In response to the private sector's protests about liquidity problems the EFF granted to the PRG by the IMF in 1983 made substantial provisions for increasing the reserves of commercial banks. Thus EC\$13.8 million from the total loan of EC\$39.7 million was earmarked for the purpose. Another EC\$14.2 million was to be used to repay old debts to the Fund, EC\$2.0 million was set aside to repay outstanding debts to the local private sector, and only EC\$9.7 million was to be used for public sector programmes. Additionally, the IMF stipulated that the government should begin to repay its debts to the state owned banks. Besides, it was not allowed to contract any new loans from the other two commercial banks (see chapter seven for further details on Grenada's 1983 IMF programme).

In an equally desperate measure to raise additional resources, the PRG introduced a spate of tax legislations in 1982.[13] Of special interest was the general increase of company tax from 50 per cent to 55 per cent. In announcing the tax package on Budget Day, Coard described the company tax as 'a carrot and stick device for ensuring greater investment in our economy by the private sector' (Government of Grenada, 1982f, pp. 128-29). It was a 'carrot' in the sense that those entrepreneurs who invested in areas that the government regarded as a priority or expanded their present investment levels in their existing operations will receive a tax rebate. The rebate will be 10-15 per cent depending on the value-added of the 'productive' activity. As Coard put it: 'for those who sit on their behinds and do nothing about reinvestment, the tax has gone up by five per cent. But for those who are interested in getting into investments either in their existing undertakings or in some new undertaking, then they will find themselves paying in reality either only 45 per cent Company Tax instead of the old 50 per cent, or 40 per cent instead of the old 50 per cent and the present 55 per cent' (p. 129).

The opening sentence of this quote is significant: 'for those who sit on their behinds and do nothing about re-investment' suggests that private sector confidence in the economy was at a low ebb. Some investors were apparently curtailing their investment level and allowing their existing capital stock to run down. The meagre rebate was not regarded by many as an incentive since consumption tax had simultaneously increased by as much as 25 per cent in some cases. The consumption tax was partly aimed at the comprador bourgeoisie. Items which the country was capable of producing felt the brunt of the new tax increases. To the PRG, they were unnecessary imports - adding nothing to the productive capacity of the Grenadian economy. Similarly, the tax aimed at discouraging imports from outside the CARICOM region. The message was simple and clear. If Grenadian businessmen have to import, they must first seek to obtain such goods from CARICOM - otherwise they will be subjected to increased taxes.

This tax package was viewed by the private sector as a disincentive. Referring to the government's description of the taxation as 'a carrot and stick device' the GCIC's President, David Minors, argued that 'the carrot is an anaemic variety grown on the arid dry lands of the island, while the stick is a *wallaba* pole'. The President went on to note that the tax measure was likely to marginalise the private sector: 'If you are facing a situation where 55 per cent of profits goes back to Government in income tax, and 25 per cent goes to workers - which I do not object to - and inflation is running at 15 - 20 per cent annually, just to replace stocks and keep going will take up all that and still have you borrowing from the bank, far less to undertake expansion' (*Trinidad Guardian*, 9 April 1982).

The net impact of the various issues and government measures discussed so far was a poisoning of the business climate, and the creation of a sense of despondency among members of the private sector. A common question they posed among themselves was 'what next?'[14] Not surprisingly, many refused to greet the government's new **Investment Code** with a positive response, notwithstanding the fact that the Code came about largely as a result of their request for 'clear guidelines' about their role in the government's development strategy (*Barbados Advocate*, 27 February 1981).

The Grenada investment code

The rationale for the Code was clearly articulated in the opening paragraph of the investment document. It was meant to assure investors (both local and foreign) of the security of their capital; provide a formal statement of government guidelines and policies towards all forms of private capital; as well as to point out the procedures to follow for applying or enquiring about investment opportunities and related matters (Government of Grenada, 1983c, p. 1).

A central theme of the document was its over-riding emphasis on industries. The shift from traditional agriculture and comprador activities was seen as holding the key to the structural transformation of the Grenadian economy. Objectives such as the allocation of high unemployment, rising prices, sluggish growth, and adverse balance of payments position were uppermost in the minds of the drafters. This explains the comparatively stringent terms and conditions which the government imposed on businessmen, especially foreign capital. They were expected to identify with the 'national interest' of the country, a term which pervaded the Code. Private capital was thus forb idden from certain areas of activities, although the existing arrangements would remain intact. The following were demarcated for investment by the state and parastatal bodies: the development of public utilities, radio/television stations, infrastructural development, public transportation, national airlines, telecommunications, and trading in certain specified commodities. It was noted further: 'If private or external equity participation is necessary then it must be only on the invitation of the state or parastatal body, and only a minority position will be permitted. However, provisions will be made in the agreement for a transfer to full/state parastatal ownership within a stipulated time period' (ibid., p. 25).

In a similar fashion the following areas were reserved for exclusive local participation or at least majority local investment: retail and distributive trading; inland transportation; restaurants, night clubs, movie houses (that are not part of a hotel complex); travel agencies; real estate development; and primary export agriculture. Once more it was stressed that this arrangement only applied to future investment. Activities outside these two categories (state/parastatal and local participation) were open to foreign entrepreneurs on either a majority or minority ownership basis. Different forms of ownership structures were envisaged and would be permitted, viz,: (i) the foreign investors alone; (ii) joint ventures involving the foreign investors, local individuals, companies or corporations; (iii) joint ventures between the foreign investors and cooperatives;(iv) joint ventures between the foreign investors and the state; (v) joint vestures involving foreign investors, local individual companies or corporations, private sector and cooperatives; (vi) joint ventures between the foreign investors, cooperatives, local individuals, companies or corporations and the state; (vii) joint ventures between the foreign investors, the state and cooperatives.

The principles governing foreign investment were essentially the same as those outlined to the Grenada Chamber of Industry and Commerce by Finance Minister Coard in his address on 24 May 1979. However, some of these received further elaboration and were generally more clearly specified.

The document also dealt with government policy with respect to: (i) taxation, repatriation of profits and company dividends; (ii) mortgaging of company assets; (iii) technology transfers; (iv) transfer of shares; (v) liquidation procedures; (vi) investment security; (vii) hiring of expatriate labour and social responsibility of companies. Under the heading of 'hiring of expatriate labour' it noted: 'Hiring of expatriate labour will be allowed up to the extent that the skills required for that particular activity cannot be obtained locally. Grenadians in the meantime must receive the necessary training' (ibid., p. 32).

On the question of social responsibility, the document stressed that workers in all private enterprises must be allowed the right to engage in trade union activities. The entrepreneur must constantly seek to improve efficiency and improve the working environment. Additionally, he must keep up-to-date financial and accounting records and comply with 'reasonable requests' for information, explanations and clarification on matters relevant to the conduct of the company. The document concluded with the 'carrot' in the package, i.e. incentives to industry and available investment opportunities in Grenada. The incentives were essentially a modification of those that were already in place under the *Hotel Aid Ordinance* of 1954 and the *Fiscal Incentives Act* of 1974.

Under the *Hotel Aid Ordinance*, licenses were granted to personnel who proposed to operate a local venture with ten or more rooms. This license provided for the free importation of building materials, equipments used in hotel construction, and all purchases relating to the furnishing of the hotel. Income generated from hotels were also exempt from income tax for a period of ten years. Besides, any losses incurred during the tax holiday period may be offset against profits of the ensuing years (for a period not exceeding five years). *The Fiscal Incentives Act*, on the other hand, was designed to promote the establishment and expansion of manufacturing activities. It aimed to harmonise the prevailing tax incentives for industrial investment in all CARICOM countries such that none of the them would be at a disadvantage in attracting investment. The concessions to industry included exemption from custom duties on plant, equipment, machinery, spare parts, raw materials; and relief from taxes on dividends and profits for a period of up to 15 years (ibid., pp. 32-34).

The PRG altered these generous conditions to reflect the fact that they were pursuing a path of development different from the Lewis model of 'Industrialization by Invitation'. The revision began even before the Investment Code. People's Law No. 20 of 1980 reduced the length of the tax holiday period associated with the Hotel Aid Ordinance to a maximum of five years for all hotels established after April 1980. The 'blanket tax holidays', to borrow the PRG's term, associated with the Fiscal Incentives

Act were also abolished. Each proposal was now examined on 'a case by case basis'; with attention paid to questions such as their local value-added, employment potential, and implications for foreign exchange generation.

An impressive list of over 41 potential industries for local and foreign investment was drawn up by the PRG. These reflected opportunities in agriculture and forestry, tourism, and manufacturing - sectors which were pivotal to the PRG's development strategy (see Appendix 6:A:1).[15] With respect to 'protection to industry', the Code made it clear that the government was not prepared to shelter 'ineffective and stagnant (local) enterprises' against foreign competition (ibid., p. 36).

The private sector's reaction to the Code

As was to be expected, many private sector interests (local and foreign) found the government's investment Code to be unpalatable. For some it provided disincentives rather than incentives to invest.[16] A document bearing the title *Preliminary Comments on the Grenada Investment Code*, written by the United Nations' Centre on Transnational Corporations (UNCTC), embodied many of the misgivings which investors had about the Code.[17] The UNCTC document dealt with two main issues, viz, (i) the format and wording of the Code; and (ii) the general stringency of its terms and conditions.

It began by questioning the title of the document - *Grenada Investment Code*, arguing in effect that the notion of 'Code' is more likely to scare prospective investors than attracting them given its legal connotation. Terms like 'Investment Guide', 'Guide to Investors' or 'Guidelines to Investment' were offered as better alternatives. The UNCTC also questioned the government's plan to regulate domestic investment, pointing out that countries generally regulate only foreign investment, or those domestic investments which compete for incentives from the government. Moreover, such a regulation was considered to be unnecessary since no new concessions were conferred by the government.[18]

It argued further that most developing countries tend to use policy statements and administrative guidelines to monitor investment as opposed to formal laws. For example, some use a licensing system (to make it compulsory for enterprises beyond a specified size to obtain a license from the government), income tax acts and/or special regulations for particular sectors of the economy deemed to be of strategic importance. By making the Code a 'guide' instead of a 'legal instrument' the policies of the government and investment guidelines could be explained with greater clarity. This also has the virtue of permitting flexibility in implementation (UNCTC, 1982, p. 2).

The vagueness, ambiguity, and confusion of several terms and passages within the Code were also pointed out. For instance, the UNCTC advised against lumping loans and equity investments under the same category 'investment'; since both were different in nature, especially with respect to the settling of disputes. With the former, all that the host country has to do is to repay the interest and principal according to pre-arranged terms and conditions. However, the question of 'fair compensation' comes into play with the latter in the case of an expropriation. The UNCTC also found the different terms used to describe 'domestic' and 'foreign' investors to be confusing. For the sake of consistency and clarity, it advised the use of one or two terms instead of 'nationals', 'citizens', 'residents', 'local', 'internal', 'local firms', and 'local entity' for the former; and 'aliens', 'non-nationals', 'foreign', 'non- residents' and 'external' for the latter. It was also observed that in some parts of the document companies with predominant, but not total Grenadian ownership, were placed on par with those owned fully by Grenadians. This reinforced the need for clarity in definition and wording.

As for the list of activities reserved for nationals, the UNCTC questioned whether that list was only 'illustrative' since that, too, was not clear from the wording of the document. As the UNCTC put it 'in matters such as reservation of activities either for the state or for nationals, it is preferable to make the list exhaustive at any given point of time' (UNCTC, p. 17). The UNCTC document also questioned what the PRG meant by the injunction that investors must follow 'proper accounting, financial, and economic practices'. The UNCTC asked: What is an appropriate standard for accounting and financial reporting? Is this standard explained elsewhere in some government legislation? How will investors know if they are violating it? (UNCTC, p. 15).

Their most trenchant criticisms were levelled at the stringency of the terms and conditions laid down for investment, especially those relating to foreign investment. As the UNCTC put it:

> If foreign investment is to be attracted, the policies in this regard will require the careful consideration of the Government ... it would appear that too many obligations are being required of the investors, ranging from promoting industrial efficiency, minimisation of use of imported - energy and preservation of the quality of the environment, to the stabilisation of the cost of living and the transfer of appropriate and adequate technology (UNCTC, p. 8).

The foreign investor's problem is further complicated by the fact that it is not easy for him to determine whether his technology is 'adequate' or 'appropriate' to Grenada's stage of industrial development. For him to be able to answer this question he would need to have intimate knowledge about the Grenadian economy, knowledge not adequately embodied in the Code. Besides, the question of 'efficiency in production' is difficult to measure and determine *a priori* since this is affected by many factors - both internal and external; over which the investor may not have much control.

The restrictions imposed on the repatriation of profits and dividends (in the case of foreign investor) was also sharply criticised.[19] According to the UNCTC: 'A preferable approach would be not to place any general limitations on repatriation of capital. However, there could be a reservation that if in a particular case the capital being repatriated is of a heavy magnitude, the Government could indicate suitable instalment for such repatriation' (UNCTC, p. 17).

The document by the UNCTC was also critical of the absence of information relating to the procedures and mechanisms governing investment, especially with respect to the specific person or Agency to whom enquiries should be made, its powers and functions, the prescribed form on which applications should be made, number of copies to be submitted, supporting documents required, the amount of time required to process an application, the manner in which application will be approved, person to whom further enquiries can be directed, and the type of agreement to be executed by the investor. A further objection was the lack of detail on procedures for granting incentives, and the nature of particular incentives (UNCTC, p. 19).

Although acutely critical, the comments made in the UNCTC document were largely constructive in spirit. The PRG readily incorporated many of their suggestions, especially those relating to the general format, wording, and ambiguity of the Code. The final document was published by the Overseas Private Investment Corporation (OPIC) in March 1983 as the *Grenada Investment Guide*. The procedural requirements were clearly spelt out, and a clear and simply worded application form enclosed. However, the terms and conditions remained largely intact. The PRG was determined to depart radically from the model of dependent capitalism which was so widely practised in the region - with the usual adverse results (see chapter two above). The frequent reference of the UNCTC about 'practices in other developing countries' on matters such as concessions and profit repatriation was thus missing the point. For the PRG what was important was that 'the activity of any private entrepreneur should be compatible with the economic policy of the country' (Government of Grenada, 1983c, p. 23). The 'stick and carrot approach' used by the government in its investment Code was fully consistent with this premise.

But it seems as though the PRG went overboard with the 'stick' and was insufficiently generous with the 'carrot'. The issue is not whether this approach was justifiable. It clearly was, given the notoriety of private capital (especially some forms of foreign capital).[20] What was needed was a better balance between the stick and the carrot. For if the package is not sufficiently attractive foreign businessmen would be deterred from risking their resources in distant, unknown places. For it to be worth their while, the return to their capital must at least be commensurate with what they could obtain in their own countries. A foreign investor cannot be expected to move into a country to 'develop' and industrialise it in the name of altruism or to facilitate the desires of a well-intentioned, people-oriented government.

There was thus much force in the UNCTC's contention that some of the obligations in the 1981 Code were likely to scare investors rather than inducing them to invest. In a similar vein the World Bank, referring to the PRG's modification of the 1974 Fiscal Incentives Act, argued that many of the criteria used for determining the period of tax holiday were 'very subjective', especially those relating to social desirability, anti-pollution effects, and product efficiency. It thus recommended 'strengthened financial incentives to the private sector (to) encourage it to play an active role in the development process' (World Bank, 1982a, pp. 20-21).

Although the PRG did not accede to all the critics' recommendations and misgivings, the final version of the investment Code did provide a few more 'carrots', but still less than what other countries in the region were offering. An important change, for instance, was the removal of the discriminatory treatment bestowed on investors depending on whether they were local or foreign. Local investors were given more favourable concessions than their foreign counterparts, even though the latter generally incurred more risks. The final document thus provided a uniform package of tax holiday to all private investors so long as they were in the same enterprise category. The distribution of tax holiday among the different categories of enterprises was as follows: A maximum of 15 years went to category I (i.e. enterprises with 50 per cent or more value-added), 12 years to category II (those with 25-50 per cent value-added), and 10 years to category III (those with 10-25 per cent value-added).[21]

Grenada's manufacturing sector

The overwhelming importance which the PRG placed on manufacturing makes it imperative to consider the structure and characteristics of Grenada's manufacturing sector. This would help us to understand the enormity of the tasks involved and perhaps the reasons why Grenada's businessmen were happy to remain with their traditional activities.

One indicator of the undevelopment of Grenada's manufacturing sector is its infinitesimal contribution to the country's GDP. This figure consistently amounted to under six per cent before 1979. For most years it was estimated at four per cent. The composition of this sector in 1982 is presented in table 6:1 below. As pointed out in Chapter four the small agro-industrial sub-sector was added after 1979 by the PRG. Food precessing, beverages, and garment enterprises were the most significant in terms of their contribution to total production in the manufacturing sector, employment creation, and value added.

The output of these enterprises was geared overwhelmingly towards the domestic market. The notable exceptions were furniture, garment products, and the surplus produced by Caribbean Agro-Industries Limited and Grenada Agro-Industries.[22] Before the imposition of trade licences and other trade restrictions by the Chambers government in Trinidad, Grenada' manufacturing exports were marketed mainly in Trinidad.[23] An estimated 85 per cent of garments produced in Grenada and about 70 percent of goods produced by Grenada Agro-Industries were marketed externally.

The dependence of many of these enterprises on external inputs helped to give them another distinguishing feature, namely their highly capital-intensive nature. In 1987, on average, capital investment per employee was estimated at over US$3,000. In the case of Caribbean Agro-Industries Ltd, the cost of producing one job was put at US$46,000. This contrasted sharply with the more labour-intensive garment industry which created one job for every US$6,300 invested (Boatswain, 1984, pp. 33-34). Many of the highly capital-intensive enterprises also operated with considerable excess capacity. This was particularly true of Caribbean Agro-Industries Limited which specialise in producing animal feed and flour. In an interview with the operations manager in 1987, it was noted that 'The plant capacity of the flour mill is 50 tons per 24 hours but the mill is only running at roughly 60 per cent of its capacity. The feed mill is 45 tons per 24 hours but this is currently running at 65 per cent capacity' (Author's interview with Cecil Hypolite in June 1987).

The manager of this important company provided a lot of information on the practical problems and challenges which confront manufacturing enterprises in small economies like Grenada. Aspects of the experience of his firm are worth mentioning if the problems confronting manufacturing enterprises in small, peripheral economies are to be understood. First, you need highly qualified technicians with intimate knowledge of the processes involved in the production of the particular product. Thus, Caribbean Agro-Industries Ltd had to recruit a miller and other specialists from Continental Grains Ltd., a US-based enterprise. Training was also provided to local workers by Continental Grains Ltd. In the case of animal feed production, the

Table 6:1
The structure of manufacturing industries in 1982

Activity	Employment	Value added in 1000 EC$	VA* per capita in 1000 EC$
Manufacturing of food, beverages and tobacco	402	5,431	13.5
Food manufacturing	242	2,890	12
Manufacture of food products not elsewhere classified	11	34	3
Beverage industries	135	2,435	18
Tobacco manufacture	14	72	5
Textile, wearing apparel and leather industries	135	1,035	4
Manufacture of wearing apparel, except footwear	235	1,035	4
Manufacture of wood and wood products, including furniture	28	261	9
Manufacture of wood and wood products, excluding furniture	4	56	14
Manufacture of furniture and fixtures	24	205	8.5
Manufacture of paper and paper products; printing, publishing and allied industries	5	48	10
Manufacture of chemicals and chemical products	27	257	9.5
Manufacture of other chemical products	5	32	6
Manufacture of rubber products	9	50	5.5
Manufacture of plastic products not elsewhere classed	13	175	13
Manufacture of non-metallic mineral products	42	460	11
Manufacture of fabricated metal products	24	220	9

Source: *Industrial Survey of Grenada 1982* (cited in Boatswain, 1984).

* denotes value added

product must be comprised of protein and other nutrients to provide animals with a balanced diet. Contrary to the PRG's assertion, the operations manager pointed out that this industry could not be based on mere bananas, breadfruit, and cassavas since these sources are very low in the type of nutrients required by animals. Typical inputs imported by Caribbean Agro-Industries Ltd for this purpose were soya meal, corn, fish meal and feed concentrates. The manager noted further that even if these products could be produced in Grenada, Grenada would not be able to satisfy the firm's demands, on account of the country's small size. For example, his firm typically imports 8,000 tons of wheat each year from the US and France.

The importance of marketing was also stressed by the manager of Caribbean Agro-Industries. The difficulties faced by new enterprises in gaining a market share in existing markets can be formidable. As he put it 'It is very easy for politicians and academics to say we must industrialise because they don't know what industrialization requires in practical terms. No one had confidence in our products since we were new to the scene. We had to compete even in the Caribbean with other well established producers from Puerto Rico, Santo Domingo, Dominica and other' (Interview with Cecil Hypolite in June 1987). He pointed out that the firm was able to sell flour to Dominica's market for two years as a result of Bishop's contact with certain influential personnel in that country. With the souring of relations between the two countries, following the election of Eugenia Charles, they lost the Dominican market in 1982. Dialogue was resumed with Dominica after October 1983, with assistance from the United States. Although this resulted in the firm winning further contracts to supply flour to Dominica, lack of secure markets (and, as a consequence, excess capacity) continued to plague the company.

Many of the problems faced by Grenada Agro-Industries Ltd and the larger manufacturing enterprises in Grenada were echoed in studies on Grenada's industrial potential and possibilities, undertaken by Cerhonek (1982) and Boatswain (1984). The former study is of particular interest. Written by a Czechoslovakian development specialist, Cerhonek's policy recommendations were designed as a blue-print for the PRG's policy in the manufacturing sector in the period 1983-85. As Cerhonek put it: 'In this study the author tries to find the ways and possibilities of diversification of the economy in the next few years with the help of the workers of the macro-planning unit. This study should be used, as the first step to create a development programme in the years 1983-85 as the basis of working out the three-year state economic plan, from which the one-year plans will be derived' (Cerhonek, 1982, p. 1).

As for the importance of industrialization in the Grenadian context the author noted further that: 'the key solution to the problem of further development must be the industrialisation of the economy which can solve all the main present problems and be a motor for the whole economy, not only from an economic point of view, but also from the organizational and political view. The history of all countries which were entering the path of non-capitalist development was the industrialization' (Cerhonek, ibid., p. 4).

His proposals for industrialization were based on the following principles: (i) processing of domestic raw materials; (ii) developing labour intensive forms of production; (iii) developing less energy intensive areas of production; (iv) developing products which are not produced in large, exportable quantities in the neighbouring territories or (better yet) not produced there at all so that they will serve as market outlets; (v) developing products for which there is a high local demand, especially some of those which are currently being imported; (vi) establishing technologies with plenty value added and a tiny material consumption, even if the needed semi-products have to be imported. Taking all these principles into consideration, Cerhonek recommended the development of the following products: (i) electronics (electronic components, electronic equipment and apparatuses); (ii) agro-industry (new products - fruit juices, candied fruit, confectionery, chocolate, coconut oil and soap, by the construction of a fish processing plant, by expansion of the cigarette factory); (iii) processing of plastics (polyethylene bags), (iv) processing of wood and waste-paper (furniture, veneer from tropical woods, cartons from the millboard produced from the combination of waste paper and fresh cellulose); (v) textiles (woven carpets from synthetic yarn, coconut carpets); (vi) shoe industry (sandals and shoes for indoor purposes from processed domestic animal skins); (vii) expansion of the garment industry; and (viii) construction materials, cement and other related products and concrete panels (Cerhonek, ibid., p. 8).

But many fundamental issues remained unresolved and undetected despite Cerhonek's careful attempt to circumvent some of the more obvious constraints such as limited domestic market size and narrow resource endowment. Chief among the unresolved issues was the question of development finance. Unlike W.A. Lewis (see chapter two above) Cerhonek recommended that this problem should be solved largely from local sources, viz,: (i) the imposition of additional taxes, especially income tax and export duties; (ii) use of indirect means to raise further revenue from the private sector, particularly by selling bonds to them; (iii) finance from the insurance companies; (iv) revenue from existing government enterprises and commercial banks; and (v) governmental loans from overseas and profits from ECCA (Cerhonek, ibid., p. 6). This was a rather unrealistic proposal for a very mammoth problem. There might have been scope in the fifth source, but the others would certainly have heighten the conflicts between the business sector and the government. In fact, even loans from overseas were dubious, since from 1981 the government began to find it increasingly difficult to raise external loans. Moreover, this option was limited since one of the conditions imposed by the IMF package in 1983 was that the PRG should desist from contracting new loans (both concessionary and commercial loans) (see chapter seven below).

Much as the PRG wished to turn Lewis on his head they could not. For much of Lewis' analysis of the myriad obstacles to industrialization in small, underdeveloped Caribbean economies remain as valid today as they were when he wrote in the 1950s (see chapter two). His solution to the problems may be open to controversy but his analysis threw into sharp relief the magnitude of the challenge. Indeed, interviews conducted by the author as part of this study revealed that it was largely because of these objective constraints why Grenadian businessmen generally evade manufacturing activities. The 'invoice mentality' - a factor also discussed by Lewis - serves as a further constraint on manufacturing activities in Grenada. As Boatswain (1984) put it:

> The granting of political independence during the sixties and seventies did not liberate Caribbean businessmen and Grenadian in particular, to pursue new adventures in the field of manufacture. Instead, the few enterprising businessmen in existence, opted for higher margins of safety by threading along a path of cautious optimism in the retail and distributive sectors of the economy, rather than bold adventurism in the risky waters of industrial undertakings (Boatswain, pp. 4-5).

The PRG's industrial strategy was thus fraught with problems. These were not just derivatives of the physical size of the country but they were also social and historical in nature. Among the latter category of obstacles were the lack of skilled manpower, lack of an entrepreneurial culture, financial bottlenecks, and limited access to external markets. Under these circumstances it was difficult for the private sector to play a leading role in Grenada's industrial prospects. In the absence of a strong patriotic national bourgeoisie the weight of industrialization would thus have to be borne by the state sector. But this sector was no better equipped to carry this challenge. Indeed, it was precisely for this reason why the PRG rejected the total sate sector model.

An overview of the performance of the private sector

As noted before the Grenadian bourgeoisie and their external allies (especially the IMF and World Bank) were overwhelmingly preoccupied with the investment climate in revolutionary Grenada. Their fears and apprehensions waxed as the contours of the government's overall strategy became more pronounced. By 1982 it was patently clear to them that the government was committed to building a socialist state, and this was despite the pragmatism of the PRG in certain aspects of domestic and foreign policies. The constant anti-imperialist pronouncements, and the rapid and growing diplomatic relations with Eastern Bloc countries was regarded by many as conclusive evidence. Added to that was the increasingly frequent resort to 'revolutionary manners', and heavy-handedness in media and electoral policies. Thorndike (1985) summarises this point very well when he wrote: 'The Westminster model might have been justifiably discredited under Gairy but it presented far more than a parliamentary system. It stood for freedom of speech, association and publication, and an independent judiciary. Neither the private sector nor the people at large accepted the argument that they wee 'bourgeois' and, as such, unacceptable in the struggle for socialism' (pp. 98-99).

Under these circumstances it is not surprising that aggregate private sector investment fell dramatically over the PRG's period in office (see table 6.2). It plummeted from a hight of US\$5.4 million in 1980 to a low of US\$2.6 million in 1983. The post-1983 trend is also instructive. Grenada's return to the conventional political culture contributed to the dramatic upward trend in private sector investment. By 1986 an impressive US\$10.6 million (more than four hundred per cent increase over the figure for 1983) was invested by private entrepreneurs. The substantial decline in private investment in revolutionary Grenada took place despite the government's concerted efforts to stimulate private investment.[24] According to the final version of the 1982 world Bank Report:

> There have been regular consultations between the government and the private sector. These consultations have involved soliciting private sector responses to proposed Government policies (i.e. investment code, national budget/plan 1982), clarifying doubts (i.e. import licensing system, MNIB) and working out co-operative solutions to problems of mutual interest (i.e. marketing of primary product exports, identifying cheaper sources of agricultural inputs). The government continues to provide a wide range of incentives... (World Bank, 1982b, p. xii).

A more accurate picture can be gained from examining the response of the private sector in terms of their composition. In this context we should distinguish between the manufacturing bourgeoisie and the commercial bourgeoisie. The former were involved in productive activities while the latter

Table 6:2
Investment and savings 1980-1986 (US$ million)

	1980	1981	1982	1983	1984	1985	1986
Gross domestic investment	19.1	32.2	41.2	42.9	43.0	38.4	44.1
Public sector	13.7	28.9	37.6	40.3	38.5	31.0	33.5
Private sector	5.4	3.3	3.6	2.6	4.5	7.4	10.6
Gross national savings	5.8	9.0	5.5	8.1	9.8	14.2	18.8
Public	-0.3	-0.7	2.9	3.3	4.3	6.3	8.7
Private	6.1	9.7	2.6	4.8	5.5	7.9	10.1
External financing	7.9	23.2	35.7	34.8	33.2	24.2	25.3
Memorandum item							
External debt service ratio	3.0	2.7	4.5	4.6	7.7	12.2	12.6

Source: World Bank, (1984), p. 42.

were predominantly engaged in services, particularly the importation and distribution of commodities. Government policies were generally more damaging to the latter than to the former. As noted earlier, government policies were deliberately biased towards manufacturers. The aim was to shift as many businessmen as possible into manufacturing activities in order to augment foreign exchange earnings and generate employment.

Many manufacturers responded positively to the government's plea. This is not to suggest that they saw themselves as being a part of any class alliance with the government. For as Stephens and Stephens (1986) write: 'when one speaks of a class being a part of a class alliance, one generally expects that most members of the class will actively support the program and not just tolerate it' (p. 300).

The manufacturing bourgeoisie were simply promoting their own interest, not necessarily the national interest. They saw how they could increase their profits from taking advantage of the fiscal incentives which were offered by the government. The majority of the enterprises which took advantage of the incentives offered by the government pre-dated the PRG; very few new firms were established after 1979. Before 1979 investors would have had to contend with Gairy's corruption which entailed, among other things, paying out large sums of money as a *quid pro quo* for incentives. Other obstacles included an inefficient, over-centralised institutional framework for handling matters relating to private investment; poor industrial infrastructure (roads, water, electricity, telephone, port and airport facilities); and, above all, an unstable political climate. Although the political climate remained uncertain after 1979, the PRG had taken positive actions to eliminate many of these bottlenecks. Its record on infrastructural development was particularly impressive.[25]

That part of the private sector engaged in merchandising operations were the ones most bitterly opposed to the policies of the revolutionary government. But despite their furore and the government's conscious policy to marginalise them, they were determined to prolong their activities 'in the hope of better days ahead' (GCIC, 1983, p. 19). Many did business in pretty much the usual way. If there were opportunities to make profit they would increase their imports. But when the situation became less promising they would react accordingly. It must be remembered that they were operating in a virtually risk-free area. Capital tied up in commodities could be quickly recovered if the need arose. Besides, much of the capital tied up in commodities was borrowed from the banks. This method of financing their activities helped to reduce the risk even further. A good indicator of the performance of the commercial sector can be seen from the growth of bank loans to the distribution trade (see table 6:3). The table shows that the distributive trade continued to dominate commercial bank credit, rising from EC$13.8 million in 1979 to EC$26.3 million in 1982.

Coard was right when he argued that the private sector was deriving enormous benefits from the increased economic and social activities in revolutionary Grenada.[26] Using the Teacher Training programme as an example, he noted that the programme 'expanded dramatically from 50 teachers to 400. All of this means buying new furnishings, typewriters, paper, vehicles, etc. Whom do we buy books from for the school books and uniforms programme? Food for our new government hotels? Tyres for our NTS buses? The private sector' (Government of Grenada, 1983e, p. 31). One firm reportedly declared a record profit of EC$1.9 million for 1982 (ibid., p. 31). Undoubtedly, more profits would have been made had the government not imposed price controls on many imported items. As many as 72 items were subject to price control in 1981, with the maximum mark up placed at

Table 6:3
Grenada: Distribution of bank credit by sector (1976-1982)

	1976	1977	1978	1979	1980	1981	1982
Total (EC$ million)	48.8	57.9	65.2	71.4	--	69.3	92.8
Agriculture	3.4	4.3	6.3	2.4	--	5.0	3.8
Manufacturing	1.6	1.9	1.1	3.9	--	7.3	5.8
Distribution trades	13.8	17.0	18.5	22.5	--	19.8	26.3
Tourism	3.9	4.4	4.5	4.9	--	6.1	7.2
Transport	1.5	2.0	2.8	4.3	--	7.1	15.5
Public utilities	3.2	1.3	1.1	0.5	--	1.5	4.0
Building and Construction	3.1	4.9	4.1	3.3	--	6.2	5.3
Personal	8.2	12.7	14.1	17.3	--	16.3	19.4
Government	9.5	7.2	9.4	8.9	--	0.2	5.7
Other	2.6	2.2	3.3	3.3	--		

-- data not available

Source: Adapted from Ministry of Finance, Grenada. (cited in A. Boatswain, 1984, op. cit.).

7½ per cent and 15 per cent for wholesale and retail, respectively.

The main losers between 1979 and 1983 were hoteliers and other businessmen who relied overwhelmingly on tourism for their livelihood. The crisis in this sector (analyzed in the previous chapter) meant that many hotels operated with substantial excess capacity for the most part.[27] This meant declining profits - a situation over which these businessmen had virtually no control. Yet many incurred further losses as they spent large sums of money on promotional tours and advertising. As the 1982 Report of the Grenada Hotel Association put it 'In spite of a significant decline in stay-over visitors to our island during the past year, member hotels of our Association have participated in more promotional tours than ever before in the history of our Association' (Grenada Hotel Association, 1983, p. 1).

The GHA Report further noted that their plight was further aggravated by high operational cost for electricity, water, land taxes, wages, etc. (Grenada Hotel Association, ibid., p. 4). The consistent failure which their efforts met convinced many that the problem was first and foremost the political complexion of the PRG. A barrage of criticisms was thus directed at the government, although these were often made behind closed doors.[28] The air access problem and LIAT's inefficiency were also blamed for their declining fortunes, being described as 'a problem which has almost equalled the political (factor)' (Grenada Hotel Association, ibid., p. 5). They had the option of closing down their enterprises, perhaps with a view to migrating as happened in Michael Manley's Jamaica in the 1970s. But they continued operating in the hope of a recovery - a hope which has been vindicated as witnessed by the upward movement in tourist arrivals in Grenada after 1983.[29]

Some concluding remarks

There is a sense in which the PRG's experience with private capital bears some resemblance with Manley's attempt to pursue a democratic socialist path of development in Jamaica. Manley described his model as 'a third path' between the Puerto Rican Model of 'Industrialisation by Invitation' and the Cuban model which was organised along strict Marxist-Leninist lines.[30] Although his model was predicated on different theoretical premises from the theory of non-capitalist development they both shared certain common goals and policies - nationalist and egalitarian ideals, a fully self-reliant economy, a call for a new International Economic Order and a commitment to the principles of the Non-Aligned Movement. In both cases the mixed economy model (with the state sector dominant) was adopted and, as such, an alliance with the bourgeoisie was imperative.

But as is well known Manley did not succeed in his attempt to develop a working accommodation with the capitalist class. The opposition manifested itself in both the political and economic spheres. With respect to the latter, the business sector curtailed and disrupted production, created artificial shortages of basic commodities, exported capital, closed down operations and migrated *en masse*. Reflecting on the difficulty of operationalising a mixed economy the experienced statesman had this to say: 'When the private sector feels there is no threat to its class interest and that the public sector is merely engaged in productive capitalist activity for the state, all is well. But where the development of a public sector is part of an overall strategy to change the balance of relations between classes in the society, the private sector reacts differently' (Manley, 1982, p. 218).

Although the Grenadian bourgeoisie did not behave in exactly the same way as their counterparts in Jamaica, they were clearly opposed to the posture and general policies of the PRG. Too much radicalism had been introduced on both the economic and political fronts within a relatively short space of time. Confidence and morale were generally low, as we have seen, but they were prepared to stand their ground and settle for a bitter siege if necessary.

As in the Jamaican case capital was certainly exported during the period but it is difficult to quantify the full magnitude of the outflow. The lack of a national Central Bank and the institutional weaknesses of the Ministry of Finance[31] made it impossible for the movement of foreign exchange to be effectively policed. Besides, commercial banks were allowed to move funds freely within the ECCA area and to overseas banks. The foreign exchange position of the commercial banks indicated that a great deal of funds which were deposited with the commercial banks were further reinvested outside of Grenada (see table 6:4 for an observation of the foreign assets position of the banks). Referring to the scenario depicted in table 6:4, Joefield-Napier (1986) notes 'deposits outside of Grenada seem to have been used by commercial banks as hedges against any diminution of their earnings. Quite naturally, for commercial banks the precautionary motive prevailed and this dampened the increase in liquidity and in turn inflationary pressures were held in check' (p. 36).

Two other mechanisms made it easy for funds to be leaked out of the economy illegally. First, the 'national currency' (Eastern Caribbean Dollar) was also legal tender in Antigua, Dominica, Montserratt, St Kitts-Nevis, St Lucia and St Vincent and the Grenadines. Evidence gained from the author's interviews suggest that many exploited this loophole.[32] Second, the openness of the economy also helped to facilitate the outflow of currency. Through this medium it was possible to export hard currency, through over-invoicing of import bills and (to a lesser extent) under-invoicing of exports in concert with their foreign dealers. Note, too, that similar arrangements could have been made with Grenadians living overseas, many of whom make regular visits to the island. Since Grenadians were allowed to hold foreign bank accounts arrangements could easily be made for visitors to deposit hard currency into foreign bank accounts in return for the equivalent sum in local currency.

It should also be pointed out that unlike Jamaica, Grenada was less vulnerable to being manipulated by private capital since its economy was not deeply penetrated by foreign capital. Neither was it as closely integrated into the US economy as was the case with the Jamaican economy. In the latter case all the critical sectors of the economy - mining, tourism, banking, agriculture (particularly the sugar sub-sector), and the public utilities - were owned and controlled by foreign capital. But outside of the financial sector (particularly the insurance companies since two out of the four commercial banks were locally owned by 1983) foreign capital was virtually non-existent

Table 6:4
Grenada: Summary accounts of commercial banks (EC$m)

	1978	1979	1980	1981	1982	1983
Net foreign assets[1]	22.1	26.4	26.1	31.4	6.0	3.9
Domestic credit (net)	86.8	90.3	96.5	99.3	131.3	132.5
Net credit to central government	22.3	19.6	15.0	16.2	42.7	42.9
Net credit to other public sector	0.4	-1.0	-0.8	1.7	5.1	4.5
Credit to private sector	62.4	72.3	84.4	87.3	94.2	97.8
Net unclassified assets	1.7	-0.6	-2.1	-5.9	-10.7	-12.7
Liabilities to private sector	108.9	116.7	122.6	130.7	137.3	136.4
Demand deposits	22.8	28.2	30.2	26.3	26.0	23.1
Saving deposits	43.7	49.6	53.4	57.3	60.4	62.4
Time deposits	27.5	22.9	20.4	25.7	29.4	26.5
Non-residents' deposits	14.9	16.0	18.6	21.4	21.5	24.4
(Percentage change)						
Domestic credit[2]	12.3	3.2	5.3	2.3	24.5	0.9
Net credit to central government[2]	6.1	-2.5	-3.9	1.0	20.3	0.2
Net credit to rest of public sector[2]	-	-1.3	0.2	2.0	2.6	-0.4
Credit to private sector[2]	9.1	9.1	10.4	2.4	5.3	2.6
Liabilities to private sector	14.1	7.2	5.1	6.6	5.0	-0.7
(In per cent of total deposits)						
Memorandum item Net liquid assets[3]	20.3	22.6	21.3	24.0	4.4	2.9

Source: Grenada: Ministry of Finance, cited in Claremont Kirton.

[1] Includes net position with ECCA and ECCA area banks but excludes non-residents' deposits.

[2] In relation to liabilities to private sector at the start of the period.

[3] Net foreign assets excluding non-resident deposits in per cent of total deposits excluding government deposits.

in Grenada. Hence the revolutionary government mainly had to contend with local private capital.

The mixed economy schema thus had better prospects for success in Grenada. But in this regard the principal mistake of the PRG was its obsession with the application of 'revolutionary manners' to those perceived as potential saboteurs. Although the fears were probably real it was possible in many cases to handle them more cautiously. Two examples will suffice, viz, the government's media policies and the deterioration in its relations with the commercial bourgeoisie. With respect to the former, the reactionary role played by *The Gleaner* (the Jamaican daily newspaper) was uppermost in the minds of the PRG. Rumourmongering in a small society was seen as a virus which could make a government lose its credibility almost overnight. Thus when the government closed the *Torchlight* newspaper (owned by Grenada Publishers Ltd) - which was accused of telling "vicious lies" and of attempting to 'stir up the maximum amount of confusion and unrest in the country', it later went on to outlaw another paper, *The Grenadian Voice*, which was published by a private company in 1981. The paper was not permitted to publish more than one issue.[33] It was declared to be illegal for five reasons; of which the most important was stated as follows: 'this is a revolution, we live in a revolutionary society, these are revolutionary conditions and there is a revolutionary legality and they will have to abide by the laws of the revolution' (see *Caribbean Monthly Bulletin*, vol. 15, August 1982, p. 3). The paper was believed to have connections with the US Central Intelligence Agency. The Roman Catholic Church Newspaper, *Catholic Focus*, was also banned.

Even the monthly news bulletin of the Grenada Chamber of Commerce was banned. This was pushing 'revolutionary manners' too far. After all, this publication was not meant as a part of the 'news business'; which Bishop spoke about: 'If a business wishes to invest to sell flour, rice, cars or insurance that is proper investment, but don't try to sell news' (*Caribbean Monthly Bulletin*, vol. 15, August 1982, p. 1). The GCIC's bulletin was simply geared towards recording trends in the various sectors of the economy and providing a brief summary of other relevant business developments (Author's interview with Adrian Redhead in June 1987). The denial of this basic right was viewed with great displeasure and it did much to alienate this important class from the PRG. Members of the GCIC expressed the view that the PRG were using the Chamber in a 'window-dressing role'. As the President, David Minors, put it 'There have been many instances in which we could have embarrassed Government.[34] And we have gone out of our way not to do so, but we can't say the same for Government. They have used all sorts of opportunities to tear into the private sector unfairly and in an unwarranted manner' (*Trinidad Guardian*, 9 April 1982, p. 5).

Another businessman used Winston Churchill's popular dictum to express the way the PRG viewed the private sector: 'Some see private enterprise as a predatory target to be shot, others as a cow to be milked, but few are those who see it as a sturdy horse pulling the wagon'. To the PRG, the private sector was everything apart from 'a sturdy horse pulling the wagon' (Author's interview with Adrian Redhead in June 1987).

Apart from revolutionary manners - the bottomline of the hostile relationship between the private sector and the government - the government's open and provocative rhetoric about the risk-averse nature of the Grenadian bourgeoisie could have been handled better. Attaching odious labels (like 'margin gatherers' and 'invoice technocrats') and enacting resentful laws to discourage them from their previous lines of operation could only do more harm than good in an ultra-conservative society. A more patient approach - an approach which relied on education and socialising them into the virtues (for the individual businessman, worker, and nation as a whole) of a transition to manufacturing would have produced better results, at least in terms of boosting production.[35] A major reason why the manufacturing bourgeoisie performed so creditably was because of the government's unswerving support and assurance to that sector - an approach which contrasted sharply with that adopted for the commercial bourgeoisie.

Also counterproductive was the rapid rate at which the state moved into the productive spheres of the economy. Although state-led development is essential to the model of non-capitalist development, this does not mean that the state should leap into production. As we have pointed out the PRG did not yet have a well-equipped group of managers to manage such a large state sector. This contributed to the poor performance of the state sector, another development which the private sector viewed with displeasure. Besides, the rapid 'encroachment' fed the fear that the government was about to centralise the entire economy. Again, this error could have been avoided.

Viewed in this light one can understand why the Grenada Chamber of Industry and Commerce should welcome 'the liberation forces of the Caribbean and United States'; with open embrace in the wake of the October events (*Grenada Voice*, 20 November 1983). Their statement 'Second Chance for a New Beginning', issued in November 1983, not only expressed their support and gratitude to the marines but it also catalogued the various ways in which their rights and freedoms were infringed under the revolutionary government. It noted that the strategy of the private sector during the rule of the PRG 'was to prolong the survival of the private sector in the hope of better days ahead' (GCIC, 1984, pp. 18-19). The statement ended with a plea to Grenadians as a whole to subordinate individual objectives to national goals of unity and nation building.

Notes

1.   See Minutes of the various Annual General Meetings of the Grenada Chamber of Industry and Commerce (GCIC). Note GCIC is the island's leading private sector organization. It is followed by the Grenada Hotel Association (GHA) which represents hoteliers. According to the May, 1983 Report of the GCIC, it had a membership of 87 firms (represented by 146 individuals) in that year.

2.   According to the author's interviews with members of the GCIC, the government enjoyed overwhelming support from Grenadians as a whole, including the business community, in the first year of the revolution. The following extracts from the statement issued by the President of the GCIC, Mr Geoffrey Thompson, is noteworthy:

> I do believe that the new Government is sincere in its intentions to hold free and fair elections as soon as possible. If that is the case then I am confident that the democratic process will ensure that the views of all sectional interests, including the commercial sector, will be truly and fully represented (See *Barbados Advocate*, 19 March, 1979 for the full statement).

3.   The government's price control legislations also came under scathing attack since it limited the profits to be gained from trading in certain goods.

4   During the authors interviews, members of the GCIC voiced strong criticisms about the government's plan to take over this sector entirely. In fact, the full list of commodities earmarked for government purchase was brought to my attention by several members of the Chamber. Interestingly, copies of several PRG documents were prominently displayed on their shelves.

5.   The plan referred to goods which are normally utilised in the state sector. The government's intention was to develop an effective mechanism for planning the purchase and utilization of these technical and material supplies in order to achieve various economies in purchase and production. The private sector saw this list as detrimental to their interests. Some of these goods were previously handled by them. Besides they reckoned that the list was illustrative rather than exhaustive (Author's interview with Mr Patrick Clara of GCIC in June 1987).

6. The National Commercial bank consistently made a profit since its acquisition in 1979. Its profits stood at EC$120,000 in 1980 and increased to EC$1 million in 1981 (Government of Grenada, 1983e, p 71).

7. This organization was expanded in mid-1983 when the PRG purchased the Holiday Inn after much of its facilities were destroyed by fire. It is important to recall here that this Hotel comprised the bulk of the first class accommodation in the island. To the private sector the state was spreading its tentacles in all the critical sectors. They were thus suspicious of the implications of this expansion for the reproduction of private capital.

8. The establishment of the Soviet Embassy in Grenada in September 1982 was interpreted by many as a clear signal of the extent to which the PRG were committed to the Eastern political model. Gradually Grenada was coming under the orbit of communism, and this attracted further opposition from the business community (author's interviews with members of the GCIC in June 1987 regarding the significance of the Soviet Embassy). See also minutes of the GCIC and GHA for the period 1979-1984.

9. Since hard currency is lacking in Eastern countries one could not hope for much income from this source. According to a source close to the PRG, the government was prepared to accept goods from them in lieu of currency, i.e. a barter arrangement (author's interview with Bernard La Conbiniere, budget officer under the PRG, in May 1987). And there can be no doubt that the government was serious about attracting 'new tourists'. Referring to the plan to operationalise this trade a document written for the PRG by a Czechoslovakian, entitled 'A Project for Grenada's Economic Development in the period 1983-1985' noted 'The tourist trips from this country (i.e. Czechoslovakia) can be combined with the presently organised visits of Czechoslovakian tourists to Cuba' (Cerhonek, July 1982, p. 20).

10. The distinction between the preliminary version and the final version of the 1982 Word Bank report is of tremendous importance since there is such a huge contrast between the two. The preliminary version was so scathing in its criticisms of the government's development strategy and achievements of the revolution, that the Grenadian Authorities were compelled to forthrightly reject the Report. Many of the criticisms had no factual basis. The revolutionary

government thus proceeded to write their own report on the economy. This Report (written from inside) was completed by the time the World bank sent their new team of experts to collect fresh data on the Grenadian economy. The Report written by this latter mission incorporated the bulk of the one produced by the PRG It was thus positive and glowing in its account of the Grenadian economy since the revolutionary era. Incidentally, this final account has become increasingly scarce since its completion, even in Grenada itself (based on author's interviews with Bernard La Corbiniere and a number of technocrats who served under the PRG).

11. See Claremont Kirton, 'Grenada and the IMF: the PRG's EFF programme, 1983', unpublished paper (also undated), for further details.

12. On 1 October, 1983 ECCA was transformed into a regional central bank (ECCB), designed to overcome many of the limitations of its predecessor.

13. See Government of Grenada (1982f), especially pp. 126-129, for details of the various tax measures. See also Macro Planning Unit, 'Implications of the new Tax Measures in Grenada on Tax payers: Theoretical Perspectives', (Ministry of Finance, St George's Grenada) for a discussion of the incidence of these tax measures.

14. Author's interview with Mr Adrian Redhead, GCIC, in June 1987.

15. The list is worthy of examination for it provides a clear insight into the types of industries the PRG had wished to see in Grenada, and the scale of industrialization envisaged.

16. Author's interviews with Grenadian businessmen in June 1987.

17 See UNCTC (1982), p. 1 for details.

18. As we have seen the incentives offered by the PRG flowed from legislations which were already in place, i.e. the Hotel Aid Ordinance and the Fiscal Incentives Act.

19. See 'Grenada Investment Code', especially pp. 29-30, for the list of restrictions. For example, non-resident shareholders would not be allowed to repatriate more than three quarters of their share of net

profits for the first five 'profitable years'. If they chose to repatriate more than three quarters, they would be subjected to a ten per cent 'toll gate' tax (see ibid., pp 29-30).

20.　　The PRG, too, had experience of the notorious side of foreign investment. The mysterious fire at the Holiday Inn which dealt a substantial blow to the island's tourist industry was a recent case in point. Interestingly, the fire coincided with the expiry of the ten years tax holiday which this multinational corporation had obtained. (Author's interviews with personnel at the Caribbean Development Bank, and with members of GHA and GCIC, in May and June, 1987).

21.　　See Overseas Private Investment Corporation, *Grenada Investment Guide*, (March 1983), p. 3 for further details.

22.　　This is a joint-ownership enterprise (49 per cent of the shares belong to the Huggins' and 51 per to US businessmen). The firm came into operation in April 1980 but construction activities actually began in 1978. The latter date is important for as the Manager pointed out construction would not have begun had they known of the imminence of a revolution in March 1979. 'We would watch the climate first before we commit our resources' (Author's interview with Mr Hypolite in June, 1987).

23.　　The decision to impose visa requirements and trade restrictions - a clear violation of the CARICOM Treaty - was directly related to the effects of the reduction in oil prices on the Trinidadian and Tobagonian economy, dominated as it was by petroleum activities.

24.　　The evidence does not suggest any major closing down of production ventures. A prominent businessman and past president for the GCIC, David Minors, however, resigned in July 1982, and took up residence in Canada (GCIC, 'Report of the Council of Management 1983', p. 1). There is adequate evidence to demonstrate that many members of the professional strata and expatriates (who previously occupied the Westerhall Point residential area for the most part) migrated *en masse*.

25.　　An estimated EC$600 million was planned to meet what Coard described as 'the requirements and the needs to develop a real economy for Grenada, a self-sufficient economy, a dynamic economy, an economy which is able to provide the necessary material well-being for the people of the country, and to provide an infrastructure which not only restores what has been destroyed but goes well beyond that in terms of what is absolutely necessary for the foundation upon which direct production can be based' (cited in Government of Grenada, 1982b, p. 32).

26. The period 1979-1981 may be regarded as a 'boom phase'. During this period projects (especially by the state) were constantly launched, new jobs were generated (albeit many were of a seasonal nature), and grants from overseas poured in without interruption. Relative to GDP total government expenditure grew from 6.5 per cent in 1978 to 54.5 per cent in 1979, and reached 58.0 per cent in 1982 (see World Bank Report, 1984, p. 126). See also chapter 7 below.

27. For the winter 1982/1983 season, hotel capacity stood at 34 per cent compared to 40 per cent for 1981/1982 winter season. The picture was even worse for the summer period. These were 25 per cent for 1983 and 23 per cent for 1982. (Grenada Hotel Association, 1983, p. 2).

28. In a joint report on the state of Grenada's tourism written by the GHA and GCIC (sent to the PRG in January 1981), the businessmen told the government candidly that 'tourists are not particularly inclined to areas which abound with rebels, counter-revolutionaries, mercenaries, etc.; or where threats of invasion and acts of political violence seem commonplace'. The government was also advised to 'adopt new approaches to the question of foreign policy, and foreign relations, and should as an imperative, eliminate revolutionary rhetoric which antagonises and/or frightens the people we need to keep the tourist industry alive and to provide jobs for the unemployed'. See article captioned 'Revolutionary Policies have Backfired', (*Trinidad Express*, Thursday, 22 October 1981), for further details.

29. According to data compiled by the CTRC a total of 39,500 stayover visitors went to Grenada in 1984. The figure increased to 52,000 and 57,300 for 1985 and 1986, respectively. These figures contrast sharply with those for the period 1979-1983. See Chapter five above.

30. See Manley (1982), especially the four chapters under the heading 'Reaction'; and Stephens and Stephens (1986) for a detailed and comprehensive discussion of the characteristics of this path of development, and the problems encountered in pursuing it.

31.   Exchange control is administered by the Ministry of Finance. Currencies are freely allowed into the country but they must be offered for sale to a local authorised foreign exchange dealer at the prevailing rate of exchange, unless Exchange Control permission has been obtained by the Ministry of Finance to do otherwise. Grenadians are also allowed to hold external bank accounts provided they conform to the requirements of the Ministry of Finance.

32.   In an anonymous interview I was told that the PRG realized that people were exporting the local currency in huge quantities. To stem the outflow the Eastern Caribbean Currency Authority was requested to place a special mark on the notes which were printed for Grenada so that they could be readily identified in the Eastern Caribbean area. The request was implemented (Anonymous interview in June 1987). In another interview with two prominent local businessmen who also had business elsewhere in the Caribbean, they admitted that they exported currency. Their strategy was to increase their overdrafts (i.e. borrow more from the banks), while exporting the bulk of their personal funds.

33.   The paper was sponsored by 26 prominent individuals in Grenada. They included business directors, business-owners, trade unionists, a barrister, a banker, a journalist, a butcher, shopkeepers, farmers and housewives (See *Caribbean Monthly Bulletin*, Vol. 15, No. 8, August 1981, p. 2 for the full list of names).

34.   He was alluding to the many foreign trips which members of the Chamber made with the PRG to champion the cause of the country. A notable joint trip was to the Airport Co-financing Conference in Brussels in 1981. On that occasion Coard could boast 'the composition of our high level delegation to this conference is also an indication and reflection of this total support about which I speak. In addition to the Government representatives like myself and our Chairman Ambassador, our delegation includes the Vice-Minister of Finance, who is himself a businessman in his own right, a former President of the Chamber of Commerce of Grenada, and a past Director of the Caribbean Association of Industry and Commerce. It also includes the present President of the Chamber of Commerce and Industry of Grenada, the President of the Grenada Hotel Association, and the Chairman of the Tourism Board of Grenada. This would tell you what our private sector people think of the project for all sections of the private sector...' (Government of Grenada, 1981c, p. 4).

35. If the non-capitalist model is not economically successful, then it is not likely to be politically successful. Therefore, it is very important not to alienate the private sector. Their presence must be tolerated even if an alliance cannot be solidified with them. Four-and-a-half years is probably too short a time to determine whether such an alliance was possible in the Grenadian context.

7 Economic performance and the October showdown

Chapters four to six provided a backdrop against which the overall performance of the Grenadian economy under the PRG's tenure in office can be gauged. The analysis contained in those chapters is indispensable to any attempt to assess the credibility of the various, often conflicting, reports written on the Grenadian economy for this period, by both inside and outside observers. There are three notable accounts, viz, (i) the People's Revolutionary Government, (ii) International Monetary Fund, and (iii) World Bank. For ease of analysis these are treated below as the 'inside account' (i.e. the PRG's account) and the 'outside account' (i.e. the account produced by the IMF and World Bank). In this chapter, we examine the macroeconomic performance of the Grenadian economy under the PRG's stewardship, the PRG's suicidal resort to the IMF in 1983, and the role of economics in the demise of the revolution.

The 'inside' account[1]

Finance Minister and Deputy Prime Minister, Bernard Coard, began his government's first official report on the performance of the Grenadian economy by reviewing developments within the world capitalist economies: 'These economies are facing high rates of inflation, inflation rates above 12 per cent.... These economies are also facing increasing levels of unemployment and slow down in expansion of international trade. Furthermore, available information shows that, in 1981, some of the developed capitalist countries had a negative rate of growth in their economies ... In fact, they grew backwards. They showed an economic decline' (Government of Grenada, 1982e, pp. 1-2). Thus, on the PRG's own terms, one standard by which it can be judged was its ability to contain and reverse inflation and unemployment, stimulate trade, and generate economic growth.

Economic growth

According to the PRG's account, the Grenadian economy under its husbandry performed creditably on all these counts. On the question of economic growth (measured in terms of real GDP) an upward trend was reported: 2.1 per cent in 1979, 3.0 per cent in 1980, 3.1 per cent in 1981 and 5.5 per cent in 1982. Not surprisingly, the construction sector accounted for the bulk of the growth that took place during this period - reflecting the importance the government attached to the development of infrastructural activities. This was regarded as the foundation for genuine socio-economic advancement. As noted before, pride of place was accorded to the construction of the international airport.

It is not clear, however, just how much money was spent on the airport or on total capital expenditure for that matter since inconsistency is evident in even the data contained in government sources. With respect to the airport, the PRG valued it at a cost of US$70 million but the CDB put the cost as high as US$110 million (World Bank, 1984, p. 30). In their *Report on the National economy for 1982*, the PRG noted that a total of EC$237 million was spent on capital expenditure between 1979 and 1982; an amount which, in the government's assessment 'stands on its own as a remarkable achievement, and it completely overshadows the tiny amounts of money spent on capital projects during all of Gairy's 25-year dictatorship' (p. 15). The breakdown of the figure is as follows: EC$16 million for 1979 (compared to EC$8 million for 1978), EC$39.9 million for 1980, EC$79.2 million for 1981 and EC$101.5 million for 1982. Another government document, *Revised Economic Memorandum on Grenada*, also confirms this upward trend, but with different figures. These are EC$32.5 million for 1980 and EC$99.1 million for 1981.[2] This surge in capital expenditure resulted in a 10.8 per cent increase in construction activities in 1980 and a growth rate of 14.5 per cent for 1981.[3]

Balance of payments

But the picture was less encouraging for other critical sectors of the Grenadian economy, particularly tourism and agriculture. According to the PRG, the main problems they faced in these two sectors were exogenously determined. Thus agriculture was plagued by bad weather, pests, shrinking demand, and adverse terms of trade. Similarly the crisis in tourism and other tourist-related sectors was attributed to the international recession and adverse propaganda and other forms of what the PRG called 'destabilization'; a term which became a part of the lexicon of the revolution from an early stage.[4]

The sluggish performance of the critical sectors of the economy contributed in no mean way to a severe balance of payments disequilibrium. Although not much is recorded in the PRG documents on the overall performance of the external sector, much can be learnt about the Grenadian economy from the available data from this source. Thus the *Report on the National Economy for 1981* noted that total merchandise exports for 1980 and 1981 amounted to a value of EC$44.6 million and EC$51.1 million, respectively (p. 32). The figure for 1982 fell to EC$50.0 million. Merchandise imports, on the other hand, stood at EC$151.8 million for 1980, EC$159.9 million for 1981, and EC$150.9 million for 1982.[5] Net receipts from invisible exports (i.e. tourism, banking, freight, insurance and other services) were not sufficient to offset this huge deficit on the balance of trade.

As noted before, tourism (Grenada's principal invisible export) underwent an acute depression during this period. According to the PRG's figures, earnings from this critical sector declined by approximately US$3 million in 1981 alone (Government of Grenada, 1982g, p. 17). For 1981, the total deficit on the current account was a staggering US$25 million or EC$67.5 million; a figure which exceeded total earnings from merchandise/visible exports by EC$16.4 million. The persistent deficit was financed mainly by grants and loans from both bilateral and multilateral sources. A total of EC$67.4 million was received from these sources in 1982 compared to EC$58.2 million in 1981. To the PRG inflows of funds on this relatively large scale was indicative of the strength of the Grenadian economy and the government's ability to sustain it on a viable path: 'This reflects the growing confidence which other Governments and international organizations now have in our people and revolution, and in the ability of the Government to manage the economy' (Government of Grenada, 1983e, p. 16).

But the PRG did not intend to get enmeshed in 'the debt trap'. As Coard put it in an interview with Chris Searle in 1983 'we try to keep our debt service ratio within manageable bounds.'[6] A proud Coard noted that only 3 per cent of Grenada's GDP was spent on repaying the total public debt in 1982. As for the foreign component of this debt, only 3.7 per cent of the country's foreign exchange earnings was required to service it in 1982; a figure described as 'among the lowest for any country in the world'. Coard also emphasised that, unlike Gairy and many other governments, the PRG were borrowing for productive purposes rather than for consumption.

Despite the adverse developments on Grenada's balance of payment, it was reported that the economy had begun to undergo a fundamental restructuring and transformation of its external trade. This was particularly marked in the case of the composition of exports; the relative share of non-traditional exports increased sharply between 1979 and 1982. It rose from seven per cent

207

in 1979 to 36.6 per cent in 1982. Among the non-traditional exports the most significant were garments, flour and agro-industrial products. Agro-industrial exports were particularly significant since they were virtually non-existent before 1979, and were undertaken by the inexperienced state sector.

As a result of these new sources of foreign exchange, the PRG was able to cushion somewhat the debilitating effects of the crises in the tourism and (traditional) agricultural sectors. It was also able to reduce Grenada's reliance on trading arrangements with a handful of countries. In addition to western sources, trade links were established with Eastern Bloc and neighbouring CARICOM countries. By 1982 Trinidad and Tobago became the second largest source for Grenada's non-traditional exports.

The PRG also claimed some success on the import side of the trade equation, particularly with respect to the significance of food in the import bill. According to the government, the share of food items as a proportion of total imports declined consistently during the period 1979-1982. The respective figures were 30.6 per cent, 28.9 per cent, 28.2 per cent, and 27.5 per cent (Government of Grenada, 1983e, p. 25).

The social wage

In stark contrast to the patchiness of data on the external sector of the economy, the PRG documents contained ample data on what the government termed the 'social wage'. The reduction in unemployment was one dimension of the social wage. In PRG parlance the term 'social wage' was used to reflect all the benefits (direct and indirect) which came with the revolution. Coard defined it as follows:

> The social wage consists of those benefits which you don't pay for out of your wage packets, but which you get anyway. And when we add up the cost of these benefits and compare that to what our brothers and sisters in other islands actually pay for, out of their own pay packets, and what we used to pay for also before the revolution, we can see how much our social wage is adding to the buying power of our own dollars (Government of Grenada, 1982e, pp. 34-35).

Starting with unemployment, the government boasted a substantial reduction from 49 per cent when they took power in 1979 to 14 per cent in April 1982 (Government of Grenada, 1983g, p. 2). It was estimated that 72 per cent of those without jobs were females, and aged between 16 and 25. In commenting on the findings of the Census, Coard had this to say:

> It should be noted that our figure would be even lower if we counted in the same way as they do in other countries. In many developed

countries, they only count you as unemployed if you have tried to get a job within the past month. We counted the people who gave up finding a job years ago! We have not done another census since April 1982, but we know that in the state sector alone, about 500 new jobs were created after that date, so that by now the unemployment rate has certainly fallen lower[7].

As evidence of some of the jobs created since the government's tenure, Coard cited the numerous projects undertaken by the PRG, especially in construction:

> Where are the youths who used to be seen in our wellknown liming-spots, on walls and street-corners all over the country during working hours? They are working on the Eastern Main road in St David's, they are building farm roads in St Andrew's and on The West Coast, they are putting up the new Telephone Company buildings, they are rebuilding the Carenage in St George's. Last year they built the Primary Health Care Centre in St Patrick's, schools in Bonaire, Florida and Corinth, the new farms and electricity expansion in Carriacou, and the electricity system in Petit Martinique. Some are working with the National Transport Service. Others are constructing the 50 town houses in True Blue which will be a new experiment in housing in our country. Hundreds are working at the International Airport and the new asphalt plant. Others are working at the Block Factory, the Tile Factory, the Sandino prefabricated Housing Plant and at the dozens of other productive enterprises set up by the PRG during the past two years (Government of Grenada, 1983e, p. 6).

Coard also noted that the state sector alone provided 9,350 fulltime jobs. It was also claimed that considerable job opportunities were created within the private sector since: 'private business has also expanded since the revolution, because of developments in the infrastructure (roads, telephones, water, etc.), and because overall improvements in the economy have brought about better conditions for investments.' (ibid., p. 6).

The government's aim was to eliminate unemployment at all costs for in their view 'unemployment is a disease, a curse, a blight and a waste of very important and scarce resources'.[8] And as the title of Bishop's speech suggests, ultimately unemployment could only be solved by real production, not through hand-outs or unproductive activities.

Similar claims to those made about unemployment were also made about living standards of Grenadians. The benefits were mainly concentrated in the spheres of education, health and housing. Among those emphasised by Coard were: free secondary school education, free school books, lunch and uniforms (to children from impoverished backgrounds), the drive towards eradication of illiteracy, free or subsidised drugs to patients, the ruralization of certain services (particularly in health) which were previously concentrated in the urban areas, improvement of transportation services, house repair programme and the savings made by small farmers by direct sales of their produce to the MNIB.

According to the PRG, the social wage was further augmented by the reduction which took place in the level of unemployment since aggregate family income was likely to have been higher during this period. That is to say, a family which had one bread-winner before 1979 was likely to have had at least two after 1979; with a consequent rise in their standard of living.

Apart from the 'social wage' it was also asserted that the 'traditional wage' had also increased in both nominal and real terms. For example, in 1981 and 1982, money wages increased by an average of 17½ per cent and ten per cent, respectively. Real living standards also increased, reflecting the fall in the general level of prices during the period of PRG rule. Inflation fell from a rate of 23 per cent in 1980 to 10.5 per cent in 1981. The inflation rate fell further to seven percent in 1982 (Government of Grenada, 1983e, p. 9). This decline in the rate of inflation was attributed to improved price and import policies on the part of the state, as well as its policy of encouraging people to produce more and 'to buy local and eat local'.

In applauding the fairly consistent improvement in real and money wages, coupled with the benefits of the social wage, a jubilant Coard had this to say: 'And we must state boldly that this steady improvement in the living standards of our people is taking place at a time when the real wages of the working people in most capitalist countries are falling and the conditions of life are getting worse for millions of them' (ibid., p. 10).

What is striking about the PRG's review of the Grenadian economy under its husbandry was their failure to admit the severity of the structural weaknesses which continued to plague the economy, and the government's inability to continue to satisfy the material expectations of the population at large. A picture of sweetness and light was painted. To improve the credibility of their claims lengthy quotations from the 'half-hearted' 1982 World Bank Report were often cited.[9] Thus an entire presentation was made on this Report by Coard in October 1982 during a press conference. One of the excerpts which Coard stressed on this occasion read as follows: 'Grenada has been one of the very few countries in the western hemisphere that continued to experience per capita growth during 1981'.

Coard continued: 'I will read it again - "Grenada has been one of the very few countries in the Western Hemisphere". Note it does not say only Caribbean, it does not even say Caribbean and Latin America, it says the western hemisphere. In other words, they include the United States, Canada,

Britain, France, everybody. Grenada has been one of the very few countries in the western hemisphere that continued to experience per capital growth during 1981. This then, is what the World Bank report had to say' (Government of Grenada, 1982f, p. 165).

Before providing a verdict and an independent assessment on the economy, it would be helpful to present the 'outside account' as represented by the IMF and World Bank; two institutions described by Payer (1974) as Siamese twins.

The 'outside' account

Significantly, the tone and style of subsequent World Bank Reports on the Grenadian economy was more akin to the language traditionally used by the World Bank and other international organizations like the IMF. This language is characteristically formal, technical, seemingly neutral, and unemotional. Statements such as 'Grenada has been **one of the very few countries in the Western hemisphere** that continued to experience per capita growth during 1981' are, indeed, unprecedented.[10]

Although there are a few notable discrepancies (particularly with respect to aggregates such as GDP and unemployment) between the 'outside' and 'inside' reports on the Grenadian economy, the main distinguishing feature is essentially one of emphasis. Whereas the PRG emphasised the plethora of projects and programmes they initiated as well as their contribution towards the social and economic advancement of Grenadians, the World Bank and IMF concentrated on providing technical information on the various areas of the economy. Both sets of information are indispensable for evaluating the health of the Grenadian economy during this period. As such they need to be examined together before hard judgments are made about the economic and social achievements of the PRG, and the development prospects of the economy under their continued stewardship (assuming the regime had survived).

The rate of growth of GDP

Both the IMF and the World Bank reported a significantly lower growth rate than that recorded by the PRG.[11] The IMF reported an average growth in real GDP of 2.6 per cent for the period 1979-1982.[12] The figure reported by the World Bank was marginally higher at 2.95 per cent. The PRG, on the other hand, claimed a correspondingly higher figure of 3.4 per cent for the period. Interestingly, the IMF had misgivings about this modest rate of growth. Thus, it was noted: 'The Statistical Office is in the process of revising statistics on national accounts and production. Its work is at the initial stage only, but preliminary indications are that previous estimates of Grenada's GDP, including those in this report, are inflated. Therefore, national accounting estimates in this report are subject to this caveat' (IMF, 1984a, p. 1). However, the figures published later by the Statistical Office failed to confirm the IMF's contention. On the contrary, it reported a real GDP of 2.1 per cent for 1981, 5.3 per cent of 1982, and 1.4 per cent for 1983.[13]

All three reports were of one accord that the driving force behind the growth experienced during this period came from the construction sector. According to the IMF, for instance, construction surged from a fall of 2.3 per cent in 1979 to a dramatic increase of 26.2 per cent in 1982. For 1980 and 1981, the growth rates were 21.9 and 20.2 per cent, respectively. Although these figures differ somewhat from those reported by the PRG, they were generally indicative of the volume of activities in this sector during this period. However, what is more notable is the picture painted by both the IMF and the PRG of developments within the vital agricultural sector. According to the IMF, the agricultural sector grew by 6.1 per cent in 1979, fell by 5.4 per cent in 1980 and recovered somewhat in 1981 with a growth rate of 3.4 per cent. These figures contrast with the PRG's 3.0 per cent growth in 1979, 1.5 per cent decline in 1980, and 5.0 per cent growth in 1981 (IMF, 1984, p. 2).

The IMF and World Bank were also quick to underline the diminutive rate of growth achieved during this period compared to the immediate pre-revolutionary period, i.e., 1975-1978. The figures presented by the World Bank, for instance, are shown in table 7:1. Thus for 1976 real GDP stood at 3.5 per cent, reached 4.2 per cent in 1977 and peaked to 7.8 per cent in 1978; yielding an average growth rate of over five percent for 1976 to 1978. Although these figures are suggestive of a significant decline in the rate of growth of the Grenadian economy during the PRG rule, it should be affirmed that GDP figures can be notoriously misleading. It is not so much the percentage rate of growth which is important. Rather, it is the overall volume and (real) value of the output which is produced from year to year. Using the World Bank's own figures, for instance, it may be noted that nominal GDP at factor cost in 1982 was nearly three times larger than what it was in 1976. When adjusted for price changes, the real value of that output (in 1980 prices) was EC$165.2 million in 1976 compared to EC$208.3 million in 1982. Table 7.1 shows that both real GDP and per capita real GDP increased steadily under the PRG, notwithstanding the comparatively higher rate of growth in percentage terms for the immediate pre-1979 period.

Another pertinent caveat is the relatively favourable international market environment which Grenadian exports experienced before 1979. Unlike the PRG era, this was a period of rising prices for traditional crops and relative

Table 7.1
Grenada - nominal and real gross domestic product (1975-1982)

(EC$ millions)

	1975	1976	1977	1978	1979	1980	1981	1982
Nominal GDP at market prices	n/a	115.9	134.1	172.3	202.6	232.2	258.8	290.5
Nominal GDP at factor cost	84.6	96.8	110.9	141.2	165.5	195.1	221.1	245.4
Real GDP at[1] factor cost (at 1980 prices)	159.6	165.2	172.0	185.5	189.4	195.1	201.7	208.3
GDP deflator (1980 - 100)	53.0	58.6	64.1	76.1	87.4	100.0	109.6	117.8
Per capita real GDP at factor cost	1,477	1,515	1,573	1,686	1,722	1,774	1,834	1,877

Source: World Bank (1984), p. 11.

[1] The real growth in GDP in percentage terms can easily be computed from this row. For the period 1979 to 1982, these are 2.1, 3.0, 3.4 and 3.3 respectively. For comparative purposes, the pre-revolutionary trend is also worth computing. These are 3.5 per cent 4.2 per cent and 7.8 per cent for 1976 to 1978, respectively.

economic buoyancy in the economies of Grenada's main trading partners. As fortune would have it, weather conditions were also more hospitable during the pre-1979 period. So was the tourist industry, at least when measured in terms of tourist inflows into the island.

The main developments in the country's balance of payments situation for this period is shown in table 7:2. The table indicates a progressive deterioration of the current account balance during the era of the PRG; it rose from US$5.2 million in 1979 to US$33.7 million in 1982. Although airport-related imports were significant, they constituted a relatively small part of total expenditure on imports. This suggests that the traditional structure of Grenada's import bill was not radically altered during the period 1979-1983. The IMF did concede, however, that the PRG had initiated a significant degree of overseas market diversification on the scale claimed by the PRG. Had it not been for that change in the mix of exports, export earnings would have fallen even more disastrously.[14] As revealed by the IMF data, these fell from US$21.4 in 1979 to US$18.6 million in 1982. Thus although GDP may have experienced positive growth during this period, export earnings either stagnated or grew negatively.

Interestingly, table 7.2 also contains information on the outflow of funds for the payment of Cuban labour. For the period these amounted to US$17.2 million, not an exorbitant sum compared to the phenomenal contribution of the Cuban government to the development efforts of the PRG. The table also calls attention to the importance of services and remittances in the Grenadian economy. The offshore US medical school (established in 1977) consistently brought in approximately US$4 million every year of the revolution - amounting to a well-needed US$19.5 million for the period 1979 to 1983. Current transfers (of which a substantial part would represent private remittances from Grenadians working and living abroad) brought in an impressive US$49.8 million during this period.

As an indicator of the importance of foreign exchange to the economy and its associated fragility, it is important to stress at this point that even a substantial disruption in student inflows could precipitate a crisis in the Grenadian economy. The same is certainly true for migrant transfers, perhaps more so. Although difficult to measure, the magnitude of migrant inflows is believed to be substantial in the context of Eastern Caribbean economies, sometimes even exceeding the annual value of the economy's main export(s). The findings of Brana-Shute and Brana-Shute (1982) are worth noting at this point. In a random sample of 100 of the over 400 households in a village in St Vincent, the economic contribution of remittances was as follows: 26 households relied on remittances for at least 25 per cent of their support, 38 households received less than 25 per cent of their support in the form of remittances, and 36 households received no remittances. While 74 of the 100 households found the primary source of their support from the economic efforts of resident household members, only 31 of these received no

Table 7:2
Grenada: summary of balance of payments (1979-1983)

	1979	1980	1981	1982	1983
	(In millions of US dollars)				
Current account	-5.2	-13.3	-23.4	-33.7	-29.0
Merchandise trade	-25.9	-36.9	-41.7	-46.5	-45.7
Exports	(21.4)	(17.4)	(19.0)	(18.6)	(18.9)
Imports	(-47.3)	(-54.1)	(-60.7)	(-65.1)	(-64.6)
of which: airport	-3.6	-3.9	-6.4	-8.6	-8.5
Interest on public debt	-0.4	-0.5	-0.6	-0.9	-1.2
Other factor income	0.0	0.0	0.0	0.7	1.0
Travel (net)	13.0	14.0	11.2	10.9	11.6
Medical school	3.7	3.8	3.8	4.2	4.0
Cuban labour	--	-2.6	-5.2	-5.1	-4.3
Other nonfactor services	-4.2	-2.2	-2.2	-8.0	-5.2
Current transfers	8.0	9.6	10.4	11.0	10.8
Capital account	5.7	13.7	17.8	36.6	24.8
Official grants	6.9	12.7	12.9	16.7	12.8
Public borrowings	1.9	1.3	7.5	9.5	14.7
Commercial banks	-1.1	1.1	-0.9	9.5	-2.2
Other	-2.0	-1.4	-1.7	0.9	-0.5
Errors and Ommissions	-2.1	-0.8	-2.4	-2.6	1.9
SDR allocation	0.8	0.5	0.4	--	--
Overall balance	-0.8	0.1	-7.6	0.3	-2.3
Memorandum time	76.4	86.0	100.0	110.1	115.9
	(In per cent of GDP)				
Trade balance	-33.9	-42.9	-41.7	-42.2	-39.4
Current balance	-6.8	-15.5	-23.4	-30.6	-25.0
Overall balance	-1.0	0.1	-7.6	0.3	-2.0

Source: International Monetary Fund, 1984, p. 25.

remittances at all. In addition, although only four households were nearly entirely dependent on remittances, almost two-thirds of the households received some amount of cash from overseas. Finally nearly every household which did not receive cash from outside the island at the time of the survey has had a history of remittance contributions from current or former members (p. 277).

But as important as remittances and other services were, they were not sufficient to offset the huge current account deficit. As noted earlier by the PRG, grants and public borrowings thus took on added importance. With respect to the former a total of US$62 million poured into Grenada during the period 1979-1983, more than three times the value of the country's total visible exports for 1982. This substantial inflow was largely a consequence of the PRG's pragmatic foreign policies[15]. Cuba provided US$37 million of this sum. Other important donors were the European Development Fund (US$2.7 million), Iraq (US$7.2 million), the German Democratic Republic (GDR) (US$1.5 million), the Soviet Union (US$2.6 million), Algeria (US$2.3 million), and Syria (US$2.1 million). The amount of grants raised by the PRG dwarfed the paltry US$2.3 million raised by Gairy during the period 1975-1978 (IMF, 1984a, p. 28).

As the demand for funds soared and sources of grants began to evaporate public borrowings began to leap upwards. As seen from table 7:2, these moved from US$1.9 million in 1979 to US$9.5 million in 1982, and US$14.7 million in 1983. Loans from domestic sources also took an upward turn. In 1980 loans from domestic commercial banks amounted to US$1.1 million, but by 1982 they increased to US$9.5 million (see table 7:2).

The IMF and World Bank reports also offer insights into the structure of external loans contracted during this period. If we compare loans from the former GDR and the Soviet Union (loosely speaking, the socialist bloc) with those from western sources, an interesting picture emerges about the terms and conditions offered by both groups of countries. Loans from the Grenada Development Bank were typically granted for a period of 20 years.[16] The grace period was typically five years and the rate of interest four per cent. On the other hand, whereas loans from the GDR and USSR were contracted at a slightly lower rate of interest (i.e., 3.5 per cent), both the duration of the loans and the grace period were significantly lower. In the case of the GDR, the grace period was only one year. The GDR's loan of US$6,000 to the PRG was expected to be repaid within 9½ years. The grace period for loans from the former USSR was three years while repayment was arranged for a period of 13 years. This observation is significant, especially when juxtaposed with the unfavourable terms on which the GDR (and to a lesser extent the USSR) bought Grenada's bananas and nutmegs during a period when Grenada's agriculture was in acute crisis.

Grenada's external public debts had reached phenomenal proportions by 1983. These escalated from US$14.07 million in 1979 to US$33.7 million in 1982 and further to US$49.4 million in 1983. The potential severity of external debts become starkly evident when related to the value of Grenada's merchandise exports for this period. In 1979 visible exports were only US$21.4 million, and fluctuated narrowly between US$17.4 million and US$19.0 million for the rest of the period. In other words, external debts had more than doubled the value of Grenada's principal (merchandise) exports by 1983 (table 7:2). Indeed, commercial loans which were virtually insignificant in 1980 amounted to almost one third of total debt in 1983 (World Bank, 1986, p. 15).

Although the country's growing indebtedness was not regarded by the PRG as cause for alarm, both the World Bank and the IMF expressed concern. IMF figures show that the debt service ratio increased from a low of four per cent of GDP in 1979 to a high of 6½ per cent (of GDP) by 1983. The debt burden was expected to surge after 1983; most of the non-concessionary loans were not scheduled to be serviced until 1985. In 1985 it was expected to reach 24 per cent of GDP.[17] Besides, 'soft' loans were proving increasingly difficult to raise, making resort to non-concessionary loans imperative.

Given the increasing and persistent deficit on the public sector account during the period, one could only expect the debt burden to become more onerous. The overall deficit (after grants) climbed from EC$5 million in 1980 to EC$41.3 million in 1981, EC$55.8 million in 1982, and EC$55.9 million in 1983 (see table 7:3). Had it not been for a spate of much resented tax legislations (especially by the private sector) introduced in 1982 the public sector deficit would have been even more severe. Tax revenue peaked to EC$74.4 million in that year (table 7:3). Short of continued capital inflows from overseas on a very substantial scale (which, of course, was no longer forthcoming), a greater profitability of public sector enterprises (which was still lacking), a strong recovery of traditional agriculture and tourism as well as an increase of revenue from domestic sources on a more popular basis; only a severe curtailment of public sector expenditure could have ameliorated the alarming public sector deficit.

In fairness to the PRG, they had managed to maintain some control over current expenditure (table 7:3). Between 1979 and 1982 current expenditure increased marginally as follows: EC$53.9 million in 1979, EC$59.6 million in 1980, EC$64.4 million in 1981 and EC$71.6 in 1982. But the situation was different in the case of capital expenditure which, again, was absolutely consistent with the development strategy of the government. These escalated from EC$26.5 million in 1979 to EC$37.5 million in 1980, then to EC$74.8 million in 1981, and a record level of EC$103.6 million in 1982 (table 7:3).

Table 7:3
Grenada: summary operations of the central government (1979-1983)

(In millions of Eastern Caribbean Dollars)

	1979	1980	1981	1982	Preliminary 1983
Current revenue	55.1	57.7	63.0	74.4	81.3
Tax revenue	49.2	51.6	54.3	65.8	70.4
Non-tax revenue	5.9	6.1	8.7	8.6	10.9
Current expenditure	53.9	59.6	64.4	71.6	79.6
Current balance	1.2	-1.9	-1.4	2.8	1.7
Capital expenditure	26.5	37.5	74.8	103.6	92.2
Overall deficit	-25.3	-39.4	-76.2	-100.8	-90.5
External grants	18.6	34.4	34.9	45.0	34.6
Overall deficit after grants	-6.7	-5.0	-41.3	-55.8	-55.9
Financing	6.7	5.0	41.3	55.8	55.9
Net external borrowing	9.1	4.4	41.5	24.2	38.8
Concessionary loans	(5.0)	(3.5)	(19.9)	(18.6)	(10.9)
Non-concessionary loans	(--)	(--)	(--)	(6.3)	(27.7)
IMF purchases (net)	(1.2)	(--)	(15.6)	(-2.4)	(3.2)
Other external borrowing	(1.9)	(0.9)	(6.0)	(1.7)	(-1.5)
Net domestic borrowing	-2.4	0.6	-0.3	31.6	5.4
Commercial banks	(-2.8)	(-4.6)	(1.2)	(29.0)	(--)
Other domestic borrowing	(1.4)	(5.2)	(-1.5)	(2.6)	(--)
Build-up of arrears	-	-	-	-	11.7

(In per cent of GDP)

	1979	1980	1981	1982	1983
Current revenue	26.7	24.8	23.3	25.0	26.0
of which: tax revenue	23.9	22.2	20.2	22.1	22.5
Current expenditure	26.1	25.7	23.9	24.1	25.4
Current balance	0.6	-0.9	-0.6	0.9	0.6
Capital expenditure	12.8	16.1	27.7	34.8	29.5
Overall deficit	-12.2	-17.0	-28.3	-33.9	-28.9
External grants	9.0	14.8	13.0	15.1	11.1
Overall deficit after grants	-3.2	-2.2	-15.3	-18.8	-17.8
Financing	3.2	2.2	15.3	18.8	17.8
Net external borrowing	4.4	1.9	15.4	8.2	12.4
Net domestic borrowing	-1.2	0.3	-0.1	10.6	1.7
Build-up of arrears	-	-	-	-	3.7

Source: *International Monetary Fund,* 1984, p. 11

Both the IMF and the World Bank agreed that there was a significant measure of success on these two fronts, although doubts have been cast on the magnitude of the fall in unemployment. IMF figures reveal that the inflation rate fell consistently during the PRG's rule; it fell from 21.2 per cent in 1980 to 18.8 per cent in 1981, 7.8 per cent in 1982, and 6.1 per cent in 1983. This accords with the trend depicted by the PRG, though the figures used by both sources are different especially in the case of 1981.[18] The World Bank and IMF attributed the fall in inflation to the government's price control policies, the suppression in the rise of oil prices, increases in the supply of domestic produce, and the appreciation of the Eastern Caribbean dollar *vis-à-vis* foreign currencies (World Bank, 1984, p. 17).

There is also some evidence from the World Bank Report to suggest that there was some truth in the PRG's claim that the social wage was substantial. The preliminary 1982 World Bank Report thus cautioned: 'The rate at which new social benefits such as those in education and health are introduced requires the attention of the government, as does the number of new public sector initiatives in areas which can be left to the 'private sector' (World Bank, 1982a, pp. 17-18).

However, there is less consensus on the thorny question of unemployment. To begin with neither the World Bank nor the IMF would categorically accept the PRG's assertion that the unemployment rate was 49 per cent at the time when they took power in 1979. As the World Bank put it: 'The available data on the Grenadian labour force is inadequate for analyzing trends in employment and unemployment over the period 1975 through 1982' (World Bank, 1984, p. 17).

Indeed, doubt existed about the size of the population, let alone the size of the labour force. A population census carried out in 1981 put the population at the end of that year at 88,175. An earlier official estimate (based on birth and death records and immigration data) put the figure at 197,000 for 1981. A sample survey carried out by the University of the West Indies in October 1980 put the unemployment rate at just over 27 per cent of the labour force (World Bank, 1984, p. 17). For 1981 the IMF cited a similar figure. In April 1981, it is also noteworthy that Coard told delegates at the Aid Donors Conference in Brussels that unemployment in Grenada stood at 35 per cent. A reasonable inference is that the unemployment rate was somewhere between 27 and 35 per cent, at least up to April of 1981. Could it have fallen so drastically (to 14 per cent in April 1982), as claimed by the PRG? The World Bank's answer was simple and straightforward: 'one is unable to verify whether this was so, since the last unemployment survey report available was published in October 1980' (World Bank, ibid., p. 19).

Similarly, the IMF argued: 'no comprehensive labour survey has been undertaken to back this estimate' (IMF, 1983, p. 19).

Yet, within PRG circles, it has been claimed that the unemployment rate continued to fall during the rest of the PRG's tenure.[19] And this was despite the cash-flow crisis which severely disrupted economic activities from 1981 onwards.

A verdict

Ideally the best way to resolve the controversy on the economy is to gather the statistics from scratch and recompute the appropriate figures for the contentious areas - notably economic growth (as measured by real GDP) and unemployment. But since this feat is beyond the scope of this study, the most that we can do is to qualify some of the claims and arguments made in the various reports, especially when it is clear that statistics have been abused to support ideological positions.

Starting with the unemployment problem, it has already been established that it was likely to be between 27 per cent (based on the survey carried out by the University of the West Indies in October 1980) and 35 per cent (based on the figure Coard quoted at the Aid Donors Conference in April 1981) for much of 1981. Yet it was claimed in April of 1982 that the rate had fallen to 14 per cent. This was clearly an exaggerated claim. Many jobs were obviously created during this period, if only because of the phenomenal level of capital expenditure undertaken by the public sector. But since expenditure was concentrated on the construction sector, it follows that most of the jobs created under the PRG were of a highly seasonal nature. Thus returning to Coard's earlier remark one wonders whether the workers who built the schools in Bonaire, Florida and Corinth, feeder roads, buildings, etc., were able to find jobs once these projects were completed or interrupted on account of severe cashflow problems. If alternative (or continued) employment could not be procured then it would be misleading to conclude that an effective panacea was found for unemployment.

The question of cashflow problem deserves emphasis at this point. As already noted the multitude of projects initiated by the PRG, coupled with managerial weaknesses of many state enterprises and a host of other endogenous and exogenous factors, meant that it was impossible for the PRG to sustain all its projects financially. The airport was the only project that was regularly sustained, given its highly symbolic nature and the PRG's determination to complete it in time for the fifth anniversary of the revolution in March 1984. So severe was the liquidity problem that dues and subscriptions to regional and international organizations such as the UWI, OECS, UNESCO, PAHO, etc., went unpaid; a situation reminiscent of the

Gairy era.[20] The state of public finances during this period thus provides some indirect insights into the unemployment situation. A further clue is given by the growth pattern of private consumption expenditure for this period. The slow growth in private consumption suggests that a permanent dent was not yet made into the unemployment situation. Private consumption stood at EC$156.4 million in 1979, EC$192.4 million in 1980, EC$215.2 million in 1981, EC$244.7 million in 1982 and EC$256.5 million in 1983 (IMF, 1984a, p. 3).

The data provided by the 1981 population census is also illuminating in this regard. As previously noted, the census put the size of the population at 88,175 in 1981 and projected an increase to 90,908 in 1982. It also recorded a net outflow of 3,515 Grenadians for 1981. This migration haemorrhage, by definition, meant an improvement in the unemployment situation; although, surely, this cannot be a desirable way of ameliorating unemployment, especially when large numbers of those migrating emanated from the professional strata.[21] As a result of this 'brain drain' Grenada experienced a situation of acute labour shortage in the case of those jobs which required skilled personnel. Technocrats and others with higher level skills thus poured into Grenada during this period, many motivated by ideology and the prospects of amassing large sums of money.[22] In an effort to increase the supply of skilled labour a programme was funded by the UNDP in 1979 to attract highly qualified and experienced expatriate Grenadians back to the island. It was hoped that they would be lured by the substantial remuneration and fringe benefits which were on offer (see Project Document, UNDP, GRN/79/001/A/01/131).

Before leaving the unemployment issue, the question of productive and unproductive employment must also be raised. It is wellknown that large numbers of young people were recruited in the People's Revolutionary Army, the Militia and other NJM mass organizations. Although they were doubtless performing an invaluable service for the party, counting such persons as 'employed' did nothing more than create a distorted picture of the employment situation. This became patently clear after the October upheaval when some 3,000 soldiers and hundreds of full-time militia members were returned to civilian and 'non-political' life to boost the ranks of the unemployed.[23]

Although job opportunities increased in the public sector between 1979 and 1983, it should also be borne in mind that (contrary to what the PRG claimed) this situation did not hold true for the private sector as a whole. The reasons for this were explored earlier in chapter six. Suffice to recall that the crisis in tourism and agriculture, as well as the low morale and loss of business confidence among the private sector, were at the heart of the sluggish performance of the private sector. The 'working class labour laws' and militancy of the trade unions during this period, also operated as a constraint on expanded employment in the private sector.

As for the claim about living standards, the PRG was largely correct when it affirmed that they had succeeded in improving the welfare of Grenadians. This was largely the result of their initiatives (and external assistance received) in the critical areas of health, education and housing; areas which were in an appalling state before 1979. The government could now boast that Grenadians had access to many services which were nonexistent in other OECS states. For example, it was the only country in the OECS with a neurologist and a house repair programme. But an important qualification needs to be introduced here. The improvement in the 'social wage' was not as steady and consistent as Coard's remark would have us believe. Besides, Grenadians attached less importance to a social wage than what they attached to a traditional wage or money in their pocket. Although they welcomed the benefits which constituted the social wage, it was felt that this was a natural part of the responsibilities of the state anyway. Many were still disillusioned since it was clear to them that the social wage had virtually frozen since early 1981. The growing difficulties of mobilising external aid meant that benefits could not be delivered at the rate they were dispensed in the first 2½ years of the revolution. The people could not understand this slowdown since PRG activists had constantly reminded them that the revolution was for sustained material betterment. Their earlier gains only served to whet their appetite, an appetite which swelled with the government's propaganda and which became increasingly difficult to satisfy.

The 1986 UWI survey

A survey carried out by a team of researchers from the University of the West Indies (Cave Hill, Barbados campus) in 1986 provides some useful insights into the way Grenadians felt about important aspects of their material welfare under the PRG[24]. The main findings are summarised in table 7:4.

The respondents exhibited mixed feelings about the PRG's trackrecord; with only 53.7 per cent expressing the view that conditions had improved **in general**, 27.5 per cent felt conditions had remained the same, and the other 19.8 per cent felt they had got worse. With respect to specific PRG programmes and policies, the highest level of support went to electricity (86.7 per cent felt it improved), advancement of women's rights (85.2 per cent), housing (82.9 per cent), and agriculture (77.6 per cent). The lowest level of support went to freedom of speech (only 22.4 per cent felt it improved), water services (39.6 per cent), and roads (50.7 per cent). Among those who were most likely to say that things under the PRG had improved were young people, unemployed people, the better educated, males and

Table 7:4
Conditions which improved, remained the same,
or worsened under PRG

Factors	Improved	Same	Worse	Total N
Roads	50.7	24.0	25.3	379
Water	39.6	50.3	10.1	376
Electricity	86.7	9.0	4.3	376
Housing	82.9	11.5	5.5	365
Employment	69.4	18.3	12.3	366
Agriculture	77.6	14.6	7.8	335
Freedom of speech	22.4	17.2	60.3	343
Legal rights	60.9	13.9	25,2	294
Women	85.2	9.2	5.6	337
Other	71.9	12.5	15.6	32

Source: P. Emmanuel et al., 1986, ibid., p. 26

supporters of the Maurice Bishop Patriotic Movement[25] (Emmanuel et al., 1986, p. 27).

Although the survey did not collect information about income distribution under the PRG, it is probable that there was also some improvement in this area. Since there was some improvement in the unemployment situation (whatever the correct percentage may have been), and given the land reform policies of the state as well as its significant ownership and control of vital economic resources, then it follows that (on balance) the gap between the 'haves' and 'have-nots' would have narrowed somewhat. Although the extent of the reduction is uncertain, it is not likely to be substantial since the structure of wages by industry and occupation did not alter radically under the PRG. Wages for workers in the agricultural sector continued to lag behind those working in banks, offices, government departments, and the urban areas in general (Government of Grenada, 1983e).

As for the area of structural transformation, an important start was made by the PRG. This is reflected in the new crops and economic activities which were introduced and promoted, particularly agro-industries. The new trading links and economic relations which were established with non western countries are also worth mentioning. It is a moot point, however, whether the costs of these new relations outweighed the benefits derived from them. Among several other factors, such a calculation would have to take into consideration a number of findings already noted in this study. These include: (i) the hostility and indifference received from the United States and other Western countries; (ii) the dislocation of the tourist industry given the substantial fall in visitor-arrivals from traditional sources; (iii) the non-response of private foreign capital to the PRG's investment code; (iv) the evaporation of aid from non-western countries after the first 2½ years of the revolution; (v) the inability/failure of the socialist countries to absorb Grenada's exports on terms at least commensurate with those offered by the West, and the uncompetitive and minuscule size of their loans *vis-á-vis* western sources.[26]

Returning to the non-traditional products which were introduced and developed by the PRG, we have already established that they brought in desperately needed foreign exchange - especially at a time when tourism and traditional agricultural produce were making the young, inexperienced revolutionaries only too conscious of the **real** meaning (and consequences) of dependency and underdevelopment. But the inability of these exports to bring in foreign exchange on the scale required by the PRG, and their overwhelming and persistent reliance on **external** assistance shows just how far the PRG had left to travel before structural transformation and many of the other lofty goals of the revolution could become a reality. Even if their time was not cut short by the events of october 1983, it is doubtful whether these could have been achieved in the medium term.

Arguably the picture would have altered significantly had the PRG de-emphasised expenditure on the international airport and promote non-traditional industries on the scale it promoted the airport. It was this subordination of other sectors to the construction of the airport which the US President found 'illogical' and 'sinister'. In May 1983 President Reagan was led to remark: 'Even if we take the PRG at its word, it must remain incredible that there is no guile in the size of that Government's spending on the airport which is twice as much as expenditure on State enterprises, six times as much on agriculture, 20 times as much on education or 40 times as much on health and housing. Surely, the airport could not be that predominant a creator of national wealth or source of social remedies and facilities' (cited in *The Trinidad Guardian*, 14 May 1983, '*Sinister Airport?*').

Grenada's suicidal resort to the IMF

The PRG's resort to the Fund in 1983 was a sure sign of the faltering state of the economy by that time. In particular, it reflected the liquidity problem which engulfed the economy and the government's inability to mobilise resources from external and domestic sources on congenial terms to implement its various capital and social welfare programme.[27] Claremont

224

Kirton, a Consultant on Economic Policy and Economic Planning to the PRG between 1980 and 1983, argues that the PRG had other motives for turning to the IMF at this particular juncture. These included the belief that 'once an IMF 'seal of approval' was granted to Grenada ... a much more favourable 'economic climate' would exist allowing for increased levels of participation of both domestic and foreign capital in the country's development efforts'. The government was also of the view that its bargaining power would be greater if it approached the Fund before the crisis manifested itself fully.[28]

Whatever the motive may have been, the 1983 IMF package was unprecedented. Unlike the one-year standby arrangement in 1981 which involved only EC$9.25 million, a total of EC$39.7 million was negotiated in this later arrangement. The leverage of the Fund in dictating how these funds should be utilised was comparatively strong given the crisis in the economy. The lion's share of the EC$39.7 million, i.e. 75.6 per cent, was to be used to address what the IMF diagnosed as the main problem-areas of the economy, viz, the parlous state of the resources of commercial banks, the growing indebtedness of the government, and the stifling of the private sector. The rest was earmarked for the government's investment programme.

The conditions imposed by the Fund were geared in the main towards reducing the twin-financial disequilibria in the economy, i.e., the public sector deficit and the widening balance of payments deficit. This was the principal manifestation of the economic crisis - a crisis which the Fund attributed to the political complexion of the regime, its over-ambitious public sector investment programme and other endogenously created factors. The PRG, on the other hand, attributed the crisis to exogenous factors, such as the dislocation of the island's tourist industry by external aggression and propaganda and the recession in the world economy.

Among the conditions stipulated by the IMF were: (i) a reduction of the government in foreign trade activities (particularly its control of essential imports through the activities of the MNIB); (ii) the introduction of new and increased tax measures to augment government revenue; (iii) ceilings on the contraction of further commercial loans from both external and local sources; (iv) lower limits on the net foreign asset position of state-owned commercial banks; (v) wage restraints for public sector workers and a trimming of government expenditure levels, especially on programmes deemed to be 'non-productive'.[29]

Had it not been for the expertise of the team of negotiators which the PRG sent to Washington, the terms and conditions would have been even more stringent. Bernard La Corbiniére, budget officer under the PRG's administration, stressed the importance of **preparation** when interviewed as part of this study. He pointed out that the staff at the Ministry of Finance were fully aware of the type of issues which would dominate the discussion.

A stiff battle was expected so they armed themselves with facts and figures about the Grenadian economy as well as other regional economies[30]. Referring to the hard discussions which took place, the PRG had this to say:

> At the recent IMF meeting, unofficial reports indicate that the deliberations on Grenada's loan request created history in two major respects. The deliberations were the longest ever in the history of the IMF, much longer than it took the IMF to approve five billion (US) dollars for Mexico and six billion dollars (US) for Brazil. This is itself a clear manifestation of the US attempts to block IMF assistance to Grenada. Secondly, the deliberations on Grenada's application was the first such in the history of the IMF, on which every single member of the Executive directors spoke - an indication of the tremendous battle which took place within the IMF on little Grenada (*Free West Indian*, 21 September, 1983).

Inspite of the bargaining capability of the PRG's team and their resoluteness in putting forward the government's case, the package they left Washington with could not be regarded as entirely satisfactory. For the most part the conditions ran counter to the government's development strategy, and limited its latitude in promoting structural transformation. Further tax measures would most certainly have heightened the tensions and conflicts (which were already fever-pitched) between the government and the private sector. Since the incidence of these taxes was to be shared by all consumers, we can also expect increased tax measures to have had an adverse impact on the relationship between the government and other social forces (particularly workers and small farmers) on which it relied for political support. Already relations between the two were strained, partly as a result of the halting of several projects and programmes which had previously brought these groups considerable social and economic benefits.

The imposition of ceilings on government borrowing, wage restraints, reduction of government expenditure, and the restrictions on the controversial MNIB were just as detrimental. Although the curtailment of the role of the state in foreign trade (particularly imports) was likely to improve the relationship between the government and Grenada's comprador bourgeoisie, the gains here would have had to be counterbalanced against the resultant losses to beneficiaries (e.g., consumers who benefitted from reduced prices of basic goods from the MNIB, and foreign exchange savings from bulk buying). Apparently the PRG were of the view that the losses would have outstripped the gains. This explains why their team of negotiators argued so vociferously (though unsuccessfully) for the preservation of the MNIB as defined and organised by the revolutionary government. Referring to this IMF conditionality, Kirton writes: '(it) not only complicated the discussions

226

surrounding the preparation of the *Letter of Intent* but also threatened the entire "negotiations", in fact, this particular precondition was the subject of long and detailed discussions not only at the technical but also political level' ('Grenada's EFF Programme', p. 15).

Kirton also noted the relative unimportance of balance of payments issues, particularly currency devaluation, in the case of Grenada's Extended Fund Facility arrangement. This was one significant way in which this programme differed from standard IMF stabilization programmes. The reason for this departure from IMF orthodoxy has already been broached in Chapter six, i.e. the fact that Grenada lacked a national central bank. It could not alter the exchange rate of the Eastern Caribbean dollar singlehandedly. Notwithstanding this institutional bottleneck, the Fund insisted that the regional currency was overvalued 'and further recommended that Grenada take the initiative in mobilising other regional member states of the monetary authority (by then, a Central Bank) to review the regional exchange rate level'.[31]

If Grenada had had a national central bank the IMF would doubtless have insisted on instituting this measure, i.e. devaluation of the national currency. And as Michael Manley's experience with the IMF in the 1970s revealed clearly, devaluation can be an effective tool for dislocating an ailing economy and destabilizing a government.[32] The absence of a Central Bank was thus a blessing in disguise for Grenada. Without a central bank it was also more difficult for reactionary forces to sabotage the economy by devious means such as flooding the country with counterfeit money in the hope of undermining the value of the local currency.[33]

What emerges from the foregoing analysis is that by the end of 1981 the PRG was presiding over a faltering economy which showed no signs of abating. Not only were the balance of payments and public sector deficits getting wider, but increasingly the government became obliged to resort to measures which ran counter to its philosophy and the political\strategic requirements of the path of development it sought to chart. Its recourse to the IMF on the scale it did in mid-1983, an institution notorious for subverting the economic strategy of progressive regimes, was clear evidence of the severity of the crisis which engulfed the Grenadian economy. Equally symptomatic of the crisis was a set of domestic measures introduced in 1982. These included a spate of unpopular tax measures, rate increases on public utilities and a raising of the special deposit requirement of commercial banks from ten per cent to 20 per cent. As we have already seen, these measures did much to impair the relationship between the private sector and the PRG; a relationship which was tense and uneasy almost from the very outset, but became worse once the contours of the government's ideological orientation crystallised.

227

Although the PRG's reports on the economy (published largely for public consumption) failed to admit that the economy (and hence their entire development model) was in severe trouble, the documents confiscated by the United States in October 1983 reveal clearly that all was not well as the PRG would have us believe. The next section uses these documents to throw light on the crisis in the economy, and its political consequences.

Crisis of the party, the economy, and the October showdown

The finding that there was a parallel crisis on the economic front is significant in itself. It may be argued further that there was, indeed, some connection between the economic crisis and the crisis which developed in the party. The latter culminated into the tragic events of October 1983 and the re-assertion, in its wake, of what Thorndike (1985) calls the 'West Indian condition'.[34] The quest for the application of firm Marxist-Leninist measures was believed to be, curiously enough, the appropriate solution to the problems which the revolution faced on the economic and political fronts.

The political problems included the growing unpopularity of the revolution among the masses (as reflected in part by their poor and irregular attendance at meetings organised by the NJM and their indifference towards the mass organizations), opposition and even open resistance from the local bourgeoisie and the church, and mounting external pressure (particularly from the United States). It should be stressed that some of these problems (especially the weakening in the party's links with the masses and the despondency of the business sector) were fed, to a considerable extent, by the adverse developments in the economy. This judgment is largely based on the government records which were captured by the US marines.[35]

Line of March - September 1982

Significantly, issues relating to the economy surfaced on more than one occasion in the intense debates which took place in the NJM after the party's critical *Line of March* meeting of September 1982. On this occasion the economy inherited by the PRG was described as 'backward' and 'underdeveloped' with 'a very low level ... of technological and economic development in the country ... This low level of development of the productive forces in turn resulted in very underdeveloped class formations' (*Line of March*, pp. 32-33).

In this address, Bishop also spoke about the overwhelming petit bourgeois nature of Grenada's social structure and the almost complete lack of a working class interested in socialist solutions to their problems. In other words, Bishop was conceding that the objective realities in Grenada were not at all favourable to the construction of socialism. Accepting the classic thesis on the role of the working class in the building of a socialist society Bishop reiterated:

> We know this is so because the working class is the class that is always growing ... Again, it is the working class that is most prepared for organization and discipline because of having to work every day, having to arrive on time, having to engage in collective organization and collective bargaining in their trade unions and so on. The working class too owns no means of production, in fact owns nothing except their labour and therefore they are the ones who most of all have to fight to end the oppression that comes about as a result of the private ownership of the means of production which of course enslaves them ... and, finally ... because of their role in production (ibid., p. 36).

At this meeting the Grenada revolution was described as a 'national democratic anti-imperialist revolution'. Five tasks were agreed by the Central Committee for this stage. In order of priority, these were (i) popularising and sinking the ideas of Marxism/Leninism among the working class and working people (especially via socialism classes); (ii) the organization of the working class (principally by means of trade unions, mass organizations, sports, and culture); (iii) strengthening the Leninist character of the party (by recruiting the best elements of the working class and through developing the internal organization of the party); (iv) building the economy along the path of socialist orientation thus providing more material gains for the masses and laying the basis for the construction of socialism; and (v) developing the defence capacity of the state through expanding the militia and strengthening the influence of the party in the army (ibid., pp. 38-39).

These tasks made it clear that after more than three years in power the party had failed to make significant progress on the path they sought to chart. Nevertheless, it was believed that 'this Line of march will equip us to go into the field and to move rapidly to ensure that this first stage of the path we are on - the socialist orientation stage - is rapidly built. We believe that we have correctly defined the new tasks, required to handle the new situation that has developed'. The path chosen by the party was described as 'correct', indeed, the **only** correct one' and it was firmly believed that it 'would **certainly** bring us to our second major historical objective to seeing socialism' (ibid., p. 40, emphasis added). Party members were thus urged to become 'more professional, more disciplined, (and) more Leninist' so that the demands of the period could be met.

Bernard Coard's resignation

Then only one month after this major meeting came Bernard Coard's resignation from the party's Central Committee and Political Bureau, a decision which took some members of the party by total surprise. In retrospect, this move marked a critical turning point for from that time until October 1983 the party found itself locked into a series of fierce debates which it could not easily resolve.

At an extraordinary meeting which was convened by Bishop from 12-15 October 1982 to discuss Coard's resignation, Selwyn Strachan, Coard's spokesman at the meeting, told members that Coard's decision was taken from as early as April. The decision was mainly due to physical strain and overwork. 'Everyone was depending on him for everything especially in the area of the economy' (*'Central Committee Meeting'*, 15 September 1982 in Seabury and McDougall, p. 263). Given this overdependence on him he was concerned that should he pass away untimely the revolution could not sustain itself. The slackness and ineptitude of the Central Committee as well as the alleged undermining of his authority as Chairman of the Organising Committee were also cited as factors influencing his resignation. For these reasons he told the party that his decision was non-negotiable.

Coard was certainly not exaggerating when he noted (among his reasons for resigning) the extreme dependence on his technical skills for running the economy. Indeed, had he relinquished his post as Minister of Finance the problems in the economy would have been even more intractable. But such a development would be to the peril of the revolution as a whole, an utterly undesirable state of affairs. His withdrawal from the party, on the other hand, could only mean one thing: when problems developed in it to almost unmanageable proportions the obvious personnel to blame would be the decision-makers, particularly the chairman of the Central Committee. This, in turn, would have paved the way for a new leader, a leader who could hold the party together and defend the revolution against all threats and adversities.

The July 1983 plenary

The July plenary made it clear that these tensions in the party had reached fever-pitched proportions by mid-1983. It lasted for 6½ days, a marathon 54 hours. During this period, the party undertook critical investigation of every area of party, mass, and state work.

In the economic sphere, a host of problems and difficulties were highlighted - some of which were never publicly conceded. After analyzing the various sectors of the economy the following were noted: (i) continuous adverse effects of cash flow on capital programmes which have threatened to halt investment on critical investment projects as well as 'shaken the confidence of broad sections of the masses and provided the basis for some vicious rumours'; (ii) continued poor performance of the productive sectors of the economy, especially agro-industries, agriculture, tourism, and fisheries; and (iii) extreme difficulties in mobilising external funds and obtaining sums which were already promised. It was noted further that these difficulties meant that '1983/1984 will be difficult years and requiring maximum efforts of the party on the economic front hence the ideological work has to be stepped up to combat consequent difficulties that these two years will pose for us' (*Central Committee Report on the First Plenary Session*, 13-19 July 1983, in US State Department and Department of Defence, 1984, Document 110, p. 11).

Among the conclusions reached after deliberating these problems were (i) the establishment of a Ministry of State Enterprises to generate badly needed efficiency in the operation of productive and non-productive public enterprises; (ii) the continuation of the government's land acquisition policy; (iii) sending a Ministerial delegation to Libya to solicit funds; (iv) encouraging the private sector to explore opportunities in the area of investments by the 'Caribbean Basin Initiative'; (The Central Committee warned, however, that 'this area must be closely monitored by the party to ensure that the capitalists are not provided with an effective new base for covert activity by the USA'); and (v) ensuring that Grenada continues to receive solidarity from her CARICOM partners on the trade and investment position of the Caribbean Basin Initiative (ibid., p. 12).

Central Committee meeting, September 1983

The problems on the economic front received further elaboration in the three-day long Central Committee meeting of 14-16 September 1983. This meeting was to mark another critical turning point in the series of events which were to engulf the island.[36] All Central Committee members who were on state business overseas were instructed to return for attendance. In the event only two were absent, Hudson Austin and Ian St Bernard. No prior agenda was distributed and that offered by Maurice Bishop, Chairman of the Central Committee, was rejected on the grounds that it was 'lacking in focus'. The alternative offered by Chalkie Ventour was accepted. This agenda had three broad headings: (i) analysis of the party and revolution; (ii) analysis of the main problems confronting the Central Committee; and (iii) finding solution(s) for the way forward.

Significantly the 'comrades' at this meeting were of one accord that the revolution was in crisis. The general mood was summarised by Ewart

Layne's opening remark that: 'The revolution now faces the greatest danger since 1979. There is great dispiritiveness and dissatisfaction among the people .... The state of the party at present is the lowest it had ever been. The international prestige of the party and revolution is compromised' (*Extraordinary Meeting of the Central Committee* in US State Department and Department of Defence (1984), Document 112, p. 4).

So far as the economic dimensions of the crisis were concerned Layne went on to note 'We are faced with the tasks of managing the state sector in **great economic difficulties**, to build the economy in the face of tremendous pressure from imperialism' (ibid., p. 4; emphasis added). In more telling terms Leon Cornwall noted 'the honey moon period of the revolution is over. In the past 4½ years progress was seen in many areas and the masses were on a high, now the work is becoming much more difficult and complex' (ibid., p. 5). Cornwall noted further 'A striking feature in this period is the absence of the masses in the activities of the revolution because of the deep frustrations which exist.... All areas of mass organization work has fallen, which is related to our lack of perspective on how to implement solutions. The serious economic difficulties we face is also affecting the people' (ibid., p. 5).

Tan Bartholomew added 'The economic problems are not explained to the people and the church has grabbed a number of people in this situation.... The revolution has lost its ability to manners counters who are very active'(ibid., p. 7). He described the 300 'supporters' who attended an indoor rally in Sauteurs as 'a very weak turnout in the context of the amount of mobilisation done. **Mobilisers were actually chased in some areas**' (ibid., p. 7; emphasis added).

Chris De Riggs asserted 'there has always been a tendency for the party to pay very little attention to the economy which has relevance to the question of social benefits and the overall development of the revolution. The Central Committee needs to prepare lines of educating the people on the present situation with IMF and the present salary negotiations of the armed forces, the social problem still remains' (ibid., p. 8).

Phyllis Coard graded the mood of the party as one or even lower, and that of the masses as 1.5 (on a scale of five presumably). According to her 'All Programmes of the revolution are in a very weak condition, while propaganda work is still very bad.... The militia is nonexistent, the army is demoralised, the Comrades have genuine complains, growth in militarisation and **deep economic problem**' (ibid., pp. 8-9; emphasis added).

Prime Minister Bishop, too, voiced his concern about the state of the economy:

> We have not paid sufficient regard to the material base (of) the

country, changes in the economy, changes in social wages and the predominant petit bourgeois character of the masses and society as a whole, our propaganda positions have consistently fed economism. We have failed to point out to the masses that this period requires a number of sacrifices and if we are not prepared to build the economy through hard work we will not make it. We have to take the blame for the over-economic expectations of the people. We need to develop proper lines on these questions for the people (ibid., p. 10).

Fitzroy Bain, George Louison, and Unison Whiteman (though less forthright) also remarked on the state of the economy and the party and the impact this decline had on the mood of the masses. In Bain's words: '... the strongest supporters of the revolution are demoralised, the party has set too much high standards for the people, we had expected social benefits to do the work for us' (ibid., p. 6). In Louison's view 'sufficient weight has not been given to the objective situation and the problem in the economy which we have failed to explain to the masses'. Louison also voiced his shock at the state of the roads in the country which, according to him, 'is in the worst state it has ever been since the revolution' (ibid., p. 11). Whiteman echoed the same sentiments. 'The propaganda work', he said, 'has been too idealistic especially on the economy ... Too much time is spent on small issues instead of fundamental issues e.g. the church ... we also need to think of how to build and sustain the mass organizations in the face of economic difficulties' (ibid., pp. 11-12).

The conclusions reached at this extraordinary meeting are instructive. It was concluded that (i) 'There is a state of deep crisis in the party and revolution'; (ii) 'The main reason for these weaknesses is the functioning of the Central Committee'; (iii) 'The crisis has also become a major contributing factor to the crisis in the country and revolution and the low mood of the masses'; and (iv) 'The crisis has also been **compounded by the weakness in the material base, electrical block outs, bad roads, retrenchments and jobs as an issue**' ibid., p. 13, emphasis added).

Further evidence on the dire state of the economy comes from a letter (dated 26 September 1983) sent by the Prime Minister to Colonel Gaddafi. A desperate Bishop implored 'Our Revolution sees you, Brother Gaddafi and the Socialist People's Libyan Arab *Jamahiriya* as the **last remaining hope**, for providing the necessary finance to complete the international airport'.[37] The letter also spoke about the importance of this project in raising the prestige of the revolution.'Its completion and official opening on 13 March 1984, the fifth anniversary of our revolution will be a striking victory over US imperialism which has worked and continues to work relentlessly to stop the advances of the Grenadian revolutionary process' (Letter to Colonel

Gaddafi, 26 September 1983 in US State Department and Department of Defence, 1984).

The solutions proposed by Bishop to deal with these problems centred on five broad sets of measures, viz, (i) 'Find methods of improving the work of individual and collective leadership of the Central Committee'; (ii) 'The need to develop a perspective based on (Marxism Leninism) criterion to guide the work in the coming period'; (iii) 'Urgently find creative ways of deepening the links with, and work among the masses'; (iv) '... rationalise the work among party comrades, bearing in mind the ground swell of complaints of overwork and lack of inner party democracy'; and (v) 'The Central Committee need to develop structures for accountability bearing in mind that comrades are now demanding accounts from the party' (*Extraordinary Meeting of Central Committee*, pp. 13-14).

The joint leadership model

But for the most part these suggestions from Bishop fell on deaf ears. They did not go far enough. Calling on the Central Committee to take what he termed 'an honest, cold-blooded and scientific approach to save the party and revolution', deputy Minister of the Interior, Lt Col. Liam James, impressed the argument upon the meeting that: 'the most fundamental problem is the quality of leadership of the central committee and the party provided by Comrade Maurice Bishop' (*Extraordinary Meeting of Central Committee 14-16 September*, ibid., p. 14). James proceeded to propose what was apparently a well thoughout, ready-made solution, namely, the marriage of 'the strengths of comrades Maurice and Bernard in the form of a Joint Leadership' to arrive at the perfect leader (ibid., p. 21). It was claimed that Bishop's strength lay essentially in public relations work at home and abroad. Coard, on the other hand, was noted for his brilliance in organization and ideological development. In James' view the qualities possessed by Coard were precisely what was required for advancing the revolution at this stage.

Although the majority of the members of the Central Committee were in favour of the model of joint leadership there were some who had reservations about the proposal. George Louison, Unison Whiteman and Bishop himself were in this latter category. In Louison's view James' proposal was nothing more than 'a load of shit' (*Extraordinary Meeting of Full Members of Central Committee 25, September 1983*, in US State Department and Department of Defence, 1984, Document 113, p. 22). An indignant Louison asked 'How will it evolve?', 'what would it evolve to?' 'Is it a temporary or permanent feature?' (ibid., p. 32). Louison could not see how this proposal could actually help Bishop to overcome his weaknesses. Echoing the same view, Whiteman remarked: 'whenever a leader is missing qualities collective leadership and not joint leadership solves the problem' (ibid., p. 24).

For his part, Bishop could not come to terms with this baffling notion of Joint Leadership. Above all, he wondered about how it would be operationalised in practice, especially his 'own role and function in this model' (ibid., p. 36). Although the 25 September meeting ended on a high note with Bishop 'accepting' the model subsequent events revealed that the euphoria was shortlived. For on his return from Hungary and Czechoslovakia on 8 October (after a two week aid mission[38]) he reneged on his decision to accept joint leadership. From then on the crisis reached a point of no return; resulting in the placing of the Prime Minister under house arrest on 13 October, the incarceration of two of his staunchest supporters (Kenrick Radix and George Louison) on 16 October, the massacre of 'Bloody Wednesday' on 19 October, the imposition of a harsh four-day curfew by the 16-man Revolutionary Military Council (RMC)[39] on the entire population from 19-23 October, and the landing of the US-led forces on 25 October; dubbed by many Grenadians as 'rescue mission' day. This was a sure sign of the rejection of the revolution by the masses by this time. The euphoria that greeted it in the beginning had long since dissipated. Bishop's death was the last straw. Their mood was summed up in the slogan 'No Bishop, no revo'.

Interpreting the showdown

Opinions differ as to how to interpret the self-immolation of the revolution. Some observers have attributed partial blame on Bishop on the grounds that he should not have reneged on the joint leadership proposal. But to be fair to Bishop, he had harboured strong misgivings about the concept from the very outset; misgivings which were doubtless reinforced by the theoretical and practical doubts shared by his two travelling companions, Whiteman and Louison, who accompanied him on the aid mission to the Eastern Bloc. Fully aware of the Prime Minister's reservations, the Coards and the majority of the central committee membership stuck uncompromisingly to what they regarded as the 'solution' to the crisis encountered by the revolution.[40]

In an influential work on the rise and fall of the revolution, *Grenada: The Jewel Despoiled*, Professor Gordon Lewis rejuvenated the widely held view that the proposed joint leadership model was nothing more than a cover for Coard's preconceived plan for ousting Bishop from power. His 'resignation' from the central committee and political bureau a year earlier was the first phase of the operation. In Lewis' view the barrage of criticisms hurled at the Prime Minister by a large segment of the Central Committee and the armed forces was clear evidence of the success of Coard in manipulating this group of inexperienced revolutionary zealots, who invariably received their tutelage in Marxism-Leninism from Coard's study group Organization for Educational Advance and Research (OREL).

Referring to the plot, Lewis writes: 'The very unity and similarity of their arguments indicate a preconceived plan of action. Almost certainly it was masterminded by Coard, ambitious to become undisputed leader of the revolution (although conversations with knowledgeable Grenadians suggest that he was at times no more than a Macbeth pushed by his wife as Lady Macbeth)' (Lewis, 1987, p. 41). He argues further that the criticisms of Bishop's leadership and the general progress of the revolution were exaggerated by this ultra-left faction 'to paint a dismal diagnosis of the patient in order that they, as the doctor, could move to undertake radical surgery' (Lewis, ibid., p. 44).

There is much plausibility in this view, although it should be emphasised that Lewis has not produced sufficient evidence to support the case in its totality. So far as the alleged shortcomings of Bishop are concerned he is probably correct. For it must be recalled that only one year earlier, at the Extraordinary Meeting of the central committee (from 12-15 October 1982), members of the meeting did not regard Bishop's leadership to be so limiting as to warrant a change. An assessment undertaken by the Central Committee at that same meeting ranked his performance almost first-rate. Only one member was ranked above him and that was Selwyn Strachan, and even then Bishop earned the highest mark (100 percent) for 'relations with the masses' and tied with Strachan (90 per cent) in the area of 'work performance'. His lowest marks were recorded in the areas of 'discipline' and 'ideological level' for which he gained 50 per cent and 60 per cent, respectively (*Extraordinary Meeting of the Central Committee from 12-15 October 1982*, op. cit., p. 5). It is therefore doubtful that his performance in these areas could have dropped so abysmally in the space of only one year.[41]

Less plausible, however, is Lewis' arguments against the impending economic collapse. This is where Lewis' otherwise excellent volume is at its weakest, based as it is on partial and overselect data. To cite him:

> The prognostications about the economic collapse of the revolution seem unbelievable when compared with the available statistical evidence for the economic record of 1982-83. Coard ... had brought in comprehensive economic planning and had claimed that in 1982 the gross national product had grown by 5.5 per cent, corroborated by the World Bank report of that year. Statistics for 1983 on particular sectors were **equally encouraging**. ... It is true that foreign exchange assets accruing from exports declined in the vital traditional areas such as cocoa, nutmegs, and bananas, but ... all of the small island economies had achieved only minimal growth in 1982, due mainly to

the general worldwide fall in prices of primary commodities, certainly not the fault of any one island government. None of these indicators prove that the Grenada economy was on the verge of collapse. **What is more, the relationship between the public and private sectors remained buoyant, with both sectors enthusiastically working together**, especially in tourism promotion. Tourism in 1982 showed only a minor decline, certainly, much less than in the rival Barbados industry. ... There is nothing here to compare with the truly calamitous state, by comparison, of the Guyana economy (Lewis, pp. 42-43; emphasis added).

This conclusion is at variance with the findings which emerge from the present study on the Grenadian economy during the PRG's rule. The wealth of empirical evidence, drawn from various sources, which we have detailed above (chapters four to six) on the performance of the various sectors of the economy, and our examination of numerous macroeconomic indicators **for the entire period** of the revolution, clearly reveal that the Grenadian economy was in a parlous and crisis-ridden state. This conclusion was shared by both pro-Bishop and pro-Coard supporters alike, as evidenced by their various contributions at the Central Committee meetings examined earlier. In particular, the evidence marshalled in chapter six above makes it patently clear that it is grossly erroneous to say that 'the relationship between the public and private sectors remained buoyant with both sectors enthusiastically working together'. This was certainly not the case after the first year of the revolution when the political and ideological orientations of the NJM regime began to crystallise.

Further, although there is some credibility in Lewis' observation about the performance of other regional economies it should be noted that this type of comparison does not enlighten us in any way since it is made out of context. The process which was unfolding in Grenada had no parallel in the Commonwealth Caribbean. It was governed by a different set of economic and political dynamics. Therefore, conclusions obtained simply on the basis of straightforward comparisons of statistical data can be particularly misleading in this case.

In sum, by the latter part of 1981, the Grenadian economy was engulfed in a profound economic crisis. Although it cannot be claimed categorically that this was responsible for the parallel political crisis, it is clear that the former exacerbated the latter. In particular, adverse economic conditions did much to undermine the confidence of large segments of the population in the revolution. Significantly, in their intensive deliberations over solutions to the crisis, economics was completely subordinated to politics, as reflected in the party's insistence on firm Marxist Leninist measures. Even if the proposed joint leadership model had been accepted by the prime minister, and that the tragic events of October 1983 had not taken place, it is difficult to see how the economic crisis could have been averted. In all probability, the economy would have continued to bleed to death, thereby forcing the regime to rethink its development strategy. The IMF would have also helped to ensure this outcome.

Notes

1. The respective accounts are mainly contained in the following documents:

    (i)   People's Revolutionary Government, (a) *Report on the National Economy for 1981 and the Prospects for 1982* (1982), (b) *Report on the National Economy for 1982 and the Budget - Plan for 1983 and Beyond* (1983), (c) *Revised Economic Memorandum on Grenada* (1982), and (d) *To Construct From Morning* (1982).

    (ii) International Monetary Fund, *Grenada: Recent Ecumenic Developments* (1984).

    (iii) World Bank, (a) *Economic Memorandum on Grenada* (April 1982) (b) *Economic Memorandum on Grenada* (August 1982), and (c) *Economic Memorandum on Grenada* (volume 1, January 1984).

    Subsuming the IMF and World Bank accounts under the heading 'outside account' can be further justified by the fact that the World Bank relies overwhelmingly on statistics drawn from IMF source. Their documents, *Economic Memorandum on Grenada* (Vol. 1, 1984), which covers the entire tenure of the PRG Administration makes this clear.

2. See Government of Grenada, 1982g, p. 13. Was this another 'printing error'? Although this 'discrepancy' is not serious in this particular case (since no one can deny, or has denied, that the PRG revolutionised expenditure on productive infrastructure), it is significant when documents (especially those produced by the same source) are not internally consistent. This suggests that allowance must be made for a margin of error when interpreting more significant and sensitive data such as those on unemployment.

3. See Government of Grenada, 1982e, pp. 6-7. The figure for 1980 seems to be dubious. In any event, it is difficult to see how they arrived at this figure, especially since the table contained on p. 6 of this document notes that no data was available for growth rate in this sector for 1979. A data point for this year is obviously needed for purposes of comparison.

4.   For a 'semi-official' account of the various forms of destabilization which Grenada was subjected to during this period, see Chris Searle, (1983). Among those mentioned by Searle in the realm of 'economic destabilization' were: US' successful attempts to discourage the EEC from granting assistance to Grenada for completion of the international airport project, the US' insistence that Grenada should be excluded from the financial assistance which was given to the WINBAN territories in 1980 when the banana industry was almost dislocated as a result of hurricane and heavy rain, a US$4 million grant which was given to the CDB by the Reagan Administration on condition that Grenada should be excluded from the project; and the US' insistence that Grenada, Nicaragua, and Cuba should be excluded from the provisions of the Caribbean Basin Initiative (a US propelled 'mini-Marshall Plan').

5.   See Government of Grenada (1982e) for the data for 1980 and 1981 and Government of Grenada (1983e) for the data for 1982. Again we can detect inconsistency in the PRG documents. Thus the latter report records a figure of EC$146.7 million for the total value of imports for 1981, i.e. EC$13.2 million less than the figure originally stated.

6.   'Building The Economy', Interview by Chris Searle with Bernard Coard on Radio Free Grenada (RFG), 13 February 1983, Reproduced in NHM (UK), *Revolutionary Grenada: A Bid and Popular School*, (Spider Web, London, 1985), p. 43.

7.   Government of Grenada, (1983e), p. 6. Emphasis in the original.

8.   M. Bishop, 'Fight Unemployment through Production', speech delivered to the Conference on Unemployment, 28 June 1982, p. 1; in Bishop (1982a). Incidentally the title of this speech was one of the popular slogans in revolutionary Grenada.

9.   The origin of this Report is worth recalling at this point. See chapter six above.

10.   World Bank, 1982b, p. 18; emphasis added. The style of the language typically used by the World Bank can be illustrated with an example from their 1979 'Report on the Grenadian Economy'. Referring to the abysmal state of the treasury under the Gairy regime, it noted: 'Public Sector savings have been non-existent because of the **deteriorated state** of the Government's finances'. (p. ii) My emphasis. It is

difficult to see how any commentator on the Grenadian economy under the Gairy regime (especially in the late 1970s when corruption, mismanagement, and arbitrary financial administrative practices were at their peak) could discuss the state of the economy without making explicit reference to these corrupt practices. Yet the World Bank skilfully eschewed 'emotional' language, and ignored the fundamental causes of the 'deteriorated state' of the Government's finances.

11. One possible reason for the discrepancy may have been the use of a different base year for deflating GDP. The PRG used 1977, whereas the IMF and World Bank used 1980. Note, too, that there is a conflict, albeit not significant, between the individual entries contained in the tables provided by the IMF and the World Bank.

12. If 1983 is included this figure would fall to less than two per cent, since real GDP declined by 1.6 per cent in this year. The IMF attributed this fall largely to the disruptive effects of the October events. For this reason, the author has decided to concentrate on the years 1979 to 1982.

13. Central Statistical Office, St George's, Grenada, March 1987. Note the series began with 1981. This seems to imply agreement with the figures reported by the PRG for 1979 and 1980.

14. But unless new markets were found, non-traditional exports were also doomed, as a result of import-restrictions levied by the Trinidad and Tobago Government.

15. For a discussion on the foreign policy orientations of the PRG, see Payne (1985); and Gill (1984).

16 In the case of the feeder road project, the CDB loan was granted for as long as 25 years. Note the most favourable loan is defined as the one with (i) the longest period of repayment; (ii) the longest grace period; and (iii) the lowest rate of interest. We should also affirm here that the bulk of the funds disbursed by the CDB originated from Western sources.

17. IMF, 1984a, p. 28. According to data published in a later IMF Report, it did not quite reach 24 per cent. Estimated outstanding debt was US £47.5 million (or 92 per cent of exports) at the end of 1985 and the debt service payments for that year amounted to 16 per cent of export

proceeds and 22 per cent of current revenues. This unexpectedly 'low' debt service ration was a direct consequence of the substantial aid inflows from the US in the wake of the October Crisis (see World Bank, 1986, p.5).

18.   According to the PRG the rate of inflation in that year was 10.5 per cent, as opposed to the 18.8 per cent reported by the IMF and the World Bank.

19.   Claremont Kirton, adviser to the PRG between 1980 and 1983, claimed that unemployment fell to 12 per cent in 1982 - presumably the figure for the end of the year (see C. Kirton, 'Grenada's Extended Fund Facility with the IMF', p. 6).

20.   See *St Lucia Voice* 'interim gov't says after Inaugural Meeting: Grenada's Finances are Grim', (10 December 1983), p. 8.

21.   See R. Cole, *On the Problem of the Reverse Transfer of Technology (Brain Drain) and Human Resources in Grenada*, (undated and unpublished paper, Ministry of Finance, Grenada) for a discussion of the costs and benefits of the 'brain drain' phenomenon to Grenada. (This paper was written for the PRG.) The severity of the migration problem among skilled personnel during this period was emphasised by Mrs Beverley Steele, Resident Tutor of the UWI Extra-mural Department in Grenada. In an interview with the author, Mrs Steele noted that sine 1981 the Extra-mural Department has been unable to host its annual re-union party for graduates of UWI. According to her the graduates emigrated *en masse* as a result of both economic and political factors (Author's interview with Beverley Steele in June 1987).

22.   A significant number of these migrant workers were aligned to international development agencies and were often paid in US dollars. (Researcher's interview with personnel at the CDB and the Grenadian Treasury, May-June 1987). This huge differential in salaries and perks between expatriate workers and Grenadians was a constant source of tensions and resentment.

23.   Another major boost to the number of people unemployed since the derailment of the revolution came from the planned retrenchment of 1,800 workers from an estimated 7,000 monthly paid workers. These were to be retrenched on a phased basis. The first phase was

implemented in April 1987, at a time when thousands of school leavers were about to join the labour market. At the time of this retrenchment measure the unemployment rate was estimated by sources within the Blaize government to be 40 per cent. So unpopular was this move that a split developed within the government, resulting in the resignation of several cabinet ministers. These included Francis Alexis, George Brizan and Tilman Thomas. For further details see 'Grenada Faces Bleak Prospects', *Caribbean Contact*, June 1987, p. 6.

24. Emmanuel et al. (1986). The focus of the survey was wide-ranginging. In the authors' words it was 'designed to discover opinions and attitudes on a selected number of contemporary issues facing the society' (p. 2). These include questions about Gairy's Administration, different aspects of the PRG regime, attitudes to Grenada-US relations since the October crisis, performance of the Interim Government, and the 1984 General Elections. The study was based on a quota sample of 390 electors drawn from nine (of the 15) electoral constituencies in the island. This selection was largely based on their 'electoral histories' (Emmanuel et al., p. 4).

25. MBPM denotes Maurice Bishop Patriotic Movement. The Movement was formed after the October 1983 events, under the leadership of ex-PRG Cabinet Minister, Kenrick Radix.

26. A letter from Ambassador Richard Jacobs in July 1983 suggests clearly that the PRG had come to realise that their relation with the Eastern Bloc, particularly the Soviet Union, was not paying the sort of dividend which they had anticipated. To the Soviet Union Grenada was a small, distant country which was relatively insignificant to the overall correlation of forces. On the economic front, the limited (and non-strategic) resource endowment of the island meant that the Soviet Union had very little to gain from integrating Grenada into its economy via the Council for Mutual Economic Assistance (CMEA) - a place reserved for the USSR's closest allies (see Richard Jacobs, letter to Unison Whiteman, 11 July 1983, 'Grenada's Relations with the USSR' in United States Department of State and the Department of Defence, 1984).

27. *The Report on the National Economy For 1982* listed a total of 130 projects for which finance was being sought. Seventy-six of those was designated 'top priority projects'.

28. See C. Kirton, 'Grenada's EFF Programme with the IMF, 1983' and Government of Grenada (1983f) for further details on the nature of the 1983 Agreement between Grenada and the Fund.

29. These include the 'people-orientated' welfare programmes which were so pivotal to the government's development strategy. See C. Kirton, ibid., pp. 12-12 for further information on the conditions stipulated by the Fund.

30. La Corbiniére was also one of the technocrats which the PRG sent to Washington in August 1983 to negotiate the IMF programme. The researcher made contact with this talented St Lucian economist, now chief budget officer to the St Lucian government, in May 1987. Detailed discussions were held with him over several days on various aspects of the Grenadian economy under the PRG.

31. C. Kirton, ibid., p. 17. Kirton also noted that Grenada was pressured to accede to this request which also became formalised in the **Letter of Intent**. This move, of course, could have seriously impaired relations between Grenada and other OECS states.

32. This experience has been comprehensively documented by Girvan et al. (1980). See, especially, pp. 113-155.

33. Of course this is not to say that important social and economic achievements were not made. But did it require a commitment to soviet style socialism to achieve these? Wouldn't the model of social democracy be just as effective and, arguably, even more appropriate for Grenadian conditions?

34. See Thorndike (1985), p. 175. See, also, Sanford and Vigilante (1984); and Schoenhals and Melanson (1985) for detailed accounts of the October Crisis. For a comprehensive discussion of the role of law in the subsequent intervention/invasion in the US in Grenada see Davidson (1987).

35. Supporting evidence also came from the interviews which the author conducted with leading members of the PRG and personnel close to the party.

36. In George Louison's view, this meeting was clearly called to sling mud at particular members of the Central Committee, particularly

Maurice Bishop. See George Louison, interview, *Inter-continental Press*, 16 April 1984, p. 208.

37. Maurice Bishop, Letter to Colonel Gaddafi, 26 September 1983. Emphasis added. Bishop's letter noted that assistance was sought from Libya from as early as March. Yet six months later Libya took no steps to act, despite its earlier promise. This indicates the growing problem the PRG were having in mobilising funds from overseas.

38. Note the Prime Minister's absence from Grenada for as many as 14 days, in the midst of severe problems in the party, was clear indication of the pressing need for development assistance to mitigate the depression in the economy.

39. Significantly those who comprised the RMC were for the most part the very members who led the attack against the Prime Minister's leadership and his alleged 'petty bourgeois' traits.

40. As one source puts it 'There was no indication that the Committee was prepared to settle the crisis on any terms other than its own' (see Ambursley and Dunkerley, 1984), p. 74.

41. An interview given by George Louison, one of the few surviving supporters of the Prime Minister contains some very instructive remarks. Louison notes that Bishop's leadership was far from perfect. However, this was not the fundamental reason for the problem in the Central Committee: 'nobody wanted to admit that half of the problems within the party itself was the continued illness of a section of the Central Committee. The areas where there were substantial problems were the areas in which these people were either ill or not functioning'. Louison recounts that there were 'five or six members of the Central Committee who virtually lived in hospital over the past year'. See Interview with George Louison, *Inter-continental Press*, 16 April 1984, p. 209. The high incidence of illness among party members (largely resulting from overwork) was probably a contributing factor to Bishop's performance in the Central Committee. The tasks were numerous and the party cadres were comparatively few - for the paternalistic model of socialism which the NJM sought to impose on Grenadians.

8 Lessons for development

The Grenadian revolution was *sui generis*, it was the direct outcome of the phenomenon characterised in this book as 'Gairyism'. But once the revolution became a reality in March 1979 it was seen not merely as an opportunity to invert Gairyism but, more fundamentally, as a vehicle for constructing a new socio-economic model aimed at challenging all forms of colonial and neo-colonial domination. While 4½ years was not long enough to overcome these intractable problems, the Grenada revolution was far from being a failure. Moreover, there are a number of important lessons which can be learned from the revolution. The purpose of this concluding chapter is to draw key lessons from the PRG's development strategy for the Caribbean and wider Third World. As implied by the title of the chapter, the focus is on lessons for economic and social development.

The economic achievements

Lewis (1984) correctly argues that 'no examination of the Grenada revolution of 1979 to 1983 should end on a pessimistic note' (p. 10)[1]. The revolution was largely successful in the sphere of economics, though the same cannot be said for politics. We will summarise the economic successes before addressing the main political failures.

The PRG had succeeded in making a critical and encouraging start in the arduous task of economic reconstruction. It was resolute in its pursuit of policies geared towards achieving convergence in the pattern of domestic production and consumption *vis-à-vis* the country's resource endowment. The broadening of the country's export base was particularly impressive; as witnessed by the development of new products - eggplants, various types of nectar (tamarind, guava, banana, mango, soursop, pawpaw and coffee), pepper sauce, mango chutney, nutmeg jelly, nutmeg jam, guava cheese, and a range of fruit juices.

Positive steps were also taken to marry the idle resources of the commercial banks (with their well-known metropolitan biases) with the productive requirements of the national economy. The tasks of establishing a vibrant and dynamic agricultural, tourism, and manufacturing sector were also tackled with great enthusiasm and dedication. The findings of the 1981 Agricultural Census, for instance, were meant to provide the basis for government policies in this vital sector. Equally indicative of the government's plans for the transformation of the Grenadian economy were its *Tourism and Investment Codes*, as well as its programmes for the livestock and handicraft sectors. These plans emphasised indigenous resources, and could be seen as an attempt by the PRG to overcome the structural imbalance between production and consumption which remains an endemic feature of the Grenadian economy: it produces what it does not consume and consumes what it does not produce. And as Thomas (1974) argues in his celebrated work on socialist transformation in small, Third World economies 'It is (the convergence of) these relationships that give an economic system its internal autonomy and determine its capacity for sustaining growth and development' (p. 133).

Bold attempts were also made to diversify sources of imports, stimulate agricultural output, find new markets for exports, and new sources of aid. The Marketing and National Importing Board played an important role in restructuring Grenada's trade structure and stimulating agricultural output. Through bulk purchases and careful selection of suppliers, the MNIB succeeded in stabilizing the price of many imported goods, especially those which were mainly consumed by farmers and workers. To encourage exports, particularly export of non-traditional goods, the MNIB also provided a guaranteed market for farmers' output. Other complementary measures aimed at boosting agricultural output included provision of feeder roads, extension services, enactment of the Land Utilization Law (to bring idle land into production), measures against praedial larceny, and restrictions on agricultural imports which were in competition with local produce.

The near completion of the international airport, which had been on the national agenda since 1955, was a notable achievement. It should be recalled that the airport project was the centrepiece of the PRG's development strategy. Given the importance the PRG attached to it, it would not be unreasonable to use progress on this project as the critical performance indicator by which to evaluate the economic success or otherwise of the regime. Apart from its symbolic role, it was important as a catalyst for generating growth in the tourist industry and the other sectors of the economy. Its opening, Coard asserted in the 1983 budget, would constitute 'the beginning of a whole new economic era for our country' (p. 44)[2].

It is one of the ironies of the Grenada revolution that the PRG regime did not survive to realise the fruits of their labour in this regard. After the collapse of the revolution, there was a dramatic change of heart among many of those who were previously opposed to the airport. George Schultz, in February 1984, thus remarked: 'The question of completing the airport is very much on everybody's mind and it was discussed everywhere I went ... We expect to come to a conclusion about it soon. I must say, having landed there and looked around a little, it certainly is needed here and in one way or another, it will be completed' (cited in Ferguson, 1990, p.21). One year earlier, the US position was that 'Grenada is building a new naval base, a new air base, storage bases and barracks for troops, and training grounds. And, of course, one can believe that they are all there to export nutmeg ... It is not nutmeg that is at stake in Central America and the Caribbean, it is the United States' national security' (President Reagan, March 1983). The airport was a major factor in the growth experienced in the tourist sector after 1984; yet the PRG received no credit for this achievement. Popular calls for it to be renamed after Maurice Bishop have met with resistance from the conservative regimes which have been installed in power in the wake of the October 1983 events.   The PRG's social reforms were resoundingly successful. Their impact was felt in areas such as housing, health, and education. Many families benefited from the low cost housing project instituted by the regime and the various home improvement grants and loans which were available. Free medical and dental facilities were also provided for the first time in the island's history. Education was accorded a high priority; free primary and secondary schooling was introduced, together with help to those in need of books, uniforms, clothes and the like.   The diversification of international economic relations and of foreign policy in general was another cornerstone of the strategy to transform the economy. Stemming from the theory of non-capitalist development; the PRG's foreign policy stressed anti-imperialism and non-alignment, achievement of a New International Economic Order, promotion of world peace and co-operation, support for national liberation struggles, and pursuit of regional co-operation and integration.[3] Foreign policy relations were thus broadened to include non-traditional countries in Eastern Europe, Western Europe (France), Northern Europe (Sweden), the Middle East, Africa and Central America. Nearer home, the PRG developed a close alliance with Cuba which brought both ideological and material support. Technical assistance, scholarships, credit, aid, equipment, and (to a lesser extent) markets were provided by these new-found friends. To maximise these gains, attempts were made to maintain good relations with traditional partners in the West, but such efforts were often rebuffed.

248

The economic and political strategy of 'breaking away' from the geopolitical orbit of the West had its successes, as witnessed by the amount of aid and other material support which the PRG garnered from these new sources. An estimated US$140 million was raised in lines of credit, loans and grants during the period of the PRG's rule (Gonsalves 1985, p. 15). Had it not been for this support, many of the projects undertaken by the PRG could not have been started, let alone completed. The value of Cuba's assistance was particularly colossal. As Castro recounted in the wake of the US invasion of Grenada:

> The value of our contribution to Grenada in the form of materials, designs and labour in building the new airport came to US$60 million at international prices - over US$500 per inhabitant. It was as if Cuba with a population of over 10 million received a project worth US$5,000 million as a donation. In addition, there was the cooperation of our doctors, teachers and technicians in diverse specialities, plus an annual contribution of Cuban products worth US$3 million, or US$40 per inhabitant. It is impossible for Cuba to render material assistance on that scale to countries with significantly large populations and territories, but we were able to offer great assistance to a country like Grenada. Many other small Caribbean nations, used to the gross economic and strategic interests of colonialism and imperialism, were amazed by Cuba's generous assistance to that fraternal people. They may have thought that Cuba's selfless action was extraordinary; in the midst of the US government's dirty propaganda, some may have even found it difficult to understand (Castro, 1983 p. 102.)

The Soviet Union adopted a more cautious approach. As we have seen, the warm embrace which was expected from the Soviet Union did not materialise. Against the fondest wishes of the NJM leaders, Grenada was regarded by the Soviet Union as a small, distant island - located in an area of relatively low priority. Its small, fragile economic base (totally lacking in strategic resources) meant that it was not able to complement the Soviet economy to any significant degree. Given these realities, the Soviet Union calculated, quite correctly, that the costs of cultivating intimate relations with the NJM regime could prove to be exorbitant in both political and economic terms. This sober assessment contrasts sharply with the romanticism and adventurism which the PRG exhibited in the direction of their foreign policy. Openly defiant against the United States and strongly pro-Soviet, this foreign policy was to cost the government dearly. It certainly multiplied the odds against the regime charting the path of non-capitalist development successfully.

There are a number of lessons to be learnt from the way Grenada conducted its foreign policy during this period. First, countries in the region need to recognize the geo-political constraints they face, the fragility and vulnerability of their economies, and the close integration of their economies into the US market (especially their tourist industry). In seeking to cultivate new international relationships, there is a clear need to seek an accommodation with traditional partners. An accommodation cannot be worked out if unnecessary verbal attacks are hurled at countries perceived as the bastion of imperialism. Towards the last ten months of the PRG's rule, the regime came to realize that anti-US sloganeering was counterproductive. Thus when George Bush argued in December 1982 that the PRG regime was repressive and was effectively an Eastern bloc satellite, the government's response was uncharacteristically tactful. The response concluded with a promise to send a high level emissary to allay Bush's fears.[4] What a marked contrast to earlier anti-imperialist pronouncements such as the famous 'in nobody's backyard speech' in April 1979. Bishop's response to the criticism of his government by the then Barbadian prime minister, Tom Adams, in 1980 was also undiplomatic: 'Like an expectant dog barking for his supper ... he rushes in to please his new master Reagan like all good yard fowls by attacking Grenada' (Latin America Regional Report: Caribbean, RC-80-10, 5 December 1980).

Such offensive language is clearly counter-productive to any foreign policy aimed at structural transformation. By failing to manage geopolitics properly, the PRG were guilty of making some of the same mistakes which Manley made in the late 1970s. In both cases the foreign policy mistakes were to have a disabling effect on the economy - reduced aid inflows from western sources, negative press reports which helped to dislocate tourism, and attempts to block loans.

There is a further lesson here, for as Lewis (1987) argues the record shows that it is dangerous for Third World leaders to leave their home base unattended for too long. The frequent trips to distant places often give their opponents ample time to mastermind plots for their downfall. This happened in the case of Gairy's overthrow in March 1979. Ironically, it may well have been a factor in Bishop's downfall. In 1983 alone, trips were planned to visit Iran, Iraq, Algiers, Yugoslavia, Korea, Romania, Angola, Tanzania, Zambia, Kuwait, Saudi Arabia, Argentina, Brazil, Colombia, Austria, and Switzerland, Sweden, Hungary, and Czechoslavakia (Minutes of the Political Bureau Meeting of 5 January 1983). Judging the mood of members of the Central Committee on Bishop's return from Czechovslavakia, it is probable that the plot to strip him of real power was planned while he was on this mission to Eastern Europe.

Size and development

These radical domestic and foreign policies were pursued in a Lilliputian state; a mere 133 square miles (including the offshore Grenadine islands of Carriacou and Petit Martinique) with an estimated 110,000 people at the time of the revolution. At this point it is worth recapitulating the PRG's perspective on the issue of size and development. Though recognising the obvious limitations of small size - most notably narrow resource configuration, limited domestic market, dearth of skills (often exacerbated by migration), and problems associated with economies of scale - the PRG did not regard smallness, in itself, as a binding and effective constraint on economic transformation. Adopting the position of the New World Group (exemplified by Lloyd Best's celebrated essay 'Size and Survival') the revolutionary government regarded imperialism as the fundamental constraint.

The PRG's experience between 1979 and 1983 does lend some empirical support to this contention. The economic aggression and various forms of destabilization, aggravated by deteriorating terms of trade, to which Grenada was subjected were clear manifestations of the sinister side of imperialism and the peripheral position which it occupies in the world economy. Doubtless, these imperialist machinations and exploitative practices were far more debilitating in their effects on the country's developmental problems and prospects than the mere physical constraints of size. The carefully orchestrated campaign of 'propaganda destabilization' waged by the United States, for instance, severely reduced the autonomy of the state. In particular, it brought about a virtual dislocation of Grenada's tourist sector almost overnight. The impact of this dislocation on the economy as a whole was just as calamitous as a destructive hurricane or typhoon in a small island economy. But, unlike a hurricane, acts of external aggression and imperialist domination are 'man-made'. As such they can be avoided. Small countries have enough problems as it is without such unnecessary violations of their sovereignty. Above all, it was the constant violation of this principle (though aggravated by mistakes in foreign and domestic policy) which dogged the process which the PRG sought to develop.

The PRG challenged the assumption, which was so widely believed in the region, that small size was a 'problem', and necessarily meant helplessness in the conduct of economic affairs. The regime demonstrated unequivocally that a large measure of a country's economic performance (regardless of its size) depends on the type of policies it pursues. No country can be too small to increase (and ultimately maximise) the benefits from its available resources. Narrow resource configuration means that small countries need to rationalise the use of existing resources (financial, material, and human), rehabilitate all usable capital stock, establish linkages between the various sectors of the economy, and make concerted efforts to save foreign exchange (e.g., by the PRG's policy of encouraging Grenadians to 'buy local and eat local'; and the emphasis which the regime placed on self-help, community projects, and preventitive medicine).

The economic successes garnered by the PRG also show that there is some room for manoeuvre in the international economy, so far as modifying dependence is concerned. Even small countries have some latitude in the world economy. This evidence does not refute the substance of **dependency theory** and the **world system approach** of the Wallerstein-Amin-Frank tradition[5]. Rather, it offers important qualifications to the deterministic and pessimistic conclusions reached by such theories about the fate of peripheral economies. One is reminded of Lloyd Best's instructive remark that '... economic development is a problem of management - of timing, sequencing and manipulation in an unending effort to perceive or create, and, in any case, to exploit a multiplicity of little openings and opportunities'(Best, 1967, p. 30).

Countries, regardless of their size, have some latitude to influence economic outcomes. A lot depends on the policy options they pursue. Just as modern companies have to conduct **SWOT** analyses (i.e., an assessment of their strengths, weaknesses, opportunities and threats in the market place), if they are to compete effectively, so too do countries. The opportunities and threats are far from fixed; they will obviously vary with the buoyancy or otherwise of the world economy. What is needed is the ability to create, recognize, and exploit the little 'openings and opportunities' which are present within the domestic and international milieus amidst the various constraints. The economics of 'mendicancy' in many of these economies must be replaced by pragmatic and innovative policies, which are consciously aimed at influencing their destinies.

The significance of people

No country, least of all Caribbean and other peripheral economies, can afford to neglect the role which a highly skilled, adaptable, and well motivated labour force can play in the transformation of their economies. People are a key resource, whose importance is even more crucial in small, underdeveloped, service-oriented economies such as those in the Caribbean. If trends in advanced economies are anything to go by, it is clear that an area's human resources will become one of its most significant assets in future. For developing countries, the quality of its workforce will have direct implications for their capacity to (i) benefit from aid inflows; (ii) adopt or (more challenging) adapt new technology; (iii) use their limited natural resources to good effect; (iv) compete in markets where consumers are increasingly paying attention to quality and value for money; and (v) achieve self-sustaining development in an increasingly competitive world economy.

Perhaps more than any other government in the Commonwealth Caribbean, the PRG fully recognised the role of people in development. Their record on education and training policies speaks for itself. As noted before, education and training received high priority under the PRG, with as much as 22 per cent of the 1982-83 budget being allocated to education and training. This was further supplemented by external technical assistance. Whereas only three individuals had received university scholarships in the last year of Gairy's rule, as many as 109 received such scholarships in the first year of the revolution. In fact, the supply of university opportunities outstripped the demand for such education for much of the PRG's rule[6].

Initiatives such as the National In-Service Teacher Education Programme (NISTEP), the Community Day School Programme (CDSP), and the Centre for Popular Education (CPE) were original, and highly successful. Much can be learned from them in the quest to develop a skilled and well-motivated workforce, without committing vast outlays of money on training and education. The CSDP, for instance, bridged the gap between the world of work and the world of education. Skilled persons from all walks of life (including barefoot farmers) were brought into the schools to impart practical skills, thus helping to make the school curriculum more attuned to the needs of the economy. The PRG's insistence that 'education and training must be a continuous and lifelong process' is one which has found expression in the human resource development policies of a number of developed countries. For example, a similar theme is stressed in the National Education and Training Targets of the British government[7].

People figured prominently in the government's development strategy at another important level. As Lewis (1987) argues, 'it was not so much structure as spirit that made the revolution' (p.34). The mass organizations were the main channel through which the people were mobilised in the task of economic transformation. Their commitment and enthusiasm to this task waned only toward the end of the PRG's tenure in office. These organizations, especially the National Women's Organization and the National Youth Organization, were instrumental in co-ordinating support for voluntary projects. These included road repair programmes, house repairs and rebuilding, distribution of free milk, books, uniforms, etc. to remote villages, and other community projects. Labour was supplied by the people and raw materials were generally provided by the state. Most of this voluntary work was undertaken on week-ends, and was very popular among the beneficiaries.

Various schemes were introduced to encourage popular participation in the workplace. The repeal of anti-union legislations (such as the Essential

Services Act) and the creation of production, emulation, disciplinary, and grievance committees were all aimed at increasing worker productivity and participation. Through these committees, workers were encouraged to suggest ideas for eliminating waste, corruption, inefficiency and poor motivation. They were exhorted to 'work harder, produce more, and build Grenada'. Rewards were given for achieving production targets and for generating innovative ideas to raise productivity.

Strenuous efforts were also made to involve the people in the process of policy development and implementation. The budgetary process in 1982 exemplified the new political model which was emerging in Grenada. First, a draft budget was prepared by the government and presented to the mass organizations for discussion and comments on 29 January. This was followed up by a series of 25 Zonal and Workers' Parish Councils throughout the country in February. Another conference on the economy was held on 1 March to give Grenadians another chance to air their views or suggestions. Such consultations on areas which, in most societies, are the preserves of a handful of 'wise men and women' were seen as an important part of mobilizing the people in economic reconstruction. In contrasting the budgetary process in Grenada with the process in 'Old Mother England', the PRG noted:

> Every year we see the same ceremony of secrecy, with the Chancellor of the Exchequer hugging the tin box to his chest, then waving it daringly at the cameramen and newspaper reporters, but determined that nothing shall get out and nobody's eyes shall get in until the box is unlocked in Parliament. Then suddenly, with no participation or consultation with the people, the economy for the next 12 months is revealed and everything worthwhile is chopped! (Government of Grenada, 1982f, p. 8).[8]

Governments in the Caribbean clearly have a lot to learn from this politics and economics of mobilization and popular participation. The self-help schemes organised by the PRG through the network of mass organizations were particularly instructive. Resource constraints in small countries make it imperative to find cost-effective solutions to social and economic problems. The various repair and rehabilitation programmes could be seen as yet another attempt of the PRG to make the best use of its resources (in this case its people). It is difficult to see how dependency and other legacies from the past can be successfully tackled without effective mobilization and involvement of the people for the task of national development. Further, it must be pointed out that many of the community and other self-help projects initiated by the PRG are rooted in the traditions of Caribbean societies. What the PRG did was to formalise such practices; practices which are increasingly being swept away by the tide of 'modernization' and the prevalence of the market economy. The need for Caribbean governments to resurrect such traditions and incorporate them into their development strategies cannot be over-emphasised. Strategies based on indigenous values are more likely to succeed than those based on alien formulas, remote from the experience of the vast majority of the population.

Policy mistakes

Arguably more gains could have been made had it not been for certain inherent flaws in the formulation and implementation of the government's development strategy. The major shortcoming was the skewedness of the public sector investment programme, dominated as it was by one single project - the international airport. Had the PRG accorded the same priority to agro-industries, handicrafts, and non-traditional exports in general the economy would have been on a sounder footing and with a greater buoyancy. Correspondingly, the problems which faced the revolution in its last two years would have been less severe. As noted before, the performance of these sectors was very encouraging, but they all suffered from lack of finance.

This is not to say that the airport project was not necessary. It was a need long recognised by previous Grenadian leaders and aid donors. But since the PRG could not afford a new international airport in the first place perhaps it should have contented itself in the short-term with an upgrading of the existing facilities at Pearls as it had pledged in its 1973 manifesto. Alternatively, it could have opted to build the airport over a longer timescale. This would not only reduce the drain on the treasury but it is probable that the tensions between the government and both Washington and the Grenadian private sector would have been mitigated. As pointed out before, in its efforts to complete the project on time and faced with pressing economic problems, the government felt obliged to institute a number of stringent measures such as increased taxes, increasing the special deposit requirement of commercial banks, and introduction of airport bonds - all of which were unpopular amongst the private sector. And whilst paying such a high price for the airport, it should be stressed that an international airport, no matter how well-endowed to provide comfort for visitors, was not a sufficient condition for attracting visitors to Grenada as the PRG seemed to have thought.

Another critical flaw relates to the pace at which the PRG moved into the productive sphere of the economy in its proclamation to make the state sector dominant. Projects followed each other in rapid succession with very little thought, if any, given to the question of whether or not the state possessed the managerial, technical, and financial capacities to operate them

255

successfully. As a result of bottle-necks in all three areas, most of these state enterprises recorded huge deficits. To the private sector and other opponents of the government, these deficits were seen as symbols of failure.

The almost indiscriminate policy of revolutionary manners against those deemed to be 'counters' (many of them, without a doubt, were only critical) was also a fatal mistake. It brought about unnecessary alienation among substantial segments of the social strata on which the government's economic strategy relied for support. To the private sector, and members of the middle class in general, the infringement of civil liberties and the state's apparent monopoly of power confirmed many of their fears of socialism. As documented in chapter six, revolutionary manners, coupled with the bullying techniques used by the government to coerce the business class into the areas demarcated by the state for private sector investment, constituted the bottomline in the tense and uneasy relationship which developed between the PRG and the private sector. That this relationship could have been handled better deserves no emphasis. What danger was there, for instance, in allowing the private sector to publish its reports with news about business developments, locally and internationally?

It should be recalled that the private sector were generally supportive towards the revolution at the outset. The Grenada Chamber of Industry and Commerce went out of their way to appeal for calm, and to rally Grenadians and foreigners to support the revolution. The statement issued shortly after the insurrection described the way the coup was executed as 'civilised' and 'urged all members and all business people in Grenada to maintain a high standards of business ethics, and to co-operate with the government in all just and legal endeavours' (*Barbados Advocate*, 19 March, 1979). As a result of what economists call 'sunk' costs[9], governments (regardless of their political complexion) can safely assume that it is in the private sector's interest to co-operate with them, at least in the short-run. Experience shows that opposition and open confrontation usually come about when the interests of the private sector are threatened, and very little attempt is made to allay their fears and develop an accommodation with them.

With better planning and a more gradual and cautious entry into the productive spheres of the economy both the economic and political outcomes would have been eminently superior. The non-capitalist path of development is necessarily a gradual and prolonged process. Alliances have to be built with the various social forces which are critical to the success of the path. Socialist-orientated countries such as Angola, Mozambique, and Nicaragua during the reign of the Sandinista regime have shown just how difficult it is to build socialism in the absence of the skills and other resources of the private sector. Without their support the model cannot be successful. Hasty across-the-board transformations will make it impossible to develop an accommodation with the private sector.

The actions of the PRG contradicted their earlier admission that a large or total state sector approach was utterly impractical on account of low levels of technology, limited human resources, the lack of capital, and lack of market connections and expertise. The private sector viewed the rapid rate at which the PRG moved into the productive sphere of the economy as a clear threat to its class interests. Under these circumstances, it was difficult to work out an accommodation with the private sector. The problem was further compounded by the PRG's inability to demonstrate that it was better equipped to run the enterprises under the expanding state sector. Apart from the poor performance of most of the state enterprises, the records of the Central Committee show that the lack of managerial and organizational skills was a problem which also constrained its own inner party life[10].

Apart from domestic policy, mistakes were also made in the design and execution of foreign policy. Pledging support to a number of repressive regimes (e.g., Libya and Syria), and voting in support of the Soviet Union in the United Nations General Assembly resolution on Afghanistan in January 1980, were clear mistakes in foreign policy. As regards the latter, Cuba was the only other state in the Western hemisphere to follow suit. Most other Third World states either opposed the Soviet invasion of Afghanistan or abstained. This was a clear expression to the US of Grenada's embrace of the Soviet Union. It was a major foreign policy blunder which was to have a crippling effect on the material base of the revolution. Equally counterproductive was the excessive anti-imperialist rhetoric, directed mainly at the US. All these mistakes could have been avoided by greater pragmatism and foresight, which would have had the effect of balancing the regime on the tight-rope which it sought to tread.

Political mistakes

Perhaps the gravest political mistake was the failure of the PRG to develop an indigenous political model, grounded in Grenadian realities. The PRG ended up substituting one alien model for another; the Westminster system was rejected in favour of the political formulas, institutions, and ideology of the Communist Party of the Soviet Union (CPSU). The decision proved to be fatal given the objective constraints (internal and external) against which the model had to struggle.

Among those which need to be recalled at this point are: (i) the overwhelming petit-bourgeois nature of the island's social structure (starkly manifested in their deep attachment to land and other forms of private property); (ii) the insignificant size of the working class; (iii) the tremendous importance (and retarding influence) of religion in the social and cultural life of the population; and - last but certainly not least - (iv) geopolitical constraints given the national security concerns of the United States.

Viewed as a whole the odds against charting the path successfully were formidable. Metaphorically speaking, it was like trying to make Russian vodka from Grenadian spices. Ironically, this was recognised by the leaders of the revolution as Bishop's 'Line of March' address clearly revealsed. But in their view socialism via the non-capitalist route was possible providing they adhered to firm Marxist-Leninist measures and obtain generous moral and material support from the socialist bloc, especially the Soviet Union (perhaps on the scale of that obtained by Fidel Castro's Cuba).

This was clearly a triumph of hope over experience. The record of other Third World countries which have sought to build socialism via the path of non-capitalist development shows that this route is littered with obstacles. There is no concrete guidance in the theory of non-capitalist development on how to overcome the various obstacles, and make the critical move from the 'national liberation revolution' to the 'socialist revolution'. As Nkrumah (1970), a victim of an aborted attempt at 'non-capitalist development', put it:

> A non-capitalist road, pursued by a 'united front of progressive forces', is not even practical politics in contemporary Africa.... Either it must remain under imperialist domination via capitalism and neo-colonialism, or it must pursue a socialist path by adopting the principles of scientific socialism. ... In a neo-colonial situation, there is no half-way to socialism. Only politics of all-out socialism can end capitalist-imperialist exploitation (cited in Harris, 1975, p. 43).

The dash for socialism by the Coard faction was probably inspired by the record of all those countries which have remained stuck on the non-capitalist path. Some of these countries ended up losing patience and reverting to the system they had rejected. Mozambique's embrace of South Africa is a notable case in point. Apart from Nkrumah's Ghana, the list is long of countries which have been considered, at one time or another, to have been at the national democratic anti-imperialist stage on the way to socialism. Yet they failed to progress to the stage of socialism proper. Indeed, examples of countries which have reached the stage of scientific socialism via the non-capitalist path are hard to find.

The Grenada experience shows that the likelihood of failure is high if the objective local and geo-political constraints are ignored in the quest for fully fledged socialism. Any variant of socialism adopted must seek to preserve and respect the democratic rights and civil liberties of the population. This extends to even known dissenters. These rights cannot be simply dismissed as a bourgeois myth, as they have often been won on the basis of struggles involving loss of lives. In the case of Grenada, they were the product of struggles such as the resistance of the Caribs against European imperialism, the Fedon uprising, the labour revolts and uprisings of the 1950s, and, curiously enough, the various struggles waged against the Gairy regime in the 1970s. Those who are at the helm of the political process also have a duty to genuinely involve the people in the affairs of the country.

The authoritarian tendencies of the PRG did not sit comfortably with the 'new democracy' which was espoused by the regime as a replacement for the Westminster model of democracy. Apart from the failure to hold elections (of any sort), the PRG displayed heavy-handedness in all areas of political life. The economics of mobilization was exercised within a rigid ideological framework. The essence of this was conveyed by Bishop at a rally in June 1981: 'This is a revolution, we live in a revolutionary Grenada, this is a revolutionary condition, and there is a revolutionary legality, and they will have to abide by the laws of the revolution. When the revolution speaks it must be heard, listened to. Whatever the revolution commands, it must be carried out; when the revolution talks no parasites must bark in their corner' (cited in O'Shaughnessy, 1984, p. 94).

Bishop's *Line of March* address to the party also echoed this authoritarian tendency 'Consider how people get detained in this country. We don't go and call for ... votes. You get detained when I sign an order after discussing it with the National Security Committee of the party, or with a higher party body. Once I sign it - like it or don't like it - it's up the hill (Richmond Hill prison) for them' (*Line of March*, 1982, p. 6). The PRG were hostile towards criticisms; a growing number of critics of aspect of the government's policy and suspects were placed in detention camps, in the interest of public order and the defence of the revolution. According to one source, during the period of the PRG rule, more than 3,000 people were question, and about 300 of these were detained (Thorndike, 1985, p. 113). The radio service and press media were also tightly controlled. The closure of *The Torchlight*, the only independent newspaper in Grenada at the time, was a notable example of the government's strict media policy. The paper was seen as having a policy of printing 'anti-PRG' articles which could potentially destabilise the government. An independent assessment of past editions of the newspaper by the Caribbean Press Council did not find any clear and consistent bias. The newspaper had both criticised and supported the PRG on a number of issues (Ryan, 1984, p. 5).

Social democracy

Many of the reforms on the PRG's agenda could have been inaugurated within a social democratic framework. The Grenadian private sector and population at large were not opposed in principle to policies aimed at reducing dependence in all its various forms, rationalising the use of resources, increasing social equality, developing a sense of cultural and national identity, and pursuing a pragmatic foreign policy as a means of furthering these goals. As Bishop put it shortly after coming to power: the goals of the revolution were 'for justice, for food, for health, for housing, for clothing, for pipeborne water, for education, for people's control of our resources, for people's participation' (Radio Broadcast, March 1979). There was nothing controversial about these goals among Grenadians. The policies to achieve them would have had a better chance of succeeding if a model of social democracy had been adopted.

Arguably, this model would have attracted a better response from the tiny, but influential, private sector, whose co-operation was vital to the health of the economy. No doubt it would have also reduced, although not eliminated, the hostility and suspicion of the United States and its allies. This, in turn, would have abated the deterioration of the economy, thereby making it easier for the regime to consolidate and extend its economic and social achievements.

In sum, those who cherish socialist solutions to West Indian problems must seek to learn from the Grenadian experience. The lessons must be fully incorporated in their political programme. The cardinal lesson is that the route to socialism must be congruent with the local socio-economic, socio-cultural, and geopolitical realities. This calls for innovation, creativity, and adaptation rather than wholesale emulation of alien, authoritarian models which bear no close relationship with the concrete conditions in the region. Since economic dynamism, material advancement, and social justice constitute the bottomline of the project, every effort should be made to develop - at the very minimum - a *modus vivendi* with the US and other western states - the 'natural trading/economic partners of Caribbean economies given their close propinquity and resource endowment. The material benefits to be gained from maintaining some level of integration in the international capitalist economy should never be sacrificed in the name of 'socialist purity', especially since the international socialist system no longer offers a viable alternative.

The return to free market orthodoxy

With the collapse of the PRG in October 1983, Grenada returned to the dependent *laissez-faire* model of economic development which was pursued by the Gairy regime in the 1960s and 1970s. It is, indeed, unfortunate that none of the economic lessons assembled above have been learnt by the regimes which have been installed in power since the post-invasion period. Instead of building on the economic and social reforms introduced by the PRG, the US and its allies in Grenada and elsewhere in the Caribbean set out to dismantle the PRG's programmes, while advocating the alleged advantages of the US free market model. The result of such reactionary policies was a systematic reversal of the legacies of the revolution, aptly reflected in the title of Ferguson's book *Grenada Revolution in Reverse*[11].

Indeed, US technocrats were assigned to government ministries to personally oversee the restructuring of the state sector and other initiatives instituted by the PRG. The strategies adopted were wide-ranging and included closures, privatisation, deregulation, retrenchments and use of political pressure to deprive state enterprises of resources. Similar measures were directed at the cooperative sector which had received special support from the PRG. For example, the National Cooperative Development Agency was closed down and many of its staff were made redundant.

Galvanised into action by ideology rather than by any concern for the interests of the Grenadian people, painstaking efforts were made to create an investor's paradise in the island. This involved suppression of trade unions, tax holidays for up to 15 years, relaxation of foreign exchange controls, liberalisation of import licensing arrangements, easing credit restrictions, removal of price controls on domestically produced goods, transfer of management of the main commodity associations to the private sector, and a sharp reduction of the role of the public sector in the productive spheres of the economy. At the same time the US signalled its commitment to this free market model by injecting a substantial amount of aid into the island, so much so that by the end of 1986 Grenada joined Israel in becoming the highest per capita recipients of American aid in the world. During this period US$83 million, or almost US$900 per person, flowed into the island. It was hoped that after a few years the aid programme would be replaced by private resources, both local and foreign, as Grenada became the showcase of the free enterprise model in the Caribbean.

But the model has failed dismally, even when assessed against its own narrow criteria. Not only has it failed to attract significant foreign investment (despite the material support and political symbolism accorded to the island by the US administration) but it has also had a catastrophic impact on the economy and large segments of the population. Instead of devising policies to encourage structural adjustment, economic diversification and self-sustaining growth, dependency relations were engendered in every sphere of the economy. For the majority of Grenadians, 'the cure has been far worse than the supposed illness' (Ferguson, 1990, p.67).

Many of the progressive reforms introduced by the PRG to improve the lot of Grenadian workers and peasants were discontinued or scaled down because they were considered to be *statist*. Only a mere seven per cent of total US aid into Grenada up to 1989 was spent on education, health, agricultural research and community-based projects (Ferguson, p. 39). In the health sector, for example, administrative fees were instituted for X-rays, eye-tests, and dental check-ups. Consistent with this shift in priorities and policy outlook, the statutory maternity leave law, passed by the PRG in 1980 to promote the rights of women, was amended in 1989 to reduce employers' financial obligations by 40 per cent. The removal of price controls on basic commodities, coupled with exorbitant indirect taxes and escalating unemployment, further undermined the living standards of many Grenadians.

There is also very little to celebrate in the political arena, as witnessed by Washington's continuing inability to find a stable government to administer the island's affairs during the post-invasion period. Political wheeling and dealing produced the New National Party (NNP), which formed the government in 1984 but collapsed mid-way during its term of office. The elections that took place in 1990, following Blaize's death, were contested by five parties - none of which emerged with a clear majority. A new era of political turbulence may well be in the offing. The possibility that Gairy and his allies may stage a successful comeback is real. In an atmosphere of declining economic fortunes for the oppressed layers of the society - the group whose cause was championed by the PRG - the remnants of the New Jewel Movement (regrouped as the Maurice Bishop Patriotic Movement) can also be expected to gain increasing support. Many Grenadians, particularly the young, are still attracted to many of the social and economic programmes instituted by the PRG (Emmanuel et al., 1986).

Grenada is thus set for an uncertain economic and political future. The need for policy-makers and practitioners in development economics to find solutions to the problems in Grenada and the wider Caribbean has never been more urgent. The model of dependent capitalism pursued in Grenada during the Gairy era and resurrected after the October 1983 invasion is clearly not the panacea to the region's problems. That model has failed dismally, and continues to provide evidence of all the pitfalls associated with a dependent-capitalist development strategy. As we approach the new millennium, options for tackling the region's developmental problems must seek to draw from the lessons which this study has assembled from the PRG's development strategy. Governments in the region cannot afford to allow ideology, or memories of the tragic way in which the PRG regime ended, to obscure the economic achievements of the revolution and the important lessons which can be learned from this singular experiment.

Notes

1. Lewis (1984, 1987) contains an excellent discussion of the **political** lessons from the revolution. It is thus a useful complement to this chapter, which concentrates on **economic** lessons.

2. See Government of Grenada (1983e). This document gives further information on the economic and political significance of the international airport project.

3. The official view of the underlying principles which guided Grenada's foreign policy during this period is contained in Whiteman (1982).

4. The full text appears in *Caribbean Insight* (February 1983, p. 5).

5. For a lucid discussion of the main theoretical propositions and conclusions from these theories see Blomstrom and Hettne (1984).

6. The link between education policies and economic development is discussed in a government document entitled *Education is Production Too* (see Bishop, 1982a).

7. For a discussion of the thinking behind the *National Education and Training Targets*, and examples of vocational education and training initiatives in Britain, see the Employment Department's annual publication entitled *Labour Market and Skill Trends*.

8. See Government of Grenada (1982f) for other examples of the 'new democracy' which was emerging in Grenada during this period.

9. Simply put, sunk costs are those which cannot be recouped when a firm leaves an industry.

10. This is evident from the minutes of Central Committee meetings, as revealed by the captured documents. See US State Department and Department of Defense, 1984, for a sample of the documents. See, also, Seabury and McDougall (1984).

11. See Ferguson (1990) for a comprehensive and lucid discussion of the economic and political policies pursued in Grenada during the post-invasion period, and the role of the US in the formulation of these policies.

Appendix 4:A:1
Capital Expenditure in Agriculture for 1982 (planned and actual)

Project/Enterprise	Planned budget	Actual outturn	per cent Achieved
Feeder roads II	2600.0	1278.1	49.1
Farm roads	2088.0	2052.8	98.3
Banana rehabilitation	250.0	172.0	69.0
Land reform project (YEP)	4000.0	1057.9	26.4
Carriacou agricultural development project	400.0	126.1	31.5
fertilizer blending plant	-	10.0	-
Aerial survey	90.0	90.3	100.3
Irrigation/drainage	8.8	8.8	100.0
Soil/plant ding.lab	30.0	30.0	100.0
Carriacou sheep development	203.0	61.5	30.3
Mardigras soil conservation	264.4	276.0	104.4
Ext.agric.building	36.2	36.2	100.0
Mirabean training school	23.0	23.0	100.0
Farm machinery pool	500.0	1512.1	302.4
Planned	9858.4	5077.4	51.5
Additional	635.0	1657.4	261.0
Total	10493.4	6734.8	64.2

Source: Government of Grenada (1983e), Appendix 1, p. 140.

Appendix 5:A:1
Remarks made by visitors about Grenada's restaurants

(i)   'Services in the restaurants need to be improved'.

(ii)   'Food in most restaurants is superb, but service is certainly lacking'.

(iii)   'Food is expensive'.

(iv)   'Restaurant food poor in quantity and quality'.

(v)   'Few cafes have fresh fruit juices - food often unimaginative and in short supply'.

(vi)   'I particularly liked the seafoods, the secluded beaches and the natural beauty of the island'.

(vii)   'Lack of good restaurants in St George's and other places around the island'.

(viii)   'Not enough use of local food products in restaurants, e.g. spices and vegetables'.

(ix)   'Food in restaurants good, but service poor'.

(x)   'Restaurants were unorganized - service took much too long, although the food was good when it came'.

(xi)   'Needs more seafoods'.

(xii)   'The food I found was very good and we were able to enjoy it unlike other countries we have visited'.

Source: CTRC (1982), pp. 4-5.

Appendix 6:A:1
List of potential industries

Agriculture	1.	Fruits and vegetables processing
Foods and	2.	Sugar
Beverages	3.	Chicken parts
	4.	Gravy browning and seasoning sauces
	5.	Cocoa - related products
	6.	Mineral water

Agricultural	1.	Animal feeds
Inputs	2.	Agricultural tools and implements, processing machinery, repairs
	3.	Packaging materials

Construction	1.	Building blocks and tiles (from clay and Building materials possolanic materials
	2.	Parquet flooring (especially from coconut trunks)
	3.	Burnt lime (based on coral)
	4.	Cement - fibre roofing
	5.	Fibre - asphalt roofing (Bagasse, waste paper or other fibrous material can be formed into sheets, impregnated, corrugated, and reflected - coated.
	6.	Coconut trunk roofing tiles
	7.	Boat building

Energy:	1.	Fuel alcohol (from low-grade cane)
Non-conventional	2.	Solar energy

Tourism	1.	Hotel construction
	2.	Entertainment complexes
	3.	Condominiums
	4.	Luxury housing
	5.	Low cost tourist villages
	6.	Marine and yacht renting facilities

266

	7.	Sightseeing business
	8.	Aqua sport facilities

Other products and service	1.	Tyre remoulding
	2.	Banana fibre (can be used for garments as is currently done in the Philippines)
	3.	Coir products (brushes, ropes, etc.
	4.	Electronics assembly
	5.	Packaging materials
	6.	Can-making
	7.	Secondary wood products (e.g. furniture)
	8.	Knock-down furniture
	9.	Fibre glass products (e.g. yachts and furniture)
	10.	Garment manufacturing
	11.	Cement production
	12.	Nutmeg oil distillation
	13.	Batik artwork
	14.	Battery production
	15.	Liquid and solid detergents.

Source: Government of Grenada (1983c), pp. 39-42.

N.B. This list of possible industries was based largely on tests and studies (pre-feasibility and feasibility) carried out by specialists who served under the PRG.

Select Bibliography

Abdulah, N. (ed.) (1974), *The Social Impact of Tourism on Tobago*, Institute of Social and Economic Research, UWI, Trinidad.

Ambursley, F. 'Grenada: The New Jewel Revolution' in Ambursley, F. and Cohen, R., (eds), (1983), *Crisis in the Caribbean*, Heinemann, London.

Ambursley, F. and Dunkerly, J. (1984), *Grenada: Whose Freedom?*, Latin American Bureau Ltd, London.

Andreyev,I. (1974), *The Non-capitalist Way*, Progress Publishers, Moscow.

Baynes, R. (1977), 'The Ideal Environment for Effective Agricultural Credit in the Caribbean', (Twelfth Agricultural Conference), University of the West Indies, Trinidad.

Beckford, G. (1972), *Persistent Poverty: Underdevelopment in Plantation Economies of the Third World*, Oxford University Press, New York.

Beckford, G. and Witter, M. (1984), *Small Garden, Bitter Weed: The Political Economy of Struggle and Change in Jamaica*, Maroon Publishing House, Jamaica.

Belfon, J. (1980), 'Trends in Caribbean Tourism' in *The Courier*, 63 (3).

Benn, D. (1974), 'The Theory of Plantation Economy and Society: a Methodological critique', *Journal of Commonwealth and Comparative Politics*, 12 (4).

Bernal, R. et al. (1984), 'Caribbean Economic, Thought: The Critical Tradition', *Social and Economic Studies*, 33 (2).

Best, L. (1968), 'Outlines of a Model of Pure Plantation Economy', *Social and Economic Studies*, 12 (3).

- (1971a) 'Independent Thought and Caribbean Freedom' in Girvan, N. and Jefferson, O. (eds), *Readings in the Political Economy of the Caribbean*, New World Group, Jamaica.

- (1971b) 'Size and Survival' in Girvan, N. and Jefferson, O., (eds), *Readings in the Political economy of the Caribbean*.

Levitt, K. and Best, L. (1975), 'Character of Caribbean Economy' in Beckford, G., *Caribbean Economy: Dependence and Backwardness*, Institute of Social and Economic Research, UWI, Jamaica.

Bishop, M. (1982a), *Selected Speeches 1979-1981*, Casa De Las Americas, Havana.

- (1982b) *Forward Ever! Three Years of the Grenadian Revolution*, Pathfinder Press, Sydney.

Blackman, C. (1980), Speech to Students in Chancellor Hall, University of the West Indies, Kingston, Jamaica.

Blomstrom, M. and Hettne, B. (1984), *Development Theory in Transition*, Zed Books, London.

Boatswain, A. (1984), 'The Development of the Manufacturing Sector in Grenada 1980-2000, Problems & Prospects', Documentation and Information Centre, Grenada.

Brana-Shute, R. and Brana-Shute (1982), 'The Magnitude and Impact of Remittances in the Eastern Caribbean: A Research Note' in Stinner, W.F. et al. (eds), *Return Migration and Remittances: Developing a Caribbean Perspective*, Rise Occasional Papers No. 3., Research Institute on Immigration and Ethnic Studies, Smithsonian Institution, Washington DC.

Brewster, H. (1967), 'The Sugar Industry - Our Life or Death?', *New World Pamphlet*.

- (1973), 'Economic Dependence. A Quantitative Interpretation', *Social and Economic Studies*, 22 (1).

Brewster, H. and Thomas, C.Y. (1967), *The Dynamics of West Indian Economic Integration*, Institute of Social and Economic Research, UWI, Jamaica.

Brierly, J.S., (1974), *Small Farming in Grenada, West Indies*, Manitoba Geographical studies, University of Manitoba, Canada.

Brizan, G. (1979), 'The Grenada Peasantry and Social Revolution, 1931-1951', Working Paper No.21, Institute of Social and Economic Research, UWI, Kingston, Jamaica.

- (1984) *Grenada: Island of Conflict From Amerindians to People's Revolution 1498-1979*, Zed Books Ltd, London.

Brown B. (1979), 'A Proposed Programme for the development of the Handicraft Industry in Grenada', Documentation and Information Centre, Grenada.

- (1982), 'Report on the Handicraft Development Project for the period 15 May - 15 Dec, 1982', Documentation and Information Centre, Grenada.

Bryden, J.M. (1975), *Tourism and Development: A Case study of the Commonwealth Caribbean*, Cambridge University Press, Cambridge.

Bryden, J.M. and Faber, M. (1971), 'Multiplying The Tourist Multiplier', *Social and Economic Studies*, 20 (3).

Caribbean Development Bank (1980a), *Global Line of Credit to the Grenada Development Bank* (Project Document), CDB Documentation Centre, Barbados.

- (1980b), *Pre-investment Study-Road Construction, Grenada* (Project Document), CDB Documentation Centre, Barbados.
- (1981), *Appraisal Report on Second Central Cocoa Fermentary, Grenada* (Project Document), CDB Documentation Centre, Barbados.
- (1982a), *Grenada Farm Corporation - Agricultural Development* (Project Document), CDB Documentation Centre, Barbados.

(1982b), *Nutmeg Oil Distillery, Grenada* (Project Document), CDB Documentation Centre, Barbados.

- (1982c), *Project Identification Mission Report on Grenada* (Project Document), CDB Documentation Centre, Barbados.
- (1984), *Economic Memorandum on Grenada, 1984* (Vols. 1 and 2), CDB Documentation Centre, Barbados.

Caribbean Tourism Research Centre (1982), *Grenada Visitor Motivational Survey, Summary and Methodology* (Vol. 1), CTRC, Barbados.

- (1983), *A Study of Linkages between Tourism and Local Agriculture in Grenada, St Vincent, St Lucia, and The Bahamas*, CTRC, Barbados.
- (1986), *Grenada: Visitor Expenditure Survey, Summary*, CTRC, Barbados.
- (select years), *Caribbean Tourism Statistical Report*, CTRC, Barbados.

Castro, F. (1983), *A Pyrrhic Military Victory and a Profound Moral Defeat*, Editora Politica, Havana.

Cerhonek, J. (1982), 'A Project for Grenada's Economic Development in the Period 1983-1985', Documentation and Information Centre, Grenada.

Chernick, S. (1978), *The Commonwealth Caribbean: The Integration Experience*, The John Hopkins University Press, Baltimore.

Clarke, E.W. (1978), *Socialist Development and Public Investment in Tanzania 1964-1973*, Toronto University Press, 1978.

Coard, B. (1979a), 'Statement delivered at a Conference hosted by the CDB on 26 April 1979', Documentation and Information Centre, Grenada.

- (1979b), 'Address at the Annual General Meeting of the Grenada Chamber of Commerce, 24 May 1979', Documentation and Information Centre, Grenada.
- (1980), 'The Process of Trying to Build A New Economic and Social Development', (interview) *The Courier*, 61 (2).
- (1981), *Grenada: Let Those Who Labour Hold The Reins*, Liberation, London.
- (1985), 'Building The Economy', (Interview by Chris Searle with Bernard Coard on RFG, 13 February 1983, Reproduced in NJM (UK), *Revolutionary Grenada: A Big and Popular School*, (Spider Web, London).

Cohen, E. (1974), 'Who is a Tourist?: A Conceptual Clarification',

Sociological Review, 22 (3).

Cole, R. (undated), 'On the Problem of the reverse Transfer of Technology (Brain Drain) and Human Resources in Grenada', Documentation and Information Centre, Grenada.

Commonwealth Secretariat (1982), *Grenada - the Development of Agriculture and Fisheries to Improve Food Supplies and Nutrition*, Commonwealth Secretariat, London.

Cumper, G. (1974), 'Dependence, Development and The Sociology of Economic Thought', *Social and Economic Studies*, 23 (3).

Dabreo, D.S. (1979), *The Grenada Revolution*, M.A.P.S Publication, Castries, St Lucia.

Davidson, S. (1987), *Grenada: A Study in Politics and the Limits of International Law*, Athenaeum Press Ltd, Great Britain.

Demas, W. (1965), *The Economics of Development in Small Countries*, McGill University, McGill.

Devas, R.P. (1964), *The History of the Island of Grenada*, Careenage Press, St George's, Grenada.

Doxey, G.Y. (1975), 'A Causation Theory of Visitor-Resident Irritants, Methodology, and Research Inferences' in *The Impact of Tourism*, Sixth Annual Conference Proceedings of the Travel Research Associations, San Diego.

Dunn, P. and Watson, B, (eds) (1985), *American Intervention in Grenada: The Implications of Operation 'Urgent Fury'*, Boulder: Westview Press.

Economist Intelligence Unit (1979), *The Economic and Social Impact of International Tourism on Developing Countries*, Special Report No. 60, EIU Limited.

Emmanuel, P. (1978), *Crown Colony Politics in Grenada, 1917-1951*, Institute of Social and Economic Research, UWI, Cave Hill, Barbados.

- (1983) 'Revolutionary Theory and Political Reality in the Eastern Caribbean', *Journal of Interamerican Studies and World Affairs*, 25 (2).

Emmanuel, P. et al. (1986), *Political Change and Public Opinion in Grenada 1979- 1984*, Occasional Paper No. 19., Institute of Social and Economic Research, UWI, Cave Hill, Barbados.

Epica Task Force (1982), *Grenada: The Peaceful Revolution*, Washington, DC.

Farm and Agricultural Organization (1982), 'Assistance to Agricultural Development - Grenada' (Terminal Statement prepared for the Government of Grenada), Documentation and Information Centre, Grenada.

Ferguson, J. (1990), *Grenada: Revolution in Reverse*, Latin America Bureau, London.

Ferguson, T., 'The Potential for Increasing Agricultural Production in Grenada' in Institute of International Relations, *Independence for Grenada:*

271

Myth or Reality?, University of the West Indies, St Augustine, Trinidad.

Frank, A. G. (1967), *Capitalism and Underdevelopment in Latin America*, Monthly Review Press, New York.

- (1969), *Latin America: Underdevelopment or Revolution*, Monthly Review Press, New York.

- (1972) *Lumpenbourgeoisie Lumpendevelopment*, Monthly Review Press, New York.

- (1979) 'Economic Crisis and the State in the Third World', *Development Studies*, Discussion Paper, 30 (1).

Frucht, R. (1967), 'A Caribbean Social Type: Neither "Peasant" nor "Proletariat"', *Social and Economic Studies*, 1 (3).

Gilmore, W. (1984), *The Grenada Intervention: Analysis and Documentation*, Mansell, London.

Gill, H.S. (1984), 'The Grenada Revolution: Domestic and Foreign Policy Orientations' (Paper presented at a conference on the Grenada Revolution held at the Institute of International Relations, UWI, St Augustine, 24-25 May, 1984).

Girvan, N. (1971), *Foreign Capital and Economic Underdevelopment in Jamaica*, Institute of Social and economic Research, UWI, Jamaica.

- (1973), 'Multinational Corporations and Underdevelopment', *Social and Economic Studies*, 22 (1).

Girvan, N. and Jefferson, O. (1971), *Readings in the Political Economy of the Caribbean*, New World Group Ltd., Kingston, Jamaica.

Girvan, N. et al. (1980), 'The IMF and the Third World: The Case of Jamaica', *Development Dialogue*, 2 (2).

Gittens-Knight, E. (1946), *The Grenada Handbook and Directory*, Advocate Company, Bridgetown, Barbados.

Gold, D. (1975), 'Recent Developments in Marxist Theories of the Capitalist State', *Monthly Review*, (October and November).

Gonsalves, R. (1981), *The Non-Capitalist Path of Development: Africa and the Caribbean*, One World Publishers, London.

Green, P. (1983), 'Case Study of Grenada Farms Corporation' (Paper presented at National Workshop for Public Enterprise in Grenada, St George's).

Green, W.A. (1976), *British Slave Emancipation, The Sugar Colonies and The Great Experiment 1830-1965*, Clarendon Press, Oxford.

Grenada Chamber of Industry and Commerce (1979), 'Report of the Council of Management for the Period April 1978 - March 1979', Grenada.

- (1982), *Brief, History of the Private Sector*, Grenada.

- (1983), 'Report of the Council of Management for the Period April 1982 - March 1983', Grenada.

- (1984), 'Report of the Council of Management for the Period April 1983 -

March 1984', Grenada.

Grenada Hotel Association (1982-1986), 'Report of the President to the Annual General Meeting', Grenada.

Hall, D.(1959), *Free Jamaica 1838-1865*, Yale University Press, New Haven.

Hobsbawm, E. (1954), 'The General Crisis of the European Economy in the seventeenth Century', *Past and Present*, 5 (2).

Holder, J. (1980), 'The Role of Tourism in Caribbean Development', *The Courier*, 63 (3).

- 'Tourism The Largest Single Industry in the Caribbean', (An Interview with Holder conducted by R.D.B., Reproduced in *The Courier*, 80 (3).

Hudson, B.J. (1983), 'The Changing Caribbean: Grenada's New International Airport', *Caribbean Geography*, 1 (1).

- (1979), 'The Touristic Potential of Grenada's Historical Monuments, Buildings, Landmarks and Other Places of Scenic Beauty and Interest', Documentation and Information Centre, Grenada.

Institute for International Relations (1974), *Independence for Grenada: Myth or Reality*, University of the West Indies, St Augustine, Trinidad.

Inter-American Institute for Co-operation in agriculture (1981), *Project Profile for the Development of Grenada Farms Corporation*, Documentation and Information Centre, Grenada.

International Monetary Fund (1981), *Grenada: Recent Economic Developments*, Washington, DC.

- (1984a), *Grenada: Recent Economic Developments*, Washington, DC.

- (1984b), *Grenada: Non-Financial Public Enterprise*, Documentation and Information Centre, Grenada.

Jacobs, W.R. and Jacobs, R.I. (1980), *Grenada : The Route to Revolution*, Casa de las Americas, Havana.

James, C.L.R. (1963), *Black Jacobins*, Vintage Books, London.

Jefferson, O. (1972), *The Post-War Economic Development of Jamaica*, Institute of Social and Economic Research, Kingston, Jamaica, University of the West Indies.

Joefield-Napier, W. (1985), 'Macroeconomic Growth During the People's Revolutionary Government's Regime: An Assessment' (Paper presented at the Conference on Democracy, Development and Collective Security in the Eastern Caribbean: The Lessons of Grenada, University of Puerto Rico, 17-19 October 1985).

Kay, G. (1975), *Development and Underdevelopment: A Marxist Analysis*, Macmillan, London.

Kirton, C. (1983), 'Attempts at Economic Planning in the Early stages of transition: Some Notes on the Grenada Experience' (Conference Paper presented at the Institute of Social studies, The Hague, Netherlands, 1983).

- (undated),'Public Policy and Private Capital in the Transition to Socialism:

Grenada 1979-1983', (Mimeo., UWI, Jamaica).

- (undated), 'Grenada and the IMF: The People's Revolutionary Government's EFF Programme, 1983', (Mimeo., UWI, Jamaica).

Knight, F. (1978), *The Caribbean, The Genesis of a Fragmented Nationalism*, Oxford University Press, Oxford.

Levitt, K. (1970),'Old Mercantilism and the New', *Social and Economic Studies*, 12 (4).

Levitt, K. and Gulati, J. (1970), 'Income Effect of Spending: Mystification Multiplied: A Critical Comment on the Zinder Report', *Social and Economic Studies*, 19 (3).

Lewis, G.K. (1968), *The Growth of the Modern West Indies*, Monthly Review Press, New York.

- (1984) 'The Lessons of Grenada for the Caribbean Left' Caribbean Contact, July edition.

- (1985) 'Grenada: History and Society' (Paper presented at the Conference on Democracy, Development and Collective Security in the Eastern Caribbean, University of Puerto Rico).

- (1987) *Grenada: The Jewel Despoiled*, The Johns Hopkins University Press, Baltimore and London.

Lewis, W.A. (1949), 'Industrial Development in puerto Rico', *Caribbean Economic Review*, 1 (1).

- (1950) 'The Industrialization of the British West Indies', *Caribbean Economic Review*, 2 (1).

- (1954), 'Economic Development with Unlimited Supplies of Labour', *Manchester School of Economics and Social Studies*, 22 (2).

Lindsay, L. (1976), 'Colonialism and the Myth of Resource Insufficiency in Jamaica' in V. Lewis, (ed.), *Size, Self Determination and International relations, The Caribbean* (UWI, Mona, Jamaica, 1976).

Louison, G. (1984), 'Interview', *Inter-Continental Press*, April.

Lowenthal, D. (1972), *West Indian Societies*, Oxford University Press, London).

Mandle, J.R. (1985a), *Big Revolution Small Country: The Rise and Fall of the Grenada Revolution*, North-South Publishing Co. Inc., Lanham, Maryland.

- (1985b), 'The Role of Agriculture in Self-Reliant Development', *Social and Economic Studies*, 34 (2).

Manifesto (1973) of the Grenada National Party in Institute of International Relations (1974), *Independence for Grenada: Myth or Reality?*, UWI, Trinidad.

'Manifesto (1973) of the New Jewel Movement' in Institute of International Relations (1974), *Independence for Grenada: Myth of Reality*, UWI, Trinidad.

Manley, M. (1974), *The Politics of Change: A Jamaican Testament*, André Deutsch, London.

- (1982) *Jamaica: Struggle in the Periphery*, Third World Media Limited, London.

Marshall, D.I. (1978), *Tourism and Employment in Barbados* (Occasional Papers, Series No. 6., Institute of Social and Economic Research, University of the West Indies, Cave Hill, Barbados.

Marshall, W.K. (1968), 'Notes on Peasant Development in the West Indies since 1938', *Social and Economic Studies*, 17 (3).

Martin, J.B. (1978), *US Policy in the Caribbean*, Westview Press, Colorado.

Mathieson, A. and Wall, G. (1982), *Tourism: Economic, Physical and Social Impacts*, Longman, London and New York.

Mathieson, W.L. (1932), *British Slave Emancipation 1838-1849*, Longmans, Green and Co., London.

McIntosh, C. and Osuji, T., 'Economic Aspects of Food Production in Grenada' in Institute of International Relations, *Independence for Grenada: Myth or Reality?*.

McIntyre, A. (1971), 'Some Issues in Trade Policy in the West Indies' in Girvan, N. and Jefferson (eds), (1971).

Medlik, S. and Middleton, V.T.C. (1975), 'The Tourist Product and its Marketing' in Burkart, A.J. and Medlik, S., (eds), *The Management of Tourism*, Heinemann, London.

Melanson, R., and Schoenhals, K. (1985), *Revolution and Intervention in Grenada: The New Jewel Movement, the United States, and the Caribbean*, Boulder: Westview Press.

Melotti, U. (1977), *Marx and the Third World*, Macmillan Press Ltd, London and Basingstoke.

Munck, R. (1985), *Politics and Dependency in the Third World* (Zed Books Ltd, London.

Munslow, B. (1983), 'Is Socialism Possible in the Periphery?', *Monthly Review*, 35 (2).

Newton, A.P. (1933), *The European Nations in the West Indies*, 1493-1688, London.

Nisbet, C. (1969), 'The Relationship Between Institutional and Informal Credit Markets in Rural Chile', *Land Economics*, 45 (2).

Nitobury, E. (1984), 'The Road to revolution' in "Social Sciences Today" Editorial Board, *Grenada: History, Revolution, US Intervention*, USSR Academy of Sciences, Moscow.

Nkrumah, K. (1975), 'Class Struggle in Africa' in Harris, R., (ed.), *The Political Economy of Africa*, Schenkman Publishing Company Inc., Cambridge, Massachussettes.

Nyerere, J. (1968), *Ujamaa: Essays on Socialism*, Oxford University Press,

London and Dar es Salam.

O.A.S. Secretariat (1977), *Economic Study of Grenada*, Washington, DC.

O'Shaughnessy, H. (1984), *Grenada: Revolution, Invasion and Aftermath*, Sphere Books with the Observer, London.

Oxaal, I. (1975), 'The Dependency Economist as Grassroots Politician in the Caribbean' in Oxaal, I. (ed.), *Beyond the Sociology of Development*, Routledge Kegan Paul Ltd, London.

- (1982), *Black Intellectuals and the Dilemmas of Race and Class in Trinidad*, Schenkmann Publishing Company Inc., Massachusetts.

Packerham, R. (1986), 'Capitalist Dependency and Socialist Dependency: The Case of Cuba', *Journal of Inter-American Studies and World Affairs*, No.28.

Pantin, D. (1980), 'The Plantation Economy Model and the Caribbean', Institute of Development studies Bulletin 12.

Payer, C. (1974), *The Debt Trap: The IMF and the Third World*, Richard Clay, the Chaucer Press Ltd, Suffolk, UK.

Payne, A. (1980), *The Politics of the Caribbean Community 1961-1979: Regional Integration Amongst New States*, Manchester University Press, Manchester.

- (1981), *Change in the Commonwealth Caribbean*, Chatham House Papers, Royal Institute of International Affairs; Stephen Austin and Sons Ltd, Hertford, 1981.

- (1985), 'The Foreign Policy of the PRG' (Paper presented at a conference on Democracy, Development and Collective Security in the Eastern Caribbean, University of Puerto Rico).

- (1984) 'Dependency Theory and the Commonwealth Caribbean' in Payne, A. and Sutton, P., (eds), (1984), *Dependency Under Challenge: The Political Economy of the Commonwealth Caribbean*, Manchester University Press, Manchester.

Payne, A. et al. (1984), *Grenada: Revolution and Invasion*, Croom Helm, London and Sydney.

Pearce, J. (1982), *Under the Eagle: US Intervention in Central America and the Caribbean*, Latin American Bureau, London.

Pearce, P.L., *The Social Psychology of Tourist Behaviour*, Pergamon Press, New York.

Petras, J. (1983), 'Problems in the Transition to Socialism', *Monthly Review*, 35 (2).

Phillips, W. (1974), 'Market Prospects for Grenada's Major Exports' in Institute of International Relations, *Independence for Grenada: Myth or Reality?*.

Post, K. (1978), *Arise Ye Starvelings: The Jamaican Labour Rebellion of 1938 and its Aftermath*, Martinis Nijhoff, The Hague, Boston and London.

Qureshi, A.D. (1966), 'Social Development and Planning in Grenada', Documentation and Information Centre, Grenada.

Ragatz, L.J. (1929), *Statistics for the Study of British Caribbean Economic History 1763-1833*, Bryan Edwards Press, London.

- (1963), *The Fall of the Planter Class in the British Caribbean, 1763-1833*, Octagon Books, New York.

Rodney, W. (1972), *How Europe Underdeveloped Africa*, Dar ES Salaam: Tanzania Publishing House.

Rostow, W. (1960),*The Stages of Economic Growth*, Cambridge University Press, Cambridge.

Rottenberg, S. (1955), 'Labour Relations in an Underdeveloped Economy', *Caribbean Quarterly*, 4 (1).

Sammy, G. (1974), 'Agro-industries, Prospects for Grenada' in Institute of International Relations in *Independence For Grenada: Myth or Reality?*.

Sandford, G. and Vigilante, R. (1984), *Grenada: The Untold Story*, Madison Books, Lanham, New York and London.

Seabury, P. and McDougall, W. (eds), (1984), *The Grenada Papers: The Inside Story of The Grenadian Revolution and The Making of a Totalitarian State as told in captured documents*, Institute for Contemporary Studies, San Francisco, California.

Searle, C. (1979),'Grenada's Revolution: An Interview with B. Coard' in *Race and Class*, 21 (2).

- (1983), *Grenada: The Struggle against Destabilization* (Writers and Readers, London.

- (1984), *Words Unchained: Language and Revolution in Grenada*, Zed Books, London.

Seers, D. (1964), 'The Mechanism of na Open Petroleum Economy', *Social and Economic Studies*, 13 (2).

Shearman, P. (1987), *The Soviet Union and Cuba*, Chatham House Papers, No. 38, The Royal Institute of International Affairs, Routlege Kegan Paul, London, New York and Andover.

Sheridan, R. (1970), *The Development of the Plantations: An era of West Indian Prosperity 1750-1775*, Caribbean Universities Press, UWI, Barbados.

Singham, A.W. (1968), *The Hero and the Crowd in a Colonial Polity*, Yale University Press, New Haven.

Skokpol, D., 'Political Response to Capitalist Crisis: Neo-Marxist Theories of the State and the case of the New Deal', *Politics and Society*, 10 (2).

Slovo, J. (1974), 'A Critical Appraisal of the Non-Capitalist Path and the National Democratic State in Africa', *Marxism Today*, 18 (2).

Smith, C.A. (1987), Review of Stephens, E.H.and Stephens, J.D., (1986), *Democratic Socialism in Jamaica: The Political Movement and Social*

Transformation in Dependent Capitalism in *The Journal of Development Studies*, 23 (4).

- (1988), *The Development Strategy of the People's Revolutionary Government: the political economy of economic transformation in Grenada, 1979-1983* (doctoral dissertation submitted to Hull University, England).

- (1994) 'The Grenada Revolution in Retrospect' in Payne, A. and Sutton, P (eds), *Modern Caribbean Politics*, Johns Hopkins University Press, Baltimore.

Smith, M.G. (1965a), *Stratification in Grenada*, University of California Press, Berkeley.

- (1965b), *The Plural Society in the British West Indies*, University of California Press, Berkely.

Solodovnikov, V.G. (1969), 'The Non-capitalist Road of Development in Africa', *Marxism Today*, 13 (3).

Solodovnikov, V.G. and Bogoslovsy, V. (1975), *Non capitalist Development: An Historical Outline*, Progress Publishers, Moscow.

Stein, H. (1985), 'Theories of the State in Tanzania: A Critical Assessment', *Journal of Modern African Studies*, 23 (1).

Stephens, E.H. and Stephens, J.D. (1986), *Democratic Socialism in Jamaica: The Political Movement and Social Transformation in Dependent Capitalism*, Macmillan, London.

Stone, C. (1980),*Democracy and Clientelism in Jamaica*, Transaction Books, New Brunswick, New Jersey.

Sutton, P.K. (1983), 'Black Power in Trinidad and Tobago: The Crisis of 1970,' *Journal of Commonwealth and Comparative Politics*, 21 (2).

- (1988), 'Grenadian Callaloo: Recent Books on Grenada', *Latin American Research Review*, 23 (1).

Szentes, T. (1976), *The Political economy of Underdevelopment*, Akadé Kiado, Budapest.

Thomas, C.Y. (1965), *Monetary and Financial Arrangements in a Dependent Monetary Economy*, Kingston, Jamaica.

- (1974), *Dependence and transformation: The Economics of the Transition to Socialism*, Monthly Review Press, New York.

- (1978), 'The Non-Capitalist Path as Theory and Practice of Decolonization and Socialist Transformation', *Latin American Perspectives*, 5 (2).

Thomas, C.Y. et al. (1968), *Economic and Social Development of Grenada*, Institute of Social and Economic Research, UWI, Jamaica.

Thompsom, R. (1987), *Green Gold: Bananas and Dependency in the Eastern Caribbean*, Latin American Bureau Ltd, London.

Thorndike, T. (1985), *Grenada, Politics, Economics and Society*, Frances Pinter Publishers, London.

Tinker, H. (1974), *A new System of Slavery: The Export of Indian Labour*

Overseas 1830-1920, Oxford University Press, London.

Ulyanovsky, R. (1971), 'Marxist and Non-Marxist Socialism', *World Marxist Review*, 14 (9).

- (1974), *Socialism and the Newly Independent Nations*, Progress Publishers, Moscow.

UNDP (1979), *Project Document GRN/79/001/A/01/31*, Documentation and Information Centre, Grenada.

UNDP/ICAO (1984), *Grenada International Airport Organization and Manpower Resources Report*, Documentation and Information Centre, Grenada.

UNESCO (1982), *Education Sector Survey: An Analysis of the Education and Training System and Recommendations for its Development*, Paris.

United Nations Centre for Transnational Development (1982), *Some Preliminary Comments on the Grenada Investment Code*, Documentation and Information Centre, Grenada.

US State Department and Department of Defence (1984), *Grenada Documents: An Overview and Selection*, Washington DC.

Vahcic, A. (1983), 'The Grenada Marketing and National Importing Board', *Quarterly Journal*, 3 (4) (International Centre for Public Enterprises in Developing Countries, Ljublijana, Yugoslavia).

Watson, H. (1985), 'Non-capitalist Path and the Derailment of a Populist Revolution', paper presented at the Caribbean Studies Association Conference, 29 May - 2 June 1985.

Wells, S., *Historical and Descriptive Sketch of the Island of Grenada*, Microfilm Reel 48, UWI, Jamaica.

West India Royal Commission (1940), *1938-39 Recommendations*, Her Majesty's Stationery Office, London.

Williams, E. (1964), *Capitalism and Slavery*, André Deutsch, London.

- (1970), *From Columbus to castro: A History of the Caribbean, 1492-1969*, André Deutsch, London.

World Bank (1980), *Economic Memorandum on Grenada*, Report No. 2949-GRD, Washington, D.C.

- (1982a), *Economic Memorandum on Grenada*, Report No. 3825-GRD, Washington, DC, April.

- (1982b), *Economic Memorandum on Grenada*, Report No. 3825-GRD, Washington, DC, August.

- (1984), *Economic Memorandum on Grenada* (Vol. 1), Washington, DC.

- (1985), *Economic Memorandum on Grenada*, Washington, DC.

- (1986), *Grenada: Updating Economic Memorandum*, Report No. 6292-GRD, Washington, DC.

Zinder, H. et al. (1969), *The Future of Tourism in the Eastern Caribbean*, Washington, DC.

Grenada Government Documents and Publications

Government of Grenada (1962), *Report of the Commission of Inquiry into the Control of Expenditure in Grenada during 1961 and Subsequently*, Documentation and Information Centre, Grenada.
- (select years), *Abstract of Statistics*, Central Statistics Office, Grenada.
- (select years), *Financial Statement and Report of the Nutmeg Board*, Documentation and Information Centre, Grenada.
- (undated), *Economic and Social Survey: Agriculture (GD93)*, Documentation and Information Centre, Grenada.
- (undated), *Housing in Grenada (GD5)*, Documentation and Information Centre, Grenada.
- (undated), *Manufacturing in Grenada*, Documentation and Information Centre, Grenada.
- (undated), *Planning in Grenada: Problems and Prospects (GD56)*, Documentation and Information Centre, Grenada.
- (undated), *The Private Sector in the Economy of Grenada: A Critique*, Documentation and Information Centre, Grenada.
- (undated), *Tourism in Grenada: the Past the Present and the Future (A Summary)*, Documentation and Information Centre, Grenada.
- (1979), 'Pointe Salines Developments Ltd', Documentation and Information Centre, Grenada.
- (1980-1986), *Annual Statistical Overview*, Department of Tourism, Grenada.
- (1981a), 'The Grenada Investment Code' (Draft), Documentation and Information Centre, Grenada.
- (1981b) *Grenada: The People's Laws*, Government Printing Office, Grenada, 1981.
- (1981c), 'Proceedings of Aid Donors Conference held in Brussels at ACP House on 14 and 15 April 1981: International Airport Project - Grenada' (Documentation and Information Centre, Grenada, Mimeo., 1981).
- (1982a), *Agricultural Census - Final Report on Grenada Agricultural Census*, Government Printing Office, Grenada.
- *Carriacou And Petit Martinique: In The Mainstream Of The Revolution*, Fedon Publishers, Grenada.
- (1982b), *Grenada Is Not Alone: Speeches by the People's Revolutionary Government at the First International Conference in Solidarity with Grenada, November 1981*, Fedon Publishers, Grenada.
- (1982c), *In the Spirit of Butler: Trade Unionism In a Free Grenada*, Fedon Publishers, Grenada.
- (1982d) *Is Freedom We Making! The New Democracy in Grenada*, Government Information Service, Grenada.

- (1982e) *Report on the National Economy for 1981 and Prospects for 1982*, Government Printing Office, Grenada.
- (1982f), *To Construct from Morning: Making the People's Budget in Grenada*, Fedon Publishers, Grenada.
- (1982g) *Revised Economic Memorandum on Grenada for 1982*, Documentation and Information Centre, Grenada.
- (1982h) *Systems for Planning Grenada's Economy* (GD238, Documentation and Information Centre, Grenada.
- (1982i), *The Grenada Laws*, Government Printing Office, Grenada.
- (1983a), 'Analysis of the New Co-operative Societies, 1979-1983', Documentation and Information Centre, Grenada.
- (1983b), 'Conference of Delegates from Mass Organizations on the Economy: Suggestions and/or Recommendations', Documentation and Information Centre, Grenada.
- (1983c), *Grenada Investors' Code*, Documentation and Information Centre, Grenada.
- (1983d), 'Physical Tourism, Development, Plan Zone 1', Documentation and Information Centre, Grenada.
- (1983e), *Report on the National Economy for 1982 and the Budget-Plan for 1983 and Beyond*, Government Printing Office, Grenada.
- (1983f), *Letter of Intent*, Documentation and Information Centre, Grenada.
- (1983g), *Report on the Unemployment Census*, Documentation and Information Centre, Grenada.
- (1984), *Economic Memorandum on Grenada*, vol. 1, Documentation and Information Centre, Grenada.

New Jewel Movement (captured documents)

Central Committee Minutes: Meeting, 15-16 April 1981; Extraordinary Meeting, 12-15 October 1982; Report on First Plenary Session 13-19 July, 1983; Meeting of 26 August 1983; Extraordinary Meeting, 14-16 September 1983; Plenary Meeting, 23 September 1983; Meeting, 28 September 1983; Meeting, 12 September 1983.

Letter from Ambassador W.R. Jacobs to Unison Whiteman, July 1983, 'Grenada's Relations with the USSR'.

Letter from Maurice Bishop to Colonel Gaddafi, September 26, 1983.

'National Service and Labour Army' (undated 'progress report').

'Line of March for the Party' (Presented by Comrade Maurice Bishop Chairman, Central Committee to General Meeting of Party on Monday 13 September 1982).

Political - Economic Bureau Meetings, Minutes; 3 August 3 1983.

'Resolution on Agriculture, January 1983'
'Resolution of the People's Revolutionary Armed Forces Branch of the New Jewel Movement', 12 October 1983.
'State Trading Corporation/Socialist Countries'

Periodicals

Barbados Advocate

Caribbean Contact

Caribbean Monthly Bulletin

The Daily Gleaner

Free West Indian

Granma Weekly

The Guardian

The Nation

New York Times

Trinidad Express

Trinidad Guardian

Washington Post